Contents

>>>

Make Your Website Sell

The Ultimate Guide to Increasing Your Online Profits

JED WYLIE

Marshall Cavendish
Business

For Julie, Elise, Aaron and Theo

Copyright © 2012 Jed Wylie

Published by Marshall Cavendish Business
An imprint of Marshall Cavendish International

PO Box 65829
London EC1P 1NY
United Kingdom
info@marshallcavendish.co.uk

and

1 New Industrial Road
Singapore 536196
genrefsales@sg.marshallcavendish.com
www.marshallcavendish.com/genref

Marshall Cavendish is a trademark of Times Publishing Limited

Other Marshall Cavendish offices:
Marshall Cavendish International (Asia) Private Limited, 1 New Industrial Road, Singapore 536196 • Marshall Cavendish Corporation, 99 White Plains Road, Tarrytown NY 10591–9001, USA • Marshall Cavendish International (Thailand) Co Ltd, 253 Asoke, 12th Floor, Sukhumvit 21 Road, Klongtoey Nua, Wattana, Bangkok 10110, Thailand • Marshall Cavendish (Malaysia) Sdn Bhd, Times Subang, Lot 46, Subang Hi-Tech Industrial Park, Batu Tiga, 40000 Shah Alam, Selangor Darul Ehsan, Malaysia

The right of Jed Wylie to be identified as the author of this work has been asserted by him in accordance with the Copyright, Designs and Patents Act 1988.

The authors and publisher have used their best efforts in preparing this book and disclaim liability arising directly and indirectly from the use and application of this book. All reasonable efforts have been made to obtain necessary copyright permissions. Any omissions or errors are unintentional and will, if brought to the attention of the publisher, be corrected in future printings.

A CIP record for this book is available from the British Library

ISBN 978–981–4346–35–1

Cover design by Matt McArdle
Author photograph by Edward Moss

Printed and bound in the United Kingdom by TJ International

Introduction

◼ *THE STRATEGY*

You've come to the decision to invest in improving your website at exactly the right time. You have, quite rightly, recognised that the Internet is a very complex selling space, and in order to be effective, to outsmart your competition and to take your business to the next level, you need to find out what works and what doesn't. And that is exactly how this book will help you.

Together we are going to unlock the potential in your website so your business can achieve rapid and sustained growth for the months and years ahead, no matter what the economic weather.

For over a decade I have been at the coalface of web design and marketing as the managing director of a web design company. I've also spent the last five years intensively researching and testing the very best online techniques used by the top-performing companies.

I have taken all that knowledge and combined it into this book, along with a healthy measure of research and creativity. Plus I've packed in as many strategies, approaches, ideas, tips, and step-by-step guides as possible in order to give you the most powerful and practical advice available to turn your website into a financial success story.

However, whether you are building your website or growing an existing one, having a strategy will be fundamental to your success. In fact, you simply cannot expect to be successful without it.

Why?

Well, many web owners struggle; and struggle is a very clear message. It's the message that something is wrong. After years of working with hundreds of web owners I have noticed that the struggle is often the result of dabbling: they do a little bit of Google AdWords, have a brush with Search Engine Optimisation, flirt with improving their sales copy,[1] some even dump their entire site in the hope that their web designers will wave magic wands to make them millionaires overnight. Then they wonder why their website never really gets top-flight success.

Often this is down to the hope that by doing something different (anything different) their website will perform better. However, without a strategy – an overview of the sequential (and sometimes simultaneous) steps that need to be taken – most web owners are left floundering on the rocks.

My aim is to give you the strategy to make your online business flourish. It's not complicated, and it's not technical, so please enjoy the sense of relief that you may feel that the route to success is easier than most believe. (You are welcome to get a bit excited at this point.)

Now as soon as most people mention 'strategy,' I get nervous, as it's usually succeeded by endless business plans, policies and meetings. That is not the kind of strategy I mean. In fact, this strategy is incredibly simple because it relates to a process which, taken step by step, will build your success.

Step 1: Get Into the Web Owner's Mindset

Owning a website is more like owning another business, with all the complexities and work that entails. In fact there are so many elements to it you could easily be overwhelmed with 'stuff to do'; many web owners end up suffering from information overload to the point they are debilitated into inaction. Knowing how to run and develop your website is more about how you *think* than simply doing things on a list, so it's important for you to get your mindset right from the outset. Think of this as the same mental exercise an athlete might do before running a race – your mindset sets the foundation stones for your future.

Step 2: Find the Right Web Design Partner

Finding a good web designer can be as hard as finding your life partner. Your web designer will need to mesh with you, your business, your website's needs and even your values and principles. They will have to 'get inside' your business and your head in order

[1] 'Copy' is marketing speak for written text.

to connect with what you want. And you have to do likewise. After all, if they are about to help you represent your company online, you'll want to be sure they are right for the task.

Step 3: Plan and Build Your Website

Having got the right web design partner, it's time to build your online empire. But get it wrong here and the repercussions will be expensive and time-consuming. That's why you need to break down your web project into manageable chunks. It begins with the specification, which is where you do all of your groundwork thinking and where the website takes shape on paper. Next, those plans are fashioned into a design you can see, then turned into a working website, and finally tested and put live on the Internet.

It sounds simple but it isn't! It's a complex and detailed process, and one which typically takes a lot longer than you think. The biggest risk to you is *believing* that your web designers will do it for you. In reality they can only provide you with the framework for your site; its organisation, content, sales capability, testing and marketing are all down to you. Your designers may be able to guide you, but they certainly can't do it all for you.

Step 4: Discover the 7 Principles of Internet Marketing

Getting your website live is only half the battle. The other half is getting visitors and conversions. This is where having a keen understanding of Internet marketing will make the difference between your website just being another unproductive corporate website and one that sparkles in Internet space.

But Internet marketing is also not just about doing a bunch of things on a list. To be really successful it's vital you allow the underlying principles of why you're doing it to mould your daily activities.

Knowing these principles will save you from costly mistakes as well as help you focus your efforts in the most efficient way possible.

Step 5: Get Instant Traffic to Your Website

Your site is live, you're rapidly becoming a marketing guru; now's the time to flex your Internet muscle.

The biggest problem for new – and often existing – websites is getting traffic (or visitors). The old adage, 'Build it and they will come,' is often met by the Internet's stark response, 'No they won't.' The fear is that your website may well become the Internet's best-kept secret unless people actually visit it. If you build a hotel in the middle of nowhere with no roads, signs or advertising, you wouldn't exactly expect it to be a roaring success. The same is true of the Internet: your website is in the middle of cyber-nowhere until you build online roads, signs and advertising.

Google AdWords is a powerful marketing system that solves the traffic problem by instantly bringing relevant prospects to your website (a huge bonus if you've just launched your website). You do have to pay for the traffic, but because the system is so measurable you can quickly get your campaign into profit. If done well, this can be the cash machine for your business – that's not hyperbole, that's a fact.

Step 6: Build Lasting Relationships with Your Customers

While you're building your profitable Google AdWords campaign (and waiting to find out the best keywords for Search Engine Optimisation), you can begin to build a database of prospects that will be a constant source of revenue for years to come.

Let's start with an uncomfortable fact: the vast majority of visitors to your site will 'bounce' off it without you even knowing who they are. This means that you can't make contact with them ever again. So how do you get around this thorny problem?

The solution is to offer your visitor something of value in exchange for their email address. Imagine a page where a visitor lands and sees something of real, tangible value and is immediately available to them. All they have to do to get it is to hand over their email address. It could be anything: a free report or download, access to a special video, a 5-day email training course, free consultancy, whatever you like. The more useful and exciting the offer, the more people will sign up for it. The important fact here is that they have 'opted in' to receive more information from you as part of the deal.

Now you have their email address. At this point you don't even need to sell; just give them really useful information. The crux of this approach is that when they do want your product or service, your email is sitting in their inbox reminding them of your business. Plus, because you've been regularly sending them helpful information, you've proven your business's value and gone a long way towards building a strong relationship.

Step 7: Turn Visitors into Customers

The next step is to take your website and optimise it. This means maximising the number of prospects who become customers, and this is achieved through testing. Imagine you are looking at a page on your website that might help convince a prospect to become a customer. The question in your mind should be, 'What can I do to increase the conversions from this single page?' And how you go about doing this is by asking yourself another question, 'What happens if I change...?'

The notion of change is really centred on testing new ideas. The 'To Do' list of testing is only limited by your imagination. What is interesting is that every time you test something and it yields an increase in conversions you are effectively giving yourself a pay rise, and that makes this one of the most rewarding activities of owning a website.

Step 8: Build Lasting Traffic to Your Website

Search Engine Optimisation (SEO) is an activity that helps improve your *organic ranking* on a search engine. Your organic ranking is where you appear on the left-hand side of Google for any particular search. For example, if you sell Cornish holiday homes, you'll want to appear top of the listing when someone types in 'cornish holiday homes'. This will give you access to traffic which is both appropriate and interested in what you have to offer. More importantly, unlike Google AdWords, traffic from here is free! Getting to the top, however, can be something which requires a concerted and focused effort. More often than not, it won't 'just happen.'

It may surprise you to learn that you can only SEO your site for a small number of keywords, usually around 4–5 at a time, without turning your entire life over to the endeavour or paying a small fortune to consultants to do it for you. Nevertheless SEO is an important part in your domination of Google and even getting to the top of a Google search for a handful of keywords could be immensely profitable.

SEO is not a 5-minute job like Google AdWords; it can take months before you see the results of your labours. Hence this is one very good reason a fledgling website should not rely on it as the sole mechanism for generating traffic but for it to be seen as one element in the overall strategy.

Step 9: Analyse and Grow

Your website is really a laboratory in which you perform experiments to constantly improve the efficiency of its money-making abilities. Well, that's the theory. However, most web owners are content to set up the lab and leave it running without ever changing a thing. However, if I could prove to them that by moving a few petri dishes and the odd Bunsen burner around they could massively improve their results, then most would be interested. And that's true: it's often the minor (obvious) changes that yield the greatest result – small keys can open big doors!

As with any good science experiment you need to record the results in order to draw any conclusions and, interestingly, your website is bursting with results just waiting to be analysed.

Measuring results is critical to successful marketing; otherwise you could be throwing time and money into unprofitable activities. Put simply, you can't control and improve what you don't measure. What is wonderful about the Internet is that almost everything you do on it is measurable to one degree or another. This is especially true when you use Google Analytics – a free service offered by Google to help you analyse how visitors are interacting with your website. When you combine this facility with the other forms of conversion analysis (such as Google AdWords, the click-through rates off your emails, the number of leads you acquire per day, and so forth) then you have an extremely powerful engine you can put to work.

Measuring the success of your online laboratory will give you the insight to improve whatever is failing and magnify whatever is working. Again, this sounds like common sense and yet you'd be amazed at how many companies (often big ones) don't measure their results, let alone analyse them.

Step 10: Everything Else

As a web owner it's difficult not to be distracted by other forms of marketing. I regularly see customers flitting from one marketing approach to another in the hope that they will land on one which will make them a fortune. Such behaviour rarely produces consistent results and can lead to lots of half-tried but potentially profitable marketing tactics discarded around them. The real key to success is the intelligent application of consistency.

Many will give up a particular marketing approach either because they haven't thought it through properly or because they never fully committed to making it work. Oddly, many give up on the brink of success and do the rather British sporting thing of snatching defeat from the jaws of victory. Yet one of the immensely exciting aspects of Internet marketing is the sheer variety of tactics available to you. For example:

1. Advertising on Facebook, YouTube or LinkedIn
2. Developing a following of people on Twitter
3. Referral marketing to your existing customers
4. Advertising on Yahoo! or Bing
5. Joint ventures and affiliate marketing
6. Becoming a recognised specialist/expert on forums or blogging sites
7. Using offline techniques to support your online activities and vice versa
8. Using advanced split-testing to improve your conversions
9. Using of co-registration opt-ins
10. Developing your PR, and so on...

However, the trouble with lists like this is temptation – the temptation to drop what you're doing in the hope that something else on the list will yield a faster, better and cheaper response.

My recommendation is to follow the nine steps outlined here and pursue them as thoroughly, thoughtfully and consistently as you can. Once you feel you've made a breakthrough with any one of the marketing techniques, you can then put it on autopilot while you introduce another marketing approach. Each time you do this you build on your previous marketing victories, creating an upward spiral of online success.

TIME, TIDE AND THE INTERNET

I've done my level best to ensure that everything in this book is correct. However, the Internet waits for no man, including me and my publishers, so it's just possible that some of the information has already changed (particularly the screenshots I've used).

Don't panic though, because I'm going to make sure that you get up-to-date, leading-edge information hot off the press to keep your website super-profitable and way ahead of your competitors.

You can find out more by visiting my Make Your Website Sell VIP Golden Circle website (www.makeyourwebsitesell-vip.co.uk). More information about the site is at the end of the book.

1

CHAPTER

Get Into the Web Owner's Mindset

■ *OWNING THE INTERNET*

Congratulations!

You are a web owner. You have secured your very own piece of Internet real estate. And it's yours to grow.

You may feel that it's only a tiny plot next to the Goliath-sized continents of Google and Amazon but remember they all started off with only a domain name. Perhaps you may have already secured a significant area for yourself. At this stage it really doesn't matter because you're here and the point of this book is to help your online business flourish and grow.

And that's our starting point: growth. My intention for your online business is that whatever the situation now, in 12 months' time your website will be bigger, better and more profitable.

If you can give your website the attention it deserves it will flourish and grow, occupying more Internet real estate. More people will visit it, more will discover and link to it, more will want to hear about what you are doing and, with each passing day, the land on which your website rests will soar in value and size.

But starve your website of attention and fewer people will visit, interest will drop and it will be overlooked by other websites which will link to your competitors instead of to you. Then you'll find yourself standing in the middle of a plot whose boundaries continue to shrink until you eventually fall prey to the 'online black hole' and end up as the Internet's best-kept secret.

But that's not for you, not while you're reading this book!

Let's begin by setting the foundation stones for your future success, and that begins with your mindset.[1]

[1] You notice in this step that I'll refer to 'you,' but 'you' may also be you and your web team.

■ *THINKING LIKE AN ONLINE ENTREPRENEUR*

So much has been written about entrepreneurial thinking that I won't try to distil it here. However, there are certain behaviours I have noted about how some web owners approach the development and running of their websites which deserve a little discussion.

Let's start with the first, and most important, influencing factor to any web owner's success: belief.

Belief

Starting your online entrepreneurial activity with the right mindset and beliefs is like winning the match before you've stepped out onto the court. It's what separates the really successful businesses from the average ones.

Ask any sportsperson or sports psychologist and they'll tell you that your beliefs profoundly affect your performance. So, if self-belief affects sports people, surely it affects business people, too?

What we believe is possible in our online entrepreneurial life is the limiting factor in our success.

Let's take an example. Lots of people wish they were millionaires, but of those who *want* to become millionaires, very few actually *believe* they will be millionaires. Those that do, however, stand a far greater chance of becoming what they believe. Why? Because at a conscious and subconscious level they are doing everything they can to pursue that one objective. Now I'm not suggesting that being a millionaire should be your life's goal; I'm just using it as an example. The point is that your underlying beliefs in what you are capable of fundamentally affect the actions you take and the choices you make.

All this may seem more like some New Age incantation rather than hard-edged business-speak, but there is good reason I mention it. Owning and running a website is not for the faint-hearted. It is complex and demanding and don't let anybody tell you otherwise. Be prepared for long hours, headaches and hard work, but also be prepared for more customers, a growing bank account and a sense of achievement. Your belief that you are doing the right thing is what will see you through and keep you on course for success.

Owning a website can be a wild ride but how you handle it is totally dictated by your mindset and your beliefs. For example, many websites fail because their owners give up – they lose confidence, interest and commitment, especially in the early days of their website's life. It's easy to give up if you're struggling or faced with outright failure. However, those who believe they will succeed don't see failure as a setback but as a learning experience – they have the right mindset and they will do well because of it.

I'm telling you this because you know that success isn't a set of purely mechanical step-by-step processes. (If it were, we'd all be millionaires.) Success comes from your mindset: what you believe you can achieve and the expectations you set yourself. This mindset is as important as knowing how to Search Engine Optimise your website or write compelling sales copy.

Respect Your Website, It's Your Best Salesperson

Many companies view their website with the same enthusiasm they have for taking the bins out. They see it purely as an extension to their core business (or marketing). At worst their website is just another thing on the marketing list of stuff they need to get done. At best they have good intentions but fail to commit because they don't quite understand the intrinsic value their website can bring to their business.

This mentality results in a website that struggles to get off the ground. Often it's not because there is anything fundamentally wrong with the website, it's because the business failed to do anything with it. This is comparable to buying a Bentley and then leaving it on your driveway because you can't be bothered to find the petrol cap!

Crazy though this is, it happens a lot more often than you might think and it's partly because websites aren't tangible, physical things. If, on entering the office, the managing director kept tripping over a £10,000 piece of machinery that had never been plugged in, it wouldn't be long before questions were being asked and heads were rolling. But it is not unusual to find £10,000 invested in a website which everyone in the business (including the managing director) then completely forgets about. They forget because it's not physically under their noses.

And this happens because their website is viewed as something that needs to 'get done' so they can move on to the next task – it's a sort of 'checkbox' mentality. Successful websites don't work like that. You can't build it, forget about it and expect it to be profitable. In fact, you'll find that the closer your website is to the heart of your business, the greater its profitability. Conversely, the further to one side it is pushed the less money it will make. (You wouldn't make much money if you set up your lemonade stand in the attic.)

The way to succeed is to treat your website as though it were just as important as the top salesperson in your business. Here's why.

Your website will often be the first place people go to find out about your business, so it stands to reason that you would want to put your best foot forward to impress your visitors. Imagine you were meeting them face to face, wouldn't you want your best salesperson on the job? Wouldn't that salesperson have a title giving them a sense of their place in the organisation and a certain amount of respect? Wouldn't they be paid a salary? And wouldn't they receive ongoing training to hone their skills and earn more money for your company?

If a salesperson automatically commands all these things, doesn't it follow that your website should too? Remember that your website is selling 24 hours a day, 7 days a week, is always promoting your business and can be seen by every single one of the two billion people online. Plus it is often the first experience many will have of your business.

So, it too should have a position in the business (i.e. everyone should recognise its value). You should invest in it regularly (by spending time and/or money improving it). You should train the relevant people in your company to work with it properly (regular updates, knowing what its capabilities are, etc.).

It may seem strange anthropomorphising a website[2] but it gives you a perspective on its value and how it should be treated. If you start thinking of your website as a person in its own right, you'll find that your thinking and behaviour towards it fundamentally changes. It's a little bit like getting married – it seals the deal. Now you're thinking of your website as your spouse! You care a lot more about their success than you do about your drunken uncle who gate-crashes your Christmas dinner. In other words, the things you make succeed are those you care most about.

[2] You'll find that a lot in this book is about doing and thinking unconventionally. After all, isn't it true that in order for our businesses to stand out from the crowd we have to think differently from the crowd?

The 80/20 Rule

The 80/20 rule is one of those principles which many people seem to know about (if only vaguely) but nobody quite knows what to do with. If you're not familiar with it, let me explain.

Essentially the 80/20 rule states that 80 per cent of the effects are produced by 20 per cent of the causes. There's lots of complicated math to underpin this but it's become a proven real-life rule. For example, 80 per cent of the world's income comes from 20 per cent of its population. You spend 80 per cent of your time in 20 per cent of your house. Some 80 per cent of software crashes are caused by 20 per cent of bugs. Eighty per cent of crimes are committed by 20 per cent of criminals. You get the idea.[3]

The problem I find with the 80/20 rule, though, is that it's a bit like trigonometry – it's nice to know but it doesn't seem to have much everyday application. (Actually, I'm not sure that trigonometry *is* nice to know.)

The trick to applying the rule is to acknowledge its existence and look for its characteristic pattern. Once you spot an aspect of business life which seems to conform to the pattern, do your best to use it to your advantage and concentrate your efforts on the 20 per cent that will yield the greatest results.

So what does this all mean for your website? Well, you will find that 80 per cent of your visitors only visit 20 per cent of your website. What does that tell you about where you should focus your efforts? Focus on and improve what the majority of people are looking at. You will also find that 80 per cent of your website's revenue comes from 20 per cent of your customers (or type of customer). What does this tell you about how to increase your website's revenue? Focus on delivering products and services aimed right between the eyes of the profitable 20 per cent of customers.

Let's flip the idea around.

What would happen to your profits if you spent 80 per cent of your time focused on the things that will only give you a 20 per cent return? Well, it doesn't take a genius to work out that they'd probably dip quite sharply. Would it be good use of your energies to focus on the 80 per cent of webpages only seen by 20 per cent of your visitors? No.

Now it is unlikely that anyone would deliberately focus on the least productive parts of their business. Instead, they are more

[3] My wife wears 20 per cent of her wardrobe 80 per cent of the time – a fact I waste no time in pointing out to her whenever we go clothes shopping. Her irritatingly clever response is that 'it's never the same 20 per cent.'

likely to spend time working on the profitable 20 per cent and some time working on the unprofitable 80 per cent. In all likelihood they haven't even recognised that there is a 20 per cent. And this is what makes recognising and using the 80/20 rule so exciting.

Take some time to identify the 80/20 pattern in your online life and use that knowledge to plan your time and resources. You'll be surprised at the speed and level of results you can obtain when you focus on the high-yield activities.

The Theory of Constraints

If you like the idea that you only need to put in 20 per cent of your effort to gain 80 per cent of your results then you may also appreciate the Theory of Constraints. Essentially, this states that your online business is constrained by a series of factors which limit your success.

Think of your business as a pipe through which money flows. If we were to crimp that pipe at various points along its length we would slow the flow of money into and through your business down to a trickle. Equally, if we banged out the dents we would release the flow of money. If you visualise your online business in this way, it helps you begin to identify the constraints or bottlenecks limiting your success.

For example, a constraint may be a lack of traffic to your website, or a lack of time to invest in building a new website, or not being able to stock a top-selling product at Christmas. It could be anything – and only you will be able to sniff out where the constraints are in your online business – but being aware that they exist is critical to removing them.

The reality for all businesses (be they online or not) is that these constraints exist to various degrees, and this causes a 'throttling' of their success.

In order to identify the constraints you need to take a bird's eye view of your business – to step back from the day-to-day and, as they say, work 'on' and not 'in' the business. Looking for these limiting factors is a great exercise in developing a strategic mindset free from the everyday minutiae of running your business. Plus, the feeling of relief and excitement when you identify and remove a constraint is truly wonderful!

Action

In this book I will give you all kinds of strategies to radically improve your online profits. However, if I gave all this good stuff to 50 business people, they wouldn't all achieve the same results. Some would absorb the information and do very little with it (they may improve their online turnover by 5 per cent). Some would absorb the information and dabble with it (their turnover may improve by 25–30 per cent). And some would absorb the information and commit to it (their turnover would improve by 200–500 per cent and beyond).

What makes the difference between these three groups is not the information. It's not the business they're in. It's not even how clever they are. It's entirely down to their desire to act.

I want to make sure that you maximise every last ounce of possibility from this material. In order for you to protect the investment you've made in your website, you need the time to put all this information into practice. In other words, just reading this stuff isn't enough – you need to go out there and take action.

The coming chapters contain information that will totally transform your online business. However, my worst nightmare is that all this material remains as information on the page and never makes it into reality.

So, please give yourself the opportunity to make a massive impact on increasing your profits by taking this information and turning it into positive action. It's also worth noting that as you act on the material in these pages it will spark off your creativity and more ideas and opportunities will present themselves. As you then act on those, your success will be hugely magnified. Eventually, you will find yourself in an upward spiral of success driven by action and results.

Action and How to Use This Book

Jim Rohn described a great rule of human behaviour called the 'Law of Diminishing Intent.' Fundamentally, it states that once you decide to do something you should act immediately when your emotional desire to get the results from the actions is at its height. In other words, take action when the desire peaks because the further you get from the desire to act, so your intent to act diminishes. The curious thing about Jim Rohn's law is that he's dead right.

My hope is that as you read this book you become excited by the possibilities it presents – at the point you 'get the buzz' you should act immediately before the desire subsides. Once you get into the habit of acting when the desire is at its peak you will start to become an 'action junkie' – you'll love the buzz you get when you act, and the better the results, the more you'll want to act. It's a wonderful cycle to get into. So, I implore you to act as soon as possible, with a sense of urgency and desire for the result.

■ TIME: FRIEND OF THE WEBSITE

Most of us are what's known as 'time poor.' Often it's a struggle to get done what we *have* to get done, let alone what we *want* to get done! Put into the middle of your busy schedule the running and development of your website and you'll probably be reaching for the paracetamol.

However, your website can only survive and thrive if you dedicate time to nurturing it. If you 'dabble' with it you'll only serve to frustrate both its results and yourself. So, here are a few tips to help you become more productive with your online entrepreneurial time:

1. Set aside a certain amount of time each week to review and improve your website. This is the creative time in your entrepreneurial life and you should defend it ruthlessly. It is the time that will make you successful. This is a behaviour pattern that runs through all successful business people – they understand the need to remain focused on a single objective and not to get side-tracked.
2. Set yourself deadlines. Having a deadline gives you the sense of urgency and priority to complete what you need to do. Deadlines help set your priority list – make sure your website is on that list!
3. Remember the 80/20 rule. Use your time to focus on the most productive 20 per cent of your online life.
4. Keep a log of your daily web-related activities. At the end of the week review it and circle the time that contributed to your online success. Work to increase that time in your working week and if that proves to be a struggle, try my next tip.

5. Outsource everything you can afford to get rid of. When you hand over the mundane tasks to others it frees you to concentrate on the high-earning activities. (This is perhaps one of the strongest arguments for *not* building your website yourself!)

6. You are undoubtedly a creative person. Almost everybody is creative at one level or other. But often, what stops us from recognising our own creativity is the crap we have to deal with day to day: answering emails, making calls to colleagues, internal meetings, routine project management – these are rarely creative pastimes. Just take a moment and ask yourself what percentage of today has been purely dedicated to creative thought? Creative time is where you improve your website copy, test a different ecommerce pricing approach, try a different headline, write a new marketing email, and so on. Creative time is what gives you the ideas to test, to generate and maximise your business.

DELAYS: ENEMY OF THE WEBSITE

Procrastination, deferring, stalling, dabbling, whatever you call it, happens to many web owners every day. It's a behaviour pattern that can turn a 2-month web project into a two-year web project. It is the simple act of knowing you need to do something now but choosing to do it later. The danger, of course, being that the 'something' keeps getting delayed until it actually falls into the category of 'never getting done.'

Deferring is dangerous. It causes you to flit from one thing to another – like being unable to resist the temptation of picking up a new book before finishing the last one. More seriously, deferring to other things can stop you from making money as quickly as you might from your website.

To be honest, most of us suffer a bit from this mentality; in fact it's one of the biggest barriers to our entrepreneurial success. Why? Because deferring makes it difficult to finish what you start. The opposite is commitment to immediate action and completion of that action. As Bear Grylls puts it, 'Commitment is what is left after the initial enthusiasm is gone.' And commitment is the one thing your project needs from you in order for it to succeed.

Often web owners suffer from the deferring problem because they have too much accumulated information to wade through. Having spent several years immersed in Internet marketing, reading everything I could find, joining every mailing list going, living in web-seminars and joining courses, I can tell you in detail about information overload. Constantly looking for new information to see if there's a better way of doing something can be so overwhelming it stops you from doing anything at all. You could spend your entire life absorbing information and never getting round to actually doing anything with it. This is a big danger for anybody who is serious about owning a successful website. My advice is simple: The moment you begin putting your website together, stop reviewing any new information. Yes, it's possible you might miss some useful nugget which may help you win a few more quid but the time you spend finding it will outweigh any return.

Of course, information overload is only one of the many potholes waiting to un-wheel your wagon. The feeling that your website must be perfect before you launch it is also a danger. However, in order to be successful you don't need the perfect solution. Even if you start trading with a horrible website, you are still trading. You are doing better than those who have yet to launch their website because it's the wrong shade of green or because they haven't quite become a ninja master at Google AdWords or because the economy is not quite right or because they can't think of a business name that properly reflects their values. So, if you're waiting for the perfect photograph of the managing director or haven't quite uploaded all 99,999 products to your ecommerce store, don't worry, it doesn't matter – 80 per cent of your website's visitors will only see 20 per cent of your website anyway.[4]

[4] A caveat: Your web designers do need to be perfectionists. The last thing a web designer wants is to be cavalier or slip-shod with the technology that makes your website work. When dealing with web software it has to be right and finished in order to work properly.

When you own a website you accept that it will never be perfect. It can't be because there is no such thing on the Internet. Even if you did build the best website ever, it wouldn't last long because market conditions on the Internet change so often and so fast. You're not trying to hit the bull's eye with the first shot. The first version will be good enough to get you started, and from there you can refine and improve based on how people interact with your site. It would be a lot of wasted energy and thought trying to anticipate how that might pan out when you can make better decisions based on fact rather than guesswork.

Remember, websites take time to mature and there are going to be mistakes along the way. Every website on the Internet changes, evolves, grows and hopefully becomes better, and yours will be no different.

CONFIDENCE

Am I doing the right thing? Is my/our/their money going to be wasted? What if it all fails because I didn't do something I don't even know about yet? Most of us have the occasional thoughts like these. It's easy to suffer from a 'cold light of day' moment especially when you are in the middle of a development project like a website. It could come from finding that the competition all look very professional or that you're not top on the search engines or that your web designers have quoted more than you expected. These can all affect your confidence.

However, the one thing I feel is the most effective at killing confidence is other people's response to what you're doing: You have a great idea. You tell your best friends. They slate it (albeit nicely). You don't do it.

When people say 'no' (in whatever form) it can kill your confidence stone dead. Even though our friends and colleagues may have the best of intentions, the majority of people prefer the status quo – they are risk-averse. However, in my experience, it pays to utterly ignore the 'no' brigade. Why? Because their response is almost always based on feelings rather than facts.

And why is this so important? Because in business, half the battle is having the idea, the other half is getting it done. It scares me to think how many website ideas, worth millions to their businesses, have been dropped because the uninformed 'no' vote consigned them to the 'it won't work' bin.

The way to get your idea past them is to ask them one simple question: 'Do you know for a *fact* this idea will not work?' And when they say 'No,' you say, 'Then let's test it and find out!'

Despite your best efforts, some of your ideas will be disasters, some just 'Ok' but some will double your business. You won't know which is which until you test them. So, beware those that doubt you. They may believe they are saving you from yourself or from you making a costly mistake but often they're just stopping your business getting off the ground or increasing its profits.

■ *RUNNING A WEBSITE IN BAD TIMES*

Every so often economies suffer from 'bad times'. If you've run a business for any length of time you can expect to face this situation. So here's some thinking which may help you through it when it happens.

Many businesses that hit the bad times take the attitude of a hedgehog facing down a juggernaut – they can see it coming but believe that the best thing to do is curl up into a ball and hope the problem goes away. As you can imagine this is not a healthy position to adopt.

Often the reason why business owners react like this (and it's not just the small businesses that react this way) is because they believe what the media are saying about how bad the economic crisis really is. Anyone who's spent any time watching the news during a recession will come away with the belief that we are all doomed. So, when all we hear are dire economic forecasts (and the 'R' word) everyone's confidence suffers. The effect is that, without even being conscious of it, our thinking starts to shift: we spend less, pause or drop development projects, slash budgets all because we're fearful of the future – real or imagined. We become focused on battening down the hatches, scaling back, holding on to the cash in the bank and so forth.

Usually the first budget out of the window is marketing – it's an easy target and an immediate saving. So, companies slash their Google AdWords spending, stall their Search Engine Optimisation projects, take longer over buying decisions, and kill off their website investment. Gradually their mindset moves to believing there are fewer and fewer opportunities (and cutting back on their marketing quickly makes that a reality).

So, how can you defend yourself from this, and recession-proof your online business at the same time?

Well, it's your reaction to the bad times that affects your business but how you react is down to how you think.

You see, your ability to make money has not changed because your colleagues, friends, family and the media might tell you so. The fact that your competitors will get sucked into this mindset is actually to your advantage. As they cut back on their online marketing they make room for you to capture the ground they have retreated from. As they withdraw from the field, so your position becomes stronger, such that in a perverse way the fear of an economic slide can actually create opportunities for entrepreneurs like you.

It also gives you a choice to make about how you deal with economic doom and negativity. You can either accept it and be subject to all its harmful influences, or reject it and take the positive steps necessary to ensure continued growth for your business in the years to come. Steps like investing in your website's marketing, testing new methods of attracting customers, developing a back-end of services which retains your customers and turns them into repeat business, and so on. Time spent improving your website is time spent strengthening your entire business and its future.

Jim Rohn once remarked, 'You cannot change the direction and the forces of the wind. But you can change the setting of your own sail.' If your business was a ship in the middle of an economic storm, would you leave the ship rudderless and dive below decks, or trim your sails and, with a sense of direction, steer your ship to safe waters?

How you get there is by understanding that while your customers may not have changed, the way they think about spending their money probably has. If they're frightened by what they presume they understand about the economy, they will start to hold on to their money purely because of our inbuilt survival mechanism and the fear that they may have less money in the future. (This prompted Hyundai to launch their Assurance Program, where you could walk away from your car loan if you lost your job. This was effectively reversing the risk to the customer, enabling them to feel easier about buying the car.)

By understanding that your customer's decision-making process has changed, you can approach them differently and help them understand the value of your business (just as Hyundai did). For example:

1. Offer guarantees.
2. Emphasise the benefits of working with you.
3. Provide testimonials from others in a similar position to them.
4. Empathise with their situation.
5. Move their thinking away from the price and towards the *value* they will receive.

However, it may be that your ideal customer has changed. If the target market no longer has money to spend that doesn't mean that the money has evaporated, it means that a different group of people have it and that's a strong argument for following the money rather than doggedly following a market, especially in a downturn.

LESSONS FROM HISTORY

If you've spent more than five minutes on the Internet you'll know that there is a common myth perpetrated by many in the web design and Internet marketing industry that unbounded success awaits you tomorrow. What's disturbing is that the myth is so common that it turns into the belief that simply by *being* online, the business will succeed.

It won't.

Anyone who believes that it will should buy a lottery ticket instead of a website. But it's not surprising that the myth exists or that both individuals and businesses get hooked into believing it. After all, who wouldn't want to be instantly and fabulously wealthy?

This kind of thing has happened throughout history. Back in the 1850s, during the Gold Rush, California was overrun with prospectors hoping to make their fortune and name by striking it lucky. Such was the allure that more than 300,000 uprooted themselves in the hope of becoming rich. For the majority it was a vain hope.

It happened again in the late 1990s with the Internet dot-com boom. The Internet was seen as a new frontier waiting to be conquered. Venture capitalists went crazy pumping money into all kinds of weird and wonderful schemes. For the entrepreneur who needed backing it was a heady time. And with success stories like Google, eBay, Yahoo!, AltaVista and many more, the venture capitalists were hungry for a fast return. However, very few of the big spenders survived past the Internet crash of 2001.

What is astonishing is that most of the companies which crashed all made obvious and fundamental errors of judgement. Errors which are so simple to spot it's hard to imagine that they were overlooked by such highly intelligent people in the first place. Or was it simply that hubris and the high life blinded them?

Let's take a look at four of the top Internet catastrophes:

Fourth Place: Flooz.com

Total amount spent: us$35–50 million

The founders of Flooz (the Arabic for 'money') had the breathtakingly stupid idea that people would buy Flooz credits which could be redeemed at any participating online store. In other words you would hand over your money to a company who gave you credits which you could then use to buy things over the Internet. Incredibly, they failed to spot that there was already something we were all happily using to buy things over the Internet, called 'money.'

Really, why would you want to use that pesky money stuff – which everyone accepts – in place of Flooz credits which you could spend in up to, erm, a few stores? Needless to say it wasn't well received by the public at large.

Towards the end Flooz became embroiled in a crime syndicate and money laundering scheme uncovered by the FBI. Eventually Flooz, and its competitor Beenz.com, were simultaneously declared bankrupt in 2001.

Lesson: If an idea doesn't work in the real world, it stands little chance of success on the Internet.

Third Place: Pets.com

Total amount spent: us$82.5 million

A simple idea, buy your pet supplies online.

Imagine spending $11.8 million dollars on advertising *before* you've done any research to see if a market exists for your product. Well, Pets.com did just that. Oddly, the warning sign that the market was just not as large as they thought was clearly evidenced by its total revenue of just $619,000 despite $11.8 million on advertising. Let's put that another way: for every $1 revenue they generated, they lost $19!

What's more absurd is that in order to win the customers over they were selling their products at a loss. I honestly can't imagine how that one got past the board as it seems to be the short route to commercial suicide. And it was.

Pets.com collapsed nine months after it was launched. Yet, despite overseeing a business disaster of Biblical proportions, the

CEO managed to walk away with a $235,000 severance package.

Lesson: Testing and measuring is the essence of success. If you know what your Return on Investment is month by month, you can adjust your marketing accordingly. This allows you to expand quickly on your successes and kill off any failures before it's too late.

Second Place: Boo.com

Total amount spent: US$135 million (in just 18 months!)

At last the Brits make it into the hit list and utterly outclass the competition for the award of 'Customer, what customer?'

Boo was a fashion business selling clothes online and it was, to be fair, both amazing and ridiculous. Brilliant because it really pushed the technological boundaries of the day. They used Java-Script and Flash extensively to show 3D representations of their stock and even created an animated avatar called Miss Boo who would help you choose your clothes (the implication being that a computer could dress you better than you could).

All this impressive technology meant that the webpages were so big the customer had to wait several minutes just to get the home page started. Back then we were all still on dial-up connections (Boo hadn't noticed that). Needless to say, not enough people hung around to see the home page let alone actually buy anything.

It's astonishing that no one at Boo bothered to test how the site ran on their customers' computers.

Their financial ruin was sealed by a series of the most extraordinary business decisions imaginable, including asking staff to delay holidays in exchange for First Class flights and five-star hotels. Eventually they went from Boo to bust.

Lesson: Take the time to understand your customer, their circumstances, what they want and how they want it presented. The simplest way to do this is to ask them!

First Place: Webvan.com

Total amount spent: US$1 billion (in 1095 days – $913,242.01/day!)

Actually, this was a sensible idea, essentially an online grocery store which delivered to your door (a precursor to Wallmart.com and Tesco.com). What was less than sensible was that none of the senior executives or investors had any experience in the super-market business.

What killed them off though was the misjudged desire to grow at a supercharged rate. Everyone looked to Amazon as a model online business and saw how quickly they had created their infrastructure and assumed that was the way to go. Unfortunately, this worked for Amazon but with fatal consequences for almost everybody else who tried.

Put simply, Webvan expanded itself out of existence.

Webvan's problems were not about technology, infrastructure or how clever they were, it was the simple fact that they had far too few customers. (Only 2 per cent of web users were buying groceries online at that time.) They filed for bankruptcy in 2001 and disappeared in a blaze of banknotes.

Lesson: Even the best idea's success rests almost entirely on how well it is marketed. It's no accident that the top entrepreneurs spend about 50 per cent of their time marketing... and if they do, so should you.

No matter how meteoric the rise or impressive the investment, there are simple laws of success that govern every business, whether online or offline. Take them to heart or ignore them at your peril! They are a lesson to us of the dangers of believing that others' success should automatically result in our own. From their experience we learn that:

1. Throwing money into a website does not guarantee its success.
2. A bad business idea in the real world is still a bad business idea on the Internet.
3. The 'get rich quick' mentality is flawed.
4. All the principles for running a successful business apply to running a successful website.

Don't get me wrong. There are plenty of businesses that *appear* to make millions overnight, but in reality they've spent a good amount of time getting their online business to that position. They may have, for example, invested months or even years growing a focused list of prospects which, when they finally leverage, produce fast profits.

■ GETTING YOUR WEBSITE'S PRIORITIES RIGHT

The majority of web owners tend to view the priorities of their website build in the following order:

1. Design
2. Technology
3. Marketing

Looking at the list, it seems natural. After all that's the order of your project: get the design right, build the site and market it. But it places the emphasis of your attention and thought in entirely the wrong order. Let's look at each in turn to discover why.

Design

If design were all that mattered, Google's home page would look a lot more 'designed' than it does. Design is like incidental music in a film: it supports the storyline but doesn't tell the story. My experience indicates that most organisations spend 80 per cent of their time on design and only 20 per cent on content. (This is the equivalent of hiring John Williams to write the soundtrack to your home movies.) Design may be the outward manifestation of branding and corporate ego but it actually delivers far less commercial value than most web owners believe. After all, nobody ever bought a product or service solely on the basis of how well the website was designed.

Design is there to provide the environment and to help your visitor's eye find the important information on the page. It provides an interface for your visitor to carry out the necessary actions in order to become a customer. It communicates to your visitor that they are in the right place – you'd hardly expect to see a web design in the style of Harrods on the Disney website or vice versa). When it does these things well, you don't even notice it's there – just like the music in a film.

Technology

Well, of course, technology does matter – the last thing you need is a website that falls over every five minutes or one that you can't update – but whether you've got the best Content Management System or not will have no bearing on whether your customer buys from you. Technology for its own sake has little value; instead, it is a means to an end. For example, deciding to add a customer comments section to your blog is actually first and foremost a marketing and sales decision, which the technology then makes a reality, not the other way around.

Choosing to add technology because your competitors have it, for its own sake or because it's 'cool' will waste your money, and worse, your time which you could spend investing in...

Marketing

This is the dark horse of the three. It's the one piece in the jigsaw most businesses never think about until after their site is launched. How crazy is that? Knowing how to generate traffic to your website and then how to convert that traffic into sales is entirely about successful marketing. If you wait until the very end of your web development project before you develop your marketing you'll probably need to go back and rework many areas of your website to accommodate your new understanding.

What truly determines whether your website succeeds or fails is not the design, nor the technology but the marketing. After all, there's no point having a great website with no traffic, or great traffic with a website that can't convert its visitors into customers.

Focus on your marketing before design and technology and, if you're feeling really unconventional (all great successes are unconventional), read chapters 4 to 9 of this book first!

Ultimately, the most important facet of your online life is that *your website attracts visitors and converts them into customers.*

◼ THE STRATEGY

Although you may not have consciously noted this, the most important part of your website is you. It's your passion, belief and desire to succeed that will give heart and soul to your online endeavours. This makes you its most valuable resource. How tuned and focused your mindset is from the beginning will have a huge impact on your future success.

Everything about your website – its look and feel, structure, content, marketing ideas, and eventually outstanding success – comes directly from you. In fact, everything you create, you first create in your mind and then turn into a reality. If your mindset is the 'environment' in which your thoughts are formed, it's logical to assume that their quality will be influenced by their surroundings.

In other words, the quality of your ideas will be positively affected by you being in the right frame of mind.

CHAPTER 2

Find the Right Web Design Partner

◼ INTRODUCTION

There are many different types of websites: those that sell directly online (i.e. ecommerce sites); those that generate leads for service-based businesses; social networking sites that connect interested parties; blogging sites that convey a stream of consciousness, directories; search engines – the list is endless.

Whatever site you are building you are probably going to need a web design company to help you. And if you have serious ambitions for your site then you are probably looking for a reasonably long-term relationship with them for at least a year, and possibly several. They are a crucial component in your online success so choosing the right one can be a daunting task, especially if you're not familiar with the web design industry.

In this chapter we'll look at how you can arm yourself with all the information necessary to pick the right partner to build your website. But first let's look at why you even need a web designer in the first place.

◼ DIY OR PROFESSIONALLY DEVELOPED?

With so much professional web development software available, it's easy to be tempted into building a website yourself. However, the Internet has grown and evolved to such a degree that keeping up with its complexity and sophistication is a full-time job and has developed beyond the hobbyist's abilities. Nowadays building a professional website should only be done by professional web designers. Okay, so it will cost you some money that you could save if you learnt how to do it yourself, but consider this:

1. While you are learning how to build a website you are not working on growing your business.
2. Your value to your business, let's say as an hourly rate, is probably a lot more than that of your web designers.

The question is really whether it is a good use of your time, and I would suggest that unless you are already a web designer, your time is better spent using your existing skills to build your business.

You could go out there and buy a template website with some basic functionality. In my experience, however, these tend not to be adaptable to future business needs. I have found that the quick and dirty solutions may get you up and running fast but they tend to sacrifice flexibility and uniqueness in the process. And that's why the vast majority of serious businesses have their websites built by professional web design companies.

So, now you are left with a different problem: there are thousands of web design companies out there but which one should you choose?

Let's face it, you're about to entrust your entire online presence to a company you've never worked with before. It stands to reason you'll want to know that they're up to the job.

A BRIEF HISTORY OF WEB DESIGNERS

Let's take a moment to look at the origins of web design as this will help you get a sense of the companies you'll be dealing with.

Web design is an industry in its infancy, and like all emerging industries, the skills you start out with aren't necessarily the skills you end up with. Ten years ago developing a website was a very different proposition from what it is now. Back then ecommerce was a novelty, content management systems had barely been thought up, and for the average business, a website was nothing more than an online brochure. Even so, the brochure had to look good, which meant that the core skill of a web design company was, well, design.

Consequently most web designers started their professional lives as designers and then discovered that there was software that could build websites for them. Some even took the trouble to learn how to hand-code websites using HTML.

Now, fast-forward five years and the technology developed on the Internet has really taken hold. Ecommerce is commonplace, content management systems are getting more sophisticated and the population is discovering broadband. The advent of broadband meant that web companies could build more sophisticated websites which could even contain audio and video. This generated a new wave of web developers. These were people who could build systems using the technology on the Internet. However, they weren't really graphic designers, they were techie people. In fact, they were software engineers.

Jump forward again and today web companies are a fusion of designers and developers. The really strong businesses recognise that good designers are rarely technical and good technical people are rarely designers. This means that the bigger web design companies are split into teams of designers and developers. But their properties are still rooted in the original ambitions to make things look good and function well.

Thankfully, the days of brochure websites are long gone. Most businesses are starting to realise that their future success is going to be rooted in their ability to use their website as an effective marketing tool and not just something that looks pretty. These days, much like staff, websites are expected to earn their keep. This is forcing web designers to develop a new skill-set around Internet marketing including business consultancy. The web designer of the future will need to be an amalgam of designer, technologist and all-round business thinker – quite a demanding combination for a fledgling industry!

Incidentally, web designers are often called many things (some of them unrepeatable in polite company) including: web agencies, web developers, web companies, and so forth. All these collective terms have come to mean businesses that build websites, but it's also a catchall expression for those who supply any web-based service.

WHERE TO BEGIN YOUR SEARCH

The natural temptation is to start looking on the Internet, but actually you may already have access to great web design companies through your existing customers and suppliers.

The first thing to do is trawl your database and look at everyone's websites.[1] Note down the websites that you really like and all

[1] You'll notice that many web design companies put a link at the bottom of their customers' home pages to their website.

those that you know are really successful. Next get on the phone to your customer or supplier and ask them the following questions:

1. Was the website completed to your satisfaction?
2. Was it completed within the agreed time scales and budget?
3. What did you like/dislike about the web designers' performance?
4. Were they prepared to go the extra mile?
5. Would you use them again when you redevelop your website?

Don't forget to keep some notes.

Referrals from friends, colleagues and family are always far better than picking someone out of the phone book (although you may want to bolster your list with companies sourced from the web). What you're looking for are companies that have already demonstrated their ability through a channel you trust – via referrals, forums you use, bloggers in your industry, their own writings, etc.

▨ GETTING TO KNOW THEM

Let's start with some tough questions to ask your prospective suppliers so you can whittle down the numbers.

1: What's in Their Portfolio?

Take a long look at the web designer's portfolio – does each website in it look unique? If they all look like they've come off the production line then, unless that hits the spot, you may want to look elsewhere.

Don't be swayed by cool-looking designs. The bottom line for most businesses is whether a website makes money. So, even if you don't like the design, take a step back and look at it from the point of view of the market (or prospect) that the website is pitching to. If the web company has got it right then it will create exactly the right effect in the consumer. (It is worth asking the web designers what they would have done differently on a specific project if the client had given them a free rein. This will tell you just how much of the website was constrained and controlled by the client and give them the chance to let their ideas on how it could have been done come to the surface.)

You're looking for individuality, a clear focus on the target market and some creative ideas that give the customer an edge.

2: What Industry Sectors Have They Worked In?

A web design company that can show you websites from all kinds of different markets will be able to demonstrate their creative ability much more effectively than a company that only works in one area. The reason for this is that each industry sector comes with its own online challenges and a smart, thoughtful and creative web design business will be able to produce fresh ideas whatever the industry.

You may feel tempted to ask them if they've done any work in your sector. However, this question can be a bit of a red herring since it is an 'If they did it for them they can do it for me' line of thinking. It can mean that you bias your thinking towards these companies. However, it is worth bearing a couple of important points in mind: firstly, you wouldn't want your own site to look like a competitor's; and secondly, companies which come at an industry from a completely fresh perspective may have some new ideas.

Now I'm not suggesting that you shouldn't choose companies with experience in your industry because they could give you the inside track. However, while you might gain from their prior work, their next customer's website (i.e. your competitor) will gain from yours. It's a tricky question, but if you feel that they bring some specialist knowledge to the table then it may be worth it.

3: Does Their Own Website Sell to You?

You may be looking for them, but they still have to sell their service to you and that starts with their website. So ask yourself 'How well am I being sold to?' Does the home page engage your interest? Do they communicate the message of how they are going to help you? Does it look like they are trying to build a relationship with you? Are they doing something which their competitors aren't? Do they offer anything innovative or useful that separates them from the rest? (Perhaps a 'Call me back' form or a live chat facility?) Maybe they have a really interesting take on how to present their portfolio?

It's easy to be beguiled by lots of flashing graphics and cool things happening on screen but at the end of the day they are trying to get you to part with your money. To persuade you to do so, they're going to need to demonstrate that they are a company of substance. If they can communicate the value of their own business to you and you get a real sense of how they can help you, then this is going to be a big boost to your website.

4: Do They 'Get' Your Project?

No two clients of a web designer are the same, and as a result it's not unusual to find a wide range of industry sectors represented in their portfolio. Your business will probably be different from anything they've done before, so it's almost impossible for them to have an in-depth knowledge of your business because it's unique to you. However, if your website is to be a success, then a lot rides on their having a strong understanding of your company. And the only way they can develop that strong understanding is to ask questions – lots of them. The more questions asked and the more interest shown, the better your relationship will be in the long-term.

5: Can They Communicate Ideas?

You are looking for a business that can give you the best possible help and advice to maximise the return on your investment. So it's a good idea to watch for signs of creativity in the conversations. If you start to hear lots of interesting ideas and approaches that are relevant to your business then it's a good sign that the web designer not only has a strong sense of your business but also a variety of ideas how to represent it on your website.

Watch out for jargon and technobabble. If you're struggling to understand what they're talking about, that may be a sign that you're going to have communication problems down the line.

6: How Well Do They Project-Manage?

Producing a highly polished, perfectly functioning and successful representation of your business on time and to budget is not without its complexities. There are probably over a hundred factors to consider during your project's life cycle: buying and re-pointing domain names, search engine optimisation considerations, accessibility, usability analysis, user interfaces, navigation, copy, graphical style, coding to web standards, securing the code from hackers, marketing considerations, back-end technology choices – and that's before we even begin accounting for your specific requirements!

With so much complexity embedded in your web project it is important that your supplier has a strong sense of organisation and planning. You may even want to see evidence of a project plan or checklist to ensure all the bases are covered. (I've included one for you in Appendix II, page 337.)

This is particularly important because you don't want to find yourself having to pay extra for aspects of the development you thought were included.

7: How Big Are They?

Web design is a strange industry and still in embryonic stage. It is not unusual to find companies of only one or two employees. Now it doesn't automatically follow that the smaller the business the less capable they are – what you want to know is whether that company meshes with your style and demands.

Here are a few questions to ask so you can get a handle on their approach:

1. How long have they been working in the web design industry?
2. How quickly can they turn around updates on an existing website?
3. How much capacity (time) do they have on a weekly basis?
4. How do they prioritise their work?

8: Get Some References

Take the time to find out that the promises your web designer makes match the delivery. To that end contacting a couple of their customers is usually a good idea.

When you speak to their clients it's worth asking a few questions relating to the company's performance and abilities. You can use the questions in Where to Begin Your Search (pages 31–2) to help you.

■ *GETTING TO KNOW THEIR TECHNICAL PROWESS*

1: Do They Have the Skills to Support Your Needs?

You're aiming for a long-term relationship with your web design-ers so it helps to have an idea of your future requirements and whether they can be met.

Here are some questions you can ask to identify the range and depth of their skills:

1. Do they have Search Engine Optimisation skills – so they improve your ranking on Google?
2. Do they have Search Engine Marketing skills – using pay-per-click to advertise on search engines?
3. Do they have experience in developing ecommerce websites?
4. Do they develop Content Management Systems (CMS) for websites – so you can update your website independently of the web design company?
5. Do they provide hosting? What is the monthly cost?
6. Can they provide you with web statistics, and will they help you interpret them?
7. Do they have experience or skills in Accessibility (how easily people with disabilities can access your site) and Usability (how efficiently your visitor can interact with your site)?

2: What's Under the Bonnet of Your Website?

What makes a website work are the hundreds (often thousands) of lines of code which tell your browser software how to display the webpage.

A few years ago you could get away with writing your own website using FrontPage or Dreamweaver because the software would write the code for you. However, the Internet has become far more complex, which means that many modern websites need to be written in very specific ways which can no longer be done 'automatically.'

I won't bore you with the details but some of the buzzwords are: semantic coding, web standards[2] (for example, XHTML 1.0

[2] If you'd like to learn more about web standards, check out www.webstandards.org.

Transitional), CSS and Priority 2 AA accessibility standards.[3] If this all sounds very technical, you're right, it is, but how can you determine if the web company's code is high-quality?

Well, the good news is that there is a way in which you can see if the code they're writing is up to scratch. The body which decides how the Internet works (the World Wide Web Consortium or W3C) has an online code validator which will analyse any web address and tell you if it meets the standards. Here's where you can find it: validator.w3.org.

A word of caution: Web design standards change from time to time, so you may find a website in a web design company's portfolio that fails to validate because it was written a while ago. The best way to see if they are keeping themselves up-to-date is to check the latest addition to their portfolio.

3: Content Management Systems

You will definitely want a Content Management System (CMS) for your website. This is a piece of software, written by your web designers, that gives you control over the content of your site. It also gives you the ability to add, delete and modify pages, products and services and much more.[4]

The web design company should be offering you a CMS, so book some time for them to demo it to you. A CMS is a vital element of your website as it defines what you can change, so it's important that you get one that's easy to use and flexibly meets your needs. CMSs are a little like cars: they all do broadly the same things but have a wide variety of features and functions. In the end you'll get a sense of which is best suited to you by reviewing them individually.

A couple of things to remember here: Get a list of the functionality of each CMS (what it can do) so you can compare them, prioritise the list ('need' versus 'nice to have'), assess any cost differences, ask how customisable the CMS is.

Some web design houses use off-the-shelf CMSs to help them build websites. However, any such solution will have limitations. It is worth taking a look at the designer's portfolio to see if they suffer from all looking and functioning in the same way. In the end, let the demo be your guide to the system's suitability to your needs.

[3] If you'd like to learn more about accessibility, check out www.w3.org/WAI and www.rnib.org.uk/professionals/webaccessibility/designbuild/Pages/design_build.aspx.

[4] In case you're still awake, here's a little technical background for you. CMSs are written in many different languages, but PHP is, arguably, the most widely supported in the marketplace at the moment, largely because it is open-source software (i.e., no licence costs for using it). This has given rise to a sizeable community of developers meaning that if you opt for a PHP solution you will always be able to find someone to support your website. There are various 'flavours' of PHP so it is well worth asking exactly what type would be used (for example, 'CakePHP' or 'Ruby on Rails').

4: Who Owns the End Result?

Some web design companies are very protective of the code they use because they regard it as their intellectual property. Consequently, you can get into difficulties if you don't own the code that runs your website and you want to change suppliers. This is a point on which you need to be absolutely clear and, ideally, it should be mapped out in a contract.

The most amicable arrangement is for you to own the code but to let the web design company own the rights to use the code on other developments that may benefit their customers (especially, when you think that your website's time and costs may have been halved because the web design company has used code from other projects).

If your supplier does decide to give you the code, they may stipulate a couple of caveats – for example, that you don't resell the code or use it to support a completely different website.

5: What Are the Post-Project On-Costs?

Once your project is live you may need to pay some ongoing monthly costs. For example, some companies charge a monthly fee for using their CMS. Some charge for using online merchant services (only relevant if you're running an ecommerce store). Some charge a retainer. Some charge for hosting your website. You may also want to ask what the company's charges are for maintenance/updates to your site as well as any other services they provide, such as search engine optimisation.

Ask them the question and make sure you get them to write down an itemised list for you.

▮ GETTING TO KNOW THEIR BUSINESS SENSE

Here's the part where I'm going to introduce a more subjective but vitally important criterion for web design selection – your web designer's business sense. Remember, building a website is really about putting your business online.

Just imagine moving your business into another market like Europe. I bet you can think of at least 100 major factors you would have to think about to make it a success. And I also bet that you would seek out the best business advice you could afford to help you do it.

Here's the thing: moving your business online *is* moving it into another marketplace. This means that you may expect a level of advice and consultancy from your web designers, especially given their familiarity with the online marketplace. It's a common mistake most businesses make – assuming that because web designers build websites that they also have the knowledge about how to make them successful. Now there is no reason why you should expect that from them. After all, you would hardly expect someone building you an extension to your house to be an expert interior decorator. However, increasing numbers of web designers are recognising that they need to do more than simply build a website in order to support their customers: they need to deliver a level of 'business thinking' to the project.

Most web design companies won't automatically demonstrate this knowledge to you. The reason is that most customers are only interested in the design of their website and end up losing sight of their real business goals. This means that most web design companies emphasise design rather than business thinking. And that means that you have to do a little bit of delving to find out if they have this skill-set.

The way to kick-start this is to start asking some questions and gauge the quality of their responses. If you really want to see how committed they are, rather than doing this over the phone, get them to write it down.

Some of the questions you might want to ask are:

1. What can I do that would add value to the visitor experience?
2. What efficiencies could I gain through Internet technology?
3. What should I do differently from my current competitors' websites?
4. How can I link the website in with my existing offline business?

There are lots more questions you could ask and many of them relate specifically to your business. But what this exercise gives you is a sense of whether they would be able to provide you with a higher level of thinking than just design and technology. What it also does is help you work out whether they can bridge the gap between your business needs and the technological solutions that are out there on the Internet. The ability to see a business problem and find a technological solution is important. However, the temptation is to only ever look to technology for solutions instead of thinking in a more business-savvy way.

For example, adding a facility for users to leave comments, star rating systems, 'people who bought this also bought that' features to ecommerce sites can be tempting because many of the really successful sites use these ideas. However, if you're planning to have an ecommerce website it doesn't automatically follow that you need all of these bells and whistles or that adding them will earn you any extra money. Very often a simple, focused buying process yields the greatest return.[5]

Before you start investing your time in having all these in-depth discussions, you will probably want to narrow down the field of web design companies that you approach. So, how can you tell that they are going to give you top-line business thinking? Well, the obvious place to look is on their website. A simple thing to look for is if they offer any free help and advice. What this begins to demonstrate is their knowledge and also how prepared they are to help out upfront. Take a critical look at that information and ask yourself whether it is genuinely trying to help you or whether it is simply promotional. The free advice can come in the form of articles or free consultancy time or even podcasts and video.

You might find that they are really proactive and they have their own web design blog. You may even want to ask them if they are active on any web design forums. How they do it doesn't matter; it's the quality of the information that counts.

In the end you're looking for a business partner more than a supplier. Ideally, your web design partner should understand your business and should come up with business-focused thinking to help make your site a success.

LOCATION, LOCATION, LOCATION (OR, DOES GEOGRAPHY REALLY MATTER?)

Web design companies are ubiquitous the world over but what difference does it make if you choose someone down the road or on a different continent? Let's look at some of the key pros and cons surrounding your options.

[5] In the very early days of www.play.com that's all they did. They focused on making buying a DVD so easy and uncluttered it was a 10-second job. And they built a hugely successful multi-million-pound business based on that one principle plus free delivery. If you start to get this kind of response from your web design company then you know that they understand your website in a wider business context.

Local

By local I mean that you and your web designers can meet within an hour's travel.

Up-side...

Choosing a company on your doorstep means you get to see their setup and put faces to names. Plus you can meet with them on a regular basis (steering meetings, dealing with problems, etc.) and there's no doubt that being able to meet the team who will transform your online vision into an online reality can make you feel much more comfortable about your choice.

You might find that a local company already has a good reputation in the area by looking for past press coverage or if they are members of the Chamber of Commerce, Rotary Club, a breakfast business club, etc. Anything that helps you get a sense that they are part of a wider business community which is prepared to refer them has an obvious advantage.

Plus, they may have local knowledge of the area which might be of special value to you.

Down-side...

A big factor which may influence your choice is their price. If you live in a city, expect to pay more than in a town and if you're in the capital city, expect to pay more than everybody! So, if you think you're in a high-priced area, it may be worth casting your net further afield. (I am assuming that you will be comparing similar companies.)

However, the major disadvantage of only focusing on local web design companies is that there may not be enough choice at the quality you need. And this brings us on to...

National

Up-side...

Widening your search to national level gives you far greater choice. More choice means a higher likelihood of specialism and that means a higher probability your specific needs will be met.

First off, most companies will be prepared to meet with you (and the bigger your project the further they will travel to secure it). However, the longer the commute, the fewer face-to-face meetings you will be able to have. And this is where the whole subject descends into personal choice.

Operating at distance from your web designers means that you'll be managing the project remotely. However, it's much easier than it sounds and there are plenty of tools available on the Internet that allow for excellent levels of collaboration. (I'll show you these in the next chapter.)

The bottom-line is if you have confidence in them then their distance from you probably won't cause a problem.

Down-side...

For some, remotely project-managing their web development pushes too many panic buttons. If you are a more 'hands-on' type of person and find value in regular meetings then this may not be the solution for you.

Another disadvantage of national-level companies (and this applies to choosing an international partner too) is that local knowledge may be essential. For example, if you are running a hotel in the middle of Inverness it is unlikely that a web design company in London would have a better sense of representing your business online than one in Inverness itself.

You may also find that they may need to factor in travel, which will increase the project cost to you.

International

Up-side...

Perhaps the biggest motivator for locating your project offshore is price. With the American exchange rate always favouring the pound and with the Indian market between £8 and £12 per hour, these cost savings are hard to ignore. To make it more appealing, you will often find that offshore workers are just as clued-up and as=motivated as those in your country. In addition, if you are entering a particular overseas market, you may find that an 'in country' company has a better understanding of your prospective market.

If you are really serious about sourcing offshore for your project, you may also want to consider Russia and the Eastern Bloc countries, which are fast developing their technology skills.

Down-side...

Time zones can make management a little more tricky, and you can easily lose a day if you're not careful. So, if you're working in the States but your web designers are in the UK, you could be a full working day out of alignment with each other.

Plus, it would be ludicrous not to acknowledge the fact that there are cultural differences between your home country and everywhere else. Indeed you may find that the cultural nuances of an overseas market cloud communication and water down your project's impact. For example, if your website was selling something uniquely British, say tours around Buckingham Palace for example, you would hardly expect somebody in Delhi or Texas to be able to represent it as well as someone in the UK.

Another complication is payment. There are the usual methods, such as PayPal or SWIFT transfers (speak to your bank about this one), or you can use an escrow service. This is where you deposit money with a third party who only releases it when the job is complete. It tells the web designers you're good for the money but stops them from disappearing without producing the goods. While this can be a secure solution for all parties, it is also a chargeable service, so do factor that into your budget.

Local, national or international – no one choice is better than the other. It is entirely down to your personal preference and business context, but hopefully, by reading this through, you come to favour one over the rest.

WORKING WITH FREELANCERS: THE LOW-COST SOLUTION

I know that for many, spending money on web design is a daunting prospect. So if investing thousands simply isn't an option for you, here's a less expensive alternative to consider: outsource your project to freelancers (sub-contractors).

Freelancers are ideal if you need an uncomplicated or small website, the project doesn't demand a deep skill-set, and can be completed by one person. It's also a better solution if you are a private individual or a start-up business for whom spending several thousand pounds isn't an option.

Firstly, you should use all the information I've given you up to now in choosing your freelancer.

Your Ideal Match

The freelance web design and development market has matured, so you can easily source good people who have been at this game for some time, fit in with your personality, your business style or even your ethical beliefs. Finding someone who dovetails with your thinking can be the difference between someone 'getting' what you want and 'guessing' what you want.

It's also easier to identify people with offbeat skills because they will tend to mention them in their resume. For example, you may want someone to develop your website who speaks another language or has a background in your business specialism.

Your project splits in two: design and development. Most free-lancers typically have both abilities but you'll find they'll 'major' in one. Just remember that it's okay having a beautiful looking website but not at the expense of it working properly. Similarly, a functional but horrid-looking website isn't going to win your visitor over either. You're aiming for a balance, so check that their work demonstrates abilities in both areas.

If you find someone you really like but their designs aren't so hot, consider buying a pre-designed web template for them to work on (check out www.templatemonster.com and www.design-load.net). The downside, though, is your website may look like someone else's who also bought the same template. (You can, in some instances, buy the template outright.)

When reviewing some freelancers' work you will occasionally find that they only worked on portions of a website. That's no good to you because you want someone who can develop *complete* websites.

Most freelancers work from home, have a small core client-base, are self-motivated and will often work late for you – no commute to worry about! But one of the most attractive aspects about freelancers is their hourly charge, which is often between £20 and £40 per hour (UK rates). However, do make sure you establish a fixed cost upfront. Paying by the hour can quickly cause project costs to spiral. You also want a clear breakdown of what you are going to get for that before you commence the project.

But, life is never perfect and web design is no exception. Here are some factors to consider.

Safety in Numbers

Employing one person to perform your project has a number of inherent problems.

Firstly, your project will get shelved if they become ill, go on holiday, take compassionate leave, etc. And if they take on too many commitments you may find your project's deadlines get pushed back.

Signs of problems include missed deadlines, sudden loss of communication and explanations that can't be backed up with evidence. Plus, you can't expect them to be a jack of all trades and a master of everything. They can only offer you what's within their capabilities. (That's where employing businesses win out because they have a wider skill-set.)

There's always a risk that they disappear (like they get a full-time job) after your project is complete, leaving you without any backup. Just make sure that they have been freelancing for at least 12 months (and that they will write your site in a language that other freelancers can work with if it all goes pear-shaped!).

It's extremely rare to find someone who has amazing abilities in every area of web design/development. So, look to plug any obvious deficiencies with another freelancer's skills. (Just remember that adding more freelancers into your project means that you'll become the project manager and shoulder all the responsibilities.)

Only The Good...

Good freelancers get booked up quickly so you may have to wait to get your project underway. The same also applies for any future updates to the site. The trick is to plan when you're going to need support and build that into the freelancer's timetable. (Note they may ask for a retainer if they are to guarantee you their availability.)

Most businesses have training programmes for their employees. However, freelancers have to fund this themselves, which means you will need to check how they keep themselves up to date. For example, what are their qualifications, what's their recent experience, have they been on any training recently? Try to get a sense of whether they're still actively learning.

10-Second Summary

Here are the headlines that define a good freelancer:

1. They get back to you quickly and stay in touch (good communication is vital to your project's success – if they fail at this hurdle you'll have continuous problems).
2. They understand you and your project.
3. They have a good cross-section of clients.
4. Their own website is well constructed and interesting.
5. They're actively learning and developing their skills.
6. You like them and their work!

Where To Find A Freelancer

Here are four approaches to locating good freelancers:

1. www.odesk.com. A freelancer database plus a system that takes screen captures of the freelancer's computer to show they're working on your project!
2. www.freelancers.net. It's free to post a job and it has a good cross-section of skilled people.
3. www.elance.com. One of the biggest freelance sites out there.
4. Google 'web design freelance [your nearest town]'.
5. Another, perhaps safer, route is to be referred to a freelancer by another business. It may be well worth sending an email to your suppliers, clients, friends, etc. asking if they can recommend someone.

10 Steps to the Perfect Job Posting

If you decide to post a listing to a freelancer site, here's what you should put in your job advert:

1. Your name/company name
2. Your email/contact details
3. Describe the project (be detailed and make it sound interesting!)
4. Is this a one-off or on-going project?
5. Explain how they will fit into your business (long-term, as an addition to an existing team, etc.)
6. Describe any special requirements you have
7. Your existing web address or sites similar to yours
8. Deadlines (start and end dates) and milestones

9. Payment structure (e.g. 25 per cent upfront, 50 per cent on delivery, 25 per cent on completion)
10. Preferred source country of freelancer (if you want to limit your responses)

■ *HOW MUCH SHOULD YOUR WEBSITE COST?*

Okay, we've got to the big question which every web owner wants answered, fast!

The great advantage of having your website built for you is that you can get it to do anything you want. Unfortunately, this is also a bit of a drawback when it comes to working out the likely costs.

Let's imagine that you go to your local builders and you say, 'Build me a house.' And that's all you say. Now your builder hasn't got a clue whether you want a two-up, two-down semi-detached, or a 10-bedroom mansion. The difference in cost would be huge, but they're both still houses.

The same situation applies to your website: the more technology and functionality you add into your website, the more it will cost. The more time you spend creating a design, the more your website is going to cost. The more marketing approaches you build to support the website – you've guessed it – the more the website is going to cost.

This means there are no hard and fast rules about how much you should spend on your website. You could spend a few thousand or you could spend £20,000 or more.

Ok, not very helpful in answering the question directly but stick with me, we're getting there.

You see, the question is not how much you want to spend on your website but how much you want to get back. I think you would agree that your website isn't a status symbol – it's a piece of marketing technology and that technology has to earn its keep. There's absolutely no point in having a website unless it is going to earn you money. So spending £10,000 on a website which earns you £100,000 in return is a good investment but spending £10,000 on a website which earns you £5,000 is not. Your focus for identifying how much you are prepared to invest in your website should be based on what you think its returns should be.

Now, no matter what type of website you are building, there are certain core features that you will need. Obviously, you want your website to look unique to your business, which means a designer is going to have to spend some time coming up with a look and feel of the website which properly represents you.

Next you will need a content management system that is flexible enough to deal with all your needs, for example with the ability to upload video, audio, switch between different design styles, email marketing features and so on. You may not want all of these things right now but because they're built into the system, you have the flexibility to use them as soon as you need to.

The design and development of your website is a fairly intense process and in my experience it tends to take anything between 60 and 100 hours to complete, depending on the complexity of what is asked. And that's the crucial bit – the time it takes to complete the project. And that's the question you've got to ask your web designers when you get their quote: How many hours will my website take to complete? Then you can divide the total number of hours on the project by their total price and work out their hourly rate.

The importance of the hourly rate is that it gives you some idea of the quality of service and expertise you can expect.

Now I realise this is a controversial point and not everyone will agree with me but I'm sure you found that, with most things in life, you get what you pay for. I would say that that is true about 90 per cent of the time. And it tends to hold true when you buy services as well as products.

So it could be that what you want to achieve doesn't require an expensive solution, in which case a company with a cheap hourly rate makes sense. However, if you need a more complex solution then a company with a higher hourly rate will probably serve you better.

Here are my guidelines for you:

Low Web Design Cost: £20–£40 per hour

These are freelance rates so expect only one person to be working on your project. There are the obvious risks of only having one resource (holidays, going sick, etc.) but you can get extremely skilful, dedicated (and cheap) people to build your site.

Mid-Range Web Design Cost: £40–£65 per hour

These will typically be smaller businesses (business incubator units, partnerships, etc.). They have more resources available so all your eggs aren't in one basket. This also means they will probably have more expertise than one person can offer. Plus, these businesses tend to have more safeguards, such as backup procedures and version-control systems.

Upper-Range Web Design Cost: £65–£125 per hour

These are larger businesses often dealing with more marketing-driven websites or bigger businesses. They have the advantage of more resources (so, theoretically more expertise), which means they should deliver more technically challenging solutions. Plus expect a dedicated project manager and a whole heap of online marketing skills (Google AdWords, SEO, etc.).

Top-Price: £125+ per hour

Frankly expect perfection and tickets to Elvis's comeback tour.

WRITING A BRIEF

Once you reach the point where you've got six to eight or so web design companies[6] you want to get quotes from, send them a brief outlining the project. Going through this process will also help you when it comes to specifying the detail of your website as some of the donkey work will already have been done.

6 I know one company that got quotes from 30 web designers and met with 15 of them. This company was either very bored or very pedantic or very indecisive!

You can find a checklist of items to include in your brief in Appendix I (page 335).

THE STRATEGY

It's possible that at this point in the project you don't need a web designer, you need some advice. You might see this most obviously if you find that the proposals you're getting back are unclear, off-the-mark, have wildly varying project costs, etc. These are all symptoms that the brief may not be clear enough.

Remember that, for the most part, web designers are 'doers', not online business gurus – that's your job, not theirs. However, when it's your business it's sometimes hard to see the wood for the trees. In these situations it's best to get some outside help to specifically design the online business – a professional consultant, if you will. An external agency can help you develop the business strategy, focus your thinking and give you a sense of priority and purpose.

All this may seem costly but, believe me, setting your project off in the right direction can be well worth the cost of the advice in the long run.

Now you need to take a deep breath because, as you will see in the next chapter, your website needs you more than it needs web designers!

CHAPTER 3

Plan and Build Your Website

INTRODUCTION

In this chapter I'm going to take you through the step-by-step process of building your website. By the end of the chapter you should feel in complete command of your project and be able to anticipate any questions and problems. This is your definitive guide to building your website!

Let's start with two key factors you'll want to note:

1. The devil is in the detail. Things go wrong when everyone fails to pick up/bother with the details of the project. Any failure at this level will have an enormous impact on:
2. Time scales. Time scales get shot to pieces more often because of a lack of attention to detail, clear specification and assumptions than anything else.

Hold these two thoughts in mind as you progress through each stage of the web project.

LEGAL NASTIES

So you've engaged your web designers. You've shaken hands, given them the good news and everyone is now very excited about the next steps. But stop, don't do anything yet. Unless your mum is doing your website, you need to get some legal protection in place. (In fact, do so even if it's your mum!)

We all like to believe that we're governed by some greater 'business ethics law' and everyone's going to be jolly nice to one another, but the harsh reality of business life is that legalities are a necessary evil. The truth is that everyone (you, the web designers, any third-party relationships, your mum) need to have a contract. It should stipulate everyone's expectations – what's to be delivered, when your web designers expect to be paid, what happens if it all goes wrong, and so forth.

You may also want your web designers to sign a Non-Disclosure Agreement. This document stops them from discussing any sensitive information about your company with anyone else. This can be useful if you are launching a new product, have stock market gag clauses, or have competitors who watch your every move.

No one wants to resort to legal measures but it makes everyone feel much more comfortable if agreements are in place. It's a pretty normal part of business life, so don't worry about asking your web designers to sign one.

▨ PLANNING AND TIME SCALES

You may or may not need to create a detailed project plan. My experience of them is that the more detailed they are, the more time you spend messing with them so they mirror reality. I favour simple plans with milestones. I've already discussed the importance of deadlines so I won't reiterate the point except to say that make sure you have them in place, even if they are approximate.

Your plan should include the major headings in this chapter but if you want to get specific, take a look at my sample to-do list in Appendix II, page 339.

And now a word about the arch-enemy: time scales. There are a few things you need to know about being a web design customer that will help keep your project on track.

Firstly, time scales are elastic. Creating a design you'll love is a creative process and as such, difficult to pin to an exact deadline. If it takes a day to develop a design but you hate it, your designer is back to the drawing board and your deadline has slipped by a day. Give yourself and your designers enough time to go backwards and forward a few times until you're satisfied with the design.

Developing your Content Management System (CMS) is also a creative discipline and one in which deadlines can be difficult to predict. This is partly because technology is constantly evolving so 'knowledge' is a moving target, and partly because problem-solving (a key factor in writing software) has two curious facets:

1. You won't necessarily be able to anticipate problems
2. You won't know the solution to a problem until it's fixed

Therefore, you can't estimate the time it takes to complete something you don't know exists yet and can't define the solution to.

So when you, as a customer, ask how long it will take to build the site (a very reasonable question, by the way), the answer needs to include some project drift. Now your web designers may not give you the date you want to hear, but I recommend setting actual launch dates at least 25–33 per cent ahead of the date you all agreed to.

Secondly, you need to give yourself some thinking space, especially at the beginning of the project, where your input will be required most.

Thirdly, don't underestimate the amount of time you'll need to enter content, identify bugs, get them fixed and put the site live.

Fourthly, your project won't be the only one your web designers are working on. They too have to plan their resources, so don't expect them to be able to 'drop on' your project if you've been late with your own deadlines – they will invariably have allocated the time to someone else and you could end up losing your time-slot with them.

I'm all for getting things done quickly but there is a balance between speed and haste which every project must find.

THE SPECIFICATION PHASE

Contracts signed? Good. The next step is to begin the specification process. This is the part of the show when you decide what information you need to put on your website and how it's going to work, beginning with its structure.

Structure

Your site will have a structure to it and develops from your home page. Under your home page sit all the subsequent pages which make up your site. Think of it as an upside-down tree. You have the trunk (home page), then main branches (sections), smaller branches (sub-sections) and eventually leaves of content (pages).

Lay out your website's structure in the simplest, most obvious way possible. For example:

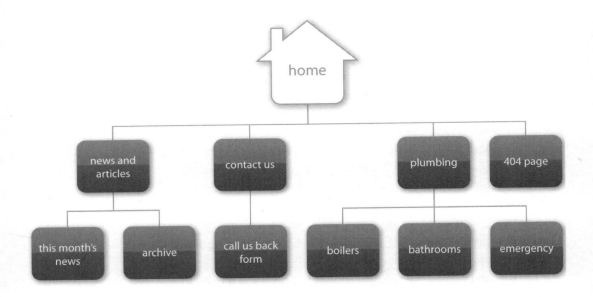

Fig 1 An example of website structure showing the hierarchy of webpages

If you're looking for a good tool to create these kinds of organisation charts then take a look at this free tool: www.slickplan.com.

Map out your structure in this way and bear in mind the following:

1. These page names will eventually become the clickable menu items on your web site so keep their names brief. The longer they are the more space your navigation will take up on the screen.

2. Remember that your visitor won't have a clue about your corporate hierarchy nor will they care, so don't let that define your structure.

3. They also won't have a clue about your product names so unless they're obvious, don't expect people to understand the difference between the PG357/8 and the PG357/9. Make sure that the descriptions mean something to a visitor who's never visited your site before.

4. Try to use keywords in the titles which are searched for on search engines. This gives you a little more 'juice' when it comes to your search engine ranking.

5. Avoid having a deep and complex site with many levels. Research indicates that visitors like to be

within three clicks of the information they are searching for. If there is no way round it, keep the structure as logical as possible so the visitor can easily navigate to the target page.

6. Don't worry too much if you don't get it finalised as your CMS should give you the ability to add/edit/delete pages and entire sections/branches of your structure. (Although getting this as close as possible will make the future processes go more smoothly.)

7. This is a minor point but a nice touch: If a user visits a part of your website for which there is no page, they will see what is called a '404 Error.' This indicates that the URL[1] which has been clicked on points to a page that doesn't exist. However, such a page can be confusing for the end user. What it offers, in fact, is a nice marketing opportunity. Try doing something with this otherwise unwelcome page. Here is an interesting article on how to make best use of it: www.smashingmagazine.com/2007/08/17/404-error-pages-reloaded. (See Hosting, page 79, for further information.)

[1] URL stands for Uniform Resource Locator, and more commonly means a web address, e.g. www.google.co.uk

Wireframing

The purpose of a wireframe is to give you something akin to the architectural drawings of your website.

Imagine you are building a house but you decide to do it without any blueprints. Now you may think you have a really clear idea of how it will look but the reality is always more complex: If you build the bathroom but forget to add in the shower you'd need to rip out what's there, re-jig the layout and re-plumb everything, costing you a lot of time and money.

Of course, very few of us are likely to build a house without detailed drawings but the same principle applies to your website. If you begin to build it without the blueprints then you run the risk that your web designers are going to charge you for unexpected changes. Having a wireframe negates all this because all the thinking is mapped out on screen before anyone actually builds anything. So, if you have a 2 a.m. moment of genius, as long as you are still in the wireframe stage it shouldn't cost you any more money to implement.

Fig 2 Sample wireframe

1. Searches database according to predefined category blocks

2. All product defined by shop database which updates automatically

3. Top three branded products by store sales

What you will notice about the wireframe is that it doesn't actually contain any real data or content. It is essentially a set of boxes which describe functionality – how the website is to work. Technically it doesn't even indicate the layout of the page although it is almost impossible for anyone to look at a wireframe without thinking that that is how the final page will be visually organised. However, try not to view it as a fixed layout because when the designers get hold of it they may change it to a more visually appealing and appropriate layout.

Wireframes should also describe what parts of the website you can modify using the CMS and what parts are fixed. For example, you will typically find that the header and footer are not editable but the main body content areas are. Make sure you mark-up which is which on the wireframe.

Let your web designers take a lead on the wireframe. They will already have experience in developing them and will probably have a template which is appropriate for your type of website.

Don't, however, leave it entirely to them to build, otherwise you will end up with the website they think is right for you and not the one you actually want! So here are a few ways in which you can contribute to the process.

Ideas (and Borrowing Them)

Your competitors are there for a reason: so you can adapt their ideas to use against them! There is no doubt that their websites will provide a rich source of ideas for you to consider (just as your new website will be a very attractive resource for them). Review your main competitors but also look on Google for those who are ranked highly for the keywords you would like to be searched against.[2]

Do be careful not to replicate their look and feel and certainly never be tempted to steal their content! You're looking for best practice (accessibility, usability, etc.), good ideas (innovative content presentation, etc.) and great marketing approaches (newsletter sign-up, etc.).

Also take a look at non-competitor websites which you like or which you think market themselves well to you. Review the methodology that they have used and integrate it into your wireframe.

And finally, remember your web brief – dig it out, along with the web designer's proposal. Now list all the ideas and approaches that you feel are worth doing (for launch with the new site) and add them into the wireframe.

[2] Don't forget that not every listing in the search results on Google will be a competitor. They could also be: directory listings, blogs, review sites, forums, pure information sites and so forth. However, they all will have some relevance in helping you generate ideas.

Clarity is Next to Godliness

Part of the wireframe's job is to convey your vision for your website to your web designers. The problem with vision is that it can be a nebulous thing and the web *developers* (the people who will actually build your website) tend to view wireframes in a very literal way. So, if you make any assumptions about how you expect certain parts of your website to work, you can't expect your web developers to interpret those assumptions in the way in which you want them to. The only way around this is to assume nothing and describe everything. Let's take an example.

Imagine you are running an ecommerce store. No doubt you'll have a page which lists products by category, which seems like a straightforward request. However, there comes a point where the web developer will need to know how the products are to be ordered on the page.

For example, they could be ordered alphabetically, by price (highest–lowest, lowest–highest), by attribute (colour, weight, etc.), popularity and so forth. Unless you specify it, the developer will probably take the default approach for them which would be displaying the products in the order in which they are entered into the database. As you can imagine, changing the approach after the system has been built may incur additional cost. This is just a small instance of where something seemingly obvious still requires a detailed level of thinking.

Sometimes, however, it is not obvious what you need to specify. My advice here is to do three things:

1. Think deeply about each page and ask yourself the basic questions of Who (is it for), What (do you want them to do), How (are they going to do it), When (do you want them to act), and Why (they should bother).
2. Take the wireframe to friends, colleagues, customers and get their thoughts.
3. Go back to the web designers and get them to ask you any technical details which they may need to know. (It's best to make sure that you also speak to one of the web developers – i.e. programmers – to get their input.)

If this all sounds like quite a lot of work, you're right, it is. But I promise that by doing it upfront you remove the likelihood of costly change requests down the line.

To help you get a sense of what you need to ask yourself so you can get the best out of the specification phase, take a look at Appendix III (page 339), where I've listed some of the more common questions.

Structuring Your Wireframe

Your wireframe doesn't need to represent every page on your website. It only needs to show those pages which are different from others. These are called templates. So, as you can imagine, your wireframe will only contain the pages which have functional or content differences between them.

For example, you can easily imagine that your services page will have one layout into which all your services will fit. Equally, your products page might contain exactly the same functions for all of your products ('Buy Now' button, related products list, etc.). Your About Us and Privacy page might also share a template layout as they are typically just plain text pages. As you go through your site structure you will naturally see that certain pages group together and can be expressed through one common template. Let's mark them up on our fictitious structure:

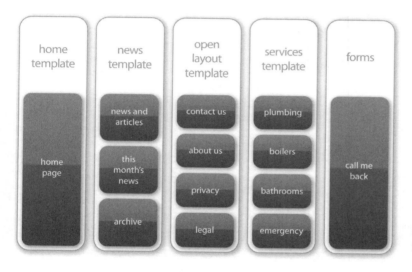

Fig 3 Common templates for your webpages

We've now reorganised our hierarchy into a table where different templates list the pages which are common to them.

In other words, we are saying that all the Services (plumbing, boilers, etc.) will share the same layout and functionality, and all the News pages will share a common template, and so forth.

This now tells you how many individual wireframe templates you need to create. There would be little point wireframing all your products if they all share a common template.

As you can see from Fig 4 we have a Home Page Template. Obviously, the home page almost always has its own template because it is unique on your site.

The template in Fig 5 shows the wireframe for the key service pages. These are the top level sections.

Fig 4 A home page wireframe

Remember that once you sign off your wireframe you are effectively saying, 'This is what I am putting on my website and this is how it works.' Any changes you make after this point could incur charges from your web designers. However, most web designers will account for some minor flexibility because when the designers get their hands on it, new things inevitably get added!

Tools for Wireframing

If you want to build a wireframe yourself there are some terrific online tools available to you:

- Protoshare (www.protoshare.com) – a great application if you want to build bigger sites which automatically 'glue' all the pages together. This means you can navigate around a

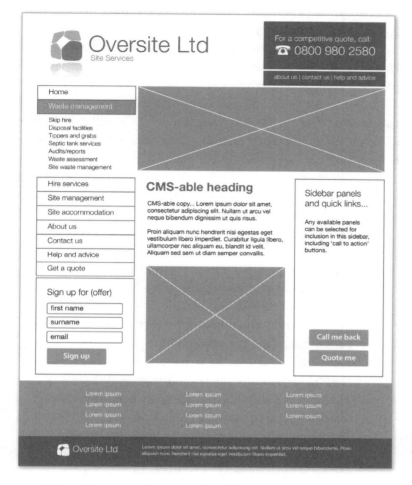

Fig 5 A services page wireframe

Protoshare wireframe as though it were a real website. Plus it's got some nice collaboration features.

- iPlotz (iplotz.com) and Balsamiq (www.balsamiq.com) – Good all-rounders that produce nice wireframes.

A Note About Accessibility

Making your site usable for people who have visual impairments or other disabilities is no longer a nicety of modern web design; it is a legal requirement.

Unfortunately, there are no clear rules defining what facilities you must provide in order for your website to be deemed accessible. However, a set of 'loose' standards has been drawn up by the World Wide Web Consortium (W3C) that helps your web designers define what accessibility tools your website provides.

The two primary standards you should be aiming for are either 'AA' or 'AAA' compliance.

Most commercial websites only need achieve AA compliance. However, if your website's demographics are likely to include people with disabilities then you should consider the AAA standard. For example, if you are an optician, best practice would suggest that you opt for the AAA standard. However, if you are a chemical manufacturer then the AA standard would probably be fine.

It seems that every web design company has different ways of approaching the standards so it's useful to ask your web designers if they cover the following:

1. Text size controls. You'll often see these text controls looking like this on the website: AAA.
2. A plain text version of the website. This is very useful for people who are using screen readers to read out the contents of your website.
3. A high visibility version of the website. This helps people who have impaired vision.
4. A dyslexia version of the website. Dyslexics find reading easier if the site is coloured a particular way.
5. The CMS has the ability to apply alt-tags. These are textual descriptions of the graphics in your website. Every time you add a graphic you should also add a description of it. This helps people who are using screen readers understand what the picture is conveying

If you'd like to understand more about this subject take a look at the following:

1. AA Compliance from W3C: www.w3.org/TR/WAI-WEBCONTENT.
2. Checklist of things to consider to make your content more accessible: www.w3.org/TR/WCAG10/full-checklist.html.
3. Advice from the Royal National Institute of Blind People: www.rnib.org.uk/professionals/webaccessibility/designbuild/Pages/design_build.aspx.

Lost in Translation

You may want your website to pitch to an international audience and so it would seem natural to have your website in different languages. A tempting solution is to use the instant translation tools available on the web but don't be beguiled by the beautiful simplicity of automatic translation systems. Having your website instantly translated by a machine into 30 different languages may sound too good to be true, because it is. No machine, no matter how sophisticated, can translate with total accuracy the subtlety of your message. Let's take a simple example…

I wrote in English this sentence 'I would like to keep chickens' and then I used Google Translate to convert it into various languages, returning to English each time.

Original English Text	*I would like to keep chickens*
Translated to French	*Je voudrais garder des poulets*
Translated back to English	*I would like to keep chickens*
Translated to German	*Ich möchte Hühner halten*
Translated back to English	*I would like to hold chickens*
Translated to Italian	*Vorrei tenere i polli*
Translated back to English	*I would want to hold the chickens*
Translated to Portuguese	*Eu quereria prender as galinhas*
Translated back to English	*I would want to arrest the hens*

So we start with 'I would like to keep chickens' and end up with 'I would want to arrest the hens.' As you can see, my original meaning has become something so completely removed from my original as to make no sense at all. The problem is I can't speak Portuguese and would have no idea what the resulting translated webpage said. Can you imagine how mangled your business message could get and what that would do to your visitor's perception of your company?

My advice is that if it's important enough for you to need your website in a different language then get a professional translation company to make sure that your message doesn't get lost in translation!

THE DESIGN PHASE

This is the cool bit, the bit everyone loves! It's the bit that turns your wireframe into a beautiful design.

When you see your wireframe blossom into a stunning design, all the hard work seems worthwhile. But before you get to enjoy the fruits of this though you've got to give your designers some direction.

The Design Brief

[3] In the past we have had clients who have been so specific they have said, 'I want it to look like Amazon's site.' Of course, simply ripping off another website's design is not a wise move especially as it removes any sense of your business's individuality in the process.

Designers love briefs and so it pays to get as much information to them as possible about your visual preferences before they produce any designs. I find a great way to begin this process is to simply list five sites that you love and five you hate.[3]

Fig 6a From wireframe...

Hand that over to the designers along with any other visual preferences you may have. I would also recommend that you make them re-read your original website brief as this will give them context for the design. Finally, I would set aside some time to talk directly with the web designer.

If you are a large organisation you may already have a style guide which specifies your corporate colours, positioning of your logo, font usage and so forth.

I've often seen design briefs which stipulate the impossible. For example, 'I want it to look cool, simple, exciting, creative, business-like and friendly.' It's almost impossible for any designer to produce something which is all these things simultaneously, especially as they can be mutually exclusive: friendly designs tend

Fig 6b ...to design!

not to be business-like, and exciting designs are rarely simple. Be careful not to create an unachievable design brief because you will inevitably end up disappointed.

Sample Content

To help your designer produce a better design you will need to provide them with some actual content. (These are the spaces in your wireframe denoted for content). This can be a tremendous help because it gives the designer the physical size of information, the written style for the website, how you intend to use headings, and so on.

You may also want to provide graphics and pictures, including your logo, your corporate font, your image library, etc.

Anything you can give them which gets the home page design closer to the finished article is going to enhance the design.

The Designs!

The home page is usually the first to get designed. It is also the most difficult to do because it sets the style and tone for the entire site.

Some web design agencies prefer gathering all the information and then producing one design, the theory being that if the brief is good enough then they should be able to get close to the bull's eye in one shot. Personally, I've never favoured that approach. I think the risk to you as a customer is that it funnels you in one direction.

An alternative approach is to request two different designs which conform to the brief but are polar opposites of each other. By polar opposites I mean that the designer has taken two totally different approaches but still maintained the integrity of the original brief. For example: multi-coloured versus monochrome, or funky versus conventional, or elaborate versus simple. So if you do have any design contradictions, they can be worked out across two designs. Typically, you will find that you like elements from both – half of which you wouldn't have known about if you'd only had one design.

The next phase is to synthesise a new design from the preferences of the first two. Once you have the third and final design (save a few tweaks here and there) you should be able to sign it off.

Here are a few pointers to help you through the process:

1. Don't panic if it's not right the first time – it's a process and can take a while for the designer to 'get' where you're coming from.

2. Be guided by your designer – they'll know how to create a design that works.

3. *But* if you hate it and it's just plain wrong, don't be afraid to say so.

4. Don't fall into the trap of wanting everything to catch your visitor's eye (headline, telephone number, text, graphics). The design should make your eye flow down the screen seeing things in an order which leads your visitor to an appropriate action.

5. Remember, less is more – don't succumb to the idea that you need everything on one page.

6. Don't keep 'trying things out' on the design. A good designer will probably have thought and tried a number of approaches before settling on the one they present to you.

7. Don't review the design according to what you like. It's how your target audience will react that's most important. Find some clients and ask for their opinions.

8. But don't get everyone and their dog to comment on the aesthetics. The old adage that a camel is a horse designed by a committee is very true. Everyone will have their own opinion and the more people you ask the more diluted the concept will become and the harder (and longer) the whole design process becomes.

And that last point leads us on to...

Design Study

Now that you've got some designs, you need to gather some feedback on them. Find a few colleagues, friends, or, better still, potential customers, show them the designs, and ask them:

1. What do we do?
2. Where's our contact information?
3. What stands out as most important?
4. What's clear?
5. What's unclear?

You can add to this list whatever is relevant to your business but the answers to these questions will be worth their weight in gold to you and certainly worth a beer for each of your participants!

Repeat this exercise between five and six times for all the pages you have designed. This usually captures about 80 per cent of the usability issues.

A great resource for getting instant feedback on your designs can be found at www.fivesecondtest.com. You upload your design, ask a question you want answered and random testers will give their feedback.

Finishing the Designs

If you find yourself wanting to make endless adjustments to the design then that signifies that something is fundamentally wrong – either with the designs or with you.[4] 'Fiddling' can really delay the project. There comes a point where you have to engage the 80/20 rule, as finding design perfection could increase the length of time it takes to complete the design phase by up to 80 per cent.

Once the home page design has been signed off then it is a relatively simple task to get the remaining pages designed in your chosen style.

Style Guides

A style guide is a very important component in the design phase and is often missed. It defines how all the visual elements appear on the screen including:

- Hyperlink colour (both before and after it is clicked)
- Heading styles. For example,

Heading 1 (Title)
Heading 2 (Subtitle)
Heading 3 (Sub-subtitle)
Body text

- Bulleted/numbered lists
- Spacings between elements on the page
- And so on…

Your designer will know what constituents make up a style guide. Make sure you see yours as part of the design sign-off process.

[4] Meant in the nicest possible way, of course!

Favicons

Here's a nice touch for your website. At the top of your web browser, where you type in website addresses, you'll sometimes see a little icon to the left. This is called a favicon and if you drag it to your desktop it will display the logo of the company. If you ask your designer, they'll create one for you which can be built into your website.

Fig 7 An example of Google's favicon

Post-Design Wireframe Jiggle

Experience shows that it is normal to find that the design phase flushes out any imperfections in the wireframe. So you might need to go back and modify the wireframe to bring it up to date with the design as there may now be functionality changes to consider.[5]

Remember that if you make changes to the wireframe it could have an impact on the overall project cost so do double check with your web designers to make sure the changes don't affect the budget.

5 This is because when the developers start to build the CMS they will initially look at the wireframes and not the design.

Licence Check

Inevitably, your designers will have used what are called 'stock' images. They are usually high-quality graphics (photographs, animations, movies, etc.) found on sites such as www.istock.com and www.shutterstock.com. It is vital that you hold a licence to use any of these images on your website.

Remember that such images are protected by copyright and anyone found in infringement is likely to face fairly aggressive demands and costs. Rather than becoming entangled in a legal battle, it's always simpler to have licence proof for your images.

I must stress that you, not your web designers, need to have the proof, as from a legal perspective *you* are ultimately responsible for the content (including graphics) of your website.

THE SITE BUILD

This is the part of the project where you get to sit back and relax while your web designers get on with the hard work of building your site. They now have:

1. The wireframe which tells them exactly how the site will be organised and how it will function
2. The designs which express how the site will look

The next step is putting the two together.

What actually happens here is rather complex, but here's a simple breakdown of what's going on behind the scenes.

Cutting the Designs to HTML

When you first see the design from the designers it will probably be in the form of a graphic, like a JPEG. However, it's just a picture and needs to be 'cut' into HTML in order for it to become a functioning webpage. That process begins with the designer handing over to the programmer a PSD[6] file. These are the 'source' or original files which contain all the design formatting, graphics, fonts, text and style guidelines.[7]

The PSD file is then carved up into individual elements and coded so that it behaves like a normal webpage (although it won't actually do much at this stage until the CMS has been added). Your programmer will then make sure that the webpage looks the same for different browsers (and different versions of the same browser).[8] This is known as browser compatibility and can take quite some time to get right. We'll talk more about this when we look at beta testing.

This is also the point where your accessibility (high visibility, dyslexia, no graphics, etc.) styles are created and browser tested.

Along with browser testing your programmer will ensure that the code conforms to the HTML standards set out by the World Wide Web Consortium.

Building the Content Management System

Now for the ultra-techy bit. At this point programmers usually geek out because this is where all the functionality defined in your specification gets turned into your CMS. In reality what they're probably doing is customising an existing 'engine.' The extent of the customisation is dependent on the nature and number of functionality requests you've made that aren't already covered by the basic engine. Unsurprisingly this, to a large degree, determines how long the coding element of the project will take.

At the end of this process you (in theory) should be able to enter content into your CMS. However, I don't recommend this for two reasons:

1. You won't be able to see your content appear on the front end of your website, making it quite difficult to judge whether you're entering anything sensible

[6] A PSD file is one generated by a product called Photoshop and is extremely popular with designers. There are other software which designers use, InDesign being one, but on the whole Photoshop is the industry standard.

[7] Here's a useful little online tool if you are trying to view PSD files: www.zamzar.com. This website will convert one file format into another. So if your web designers send you a PSD file you'll know where to go to turn it into a JPEG!

[8] The typical browsers most web design companies work to are Internet Explorer versions 7–9, Firefox 3–7, Opera 9–11 and Chrome 4–15.

2. Any changes to the system could affect (and possibly destroy) your content

Integrating the HTML with the CMS

Once the CMS is complete it needs to be integrated with the HTML. Think of this as linking the back end (the CMS) with the front end (the HTML). Essentially this involves attaching a database to the HTML, giving you the ability to add pages and content into the CMS and see them appear as a website.

■ TESTING

In theory, testing[9] should be extensive, thorough and iterative. In reality, it's often last-minute, scanty, and regularly leaves project managers crossing their fingers in hope. However, I can't overstate the importance of the process nor how not giving yourself enough time could lead to catastrophic (and public) failure.

> [9] A great article on testing can be found at en.wikipedia.org/wiki/Software_testing

I remember one project in which the deadlines were so tight that we were testing, training, bug fixing and changing the design simultaneously. Needless to say, it was a nightmare and the project ended up delayed because too many things were being done at once without any formality to the testing phase.

Ok, so what do I mean by formality? Well, firstly both you and your web designers will test the website independently of each other (alpha testing is done by the developers and beta testing is done by you). In both cases you will test every piece of functionality, making sure it is behaving itself.

I recommend that you devise a testing table (which you can share with your web designers). Here's one to start you off:

ID Date	Front-End / CMS	Bug / Interpretation of Spec / Change Request	Comments	Reference URL	Resolved
1/03	CMS	Bug	Can't rename a page	test.newwebsite.co.uk/admin	✓
2/03	F/E	Interpretation of Spec	Thought we'd suggested that News Items should be categorised?	test.newwebsite.co.uk/news	✗
3/03	F/E	Change Request	Can we add another news item to the summary on the home page?	test.newwebsite.co.uk/	✗

Alpha Testing

Usually web designers will test the website before you see it. This just makes sure they have ironed out any obvious omissions or bugs. Ideally this should be done by someone who has had nothing to do with the project, as a fresh pair of eyes often spots things that have been missed.

It might be useful for you to request a copy of their alpha test results just to cross-check any functionality you (or they) may have missed. Be prepared for them not to have extensive records listing every aspect of the system – they may have tested elements many times before. Although, if one is being pedantic, it should be tested again, the likelihood of something failing which has worked in ten other projects is probably quite remote. You may end up with just a list of elements that were tested but which differed from the standard or core CMS.

Browser Compatibility

There are many different browsers on the market today: Internet Explorer, Firefox, Opera, Chrome and Safari to name but a few. Each interprets HTML slightly differently, which results in your webpage looking slightly different in each one. To complicate matters further there are various versions of each of these browsers still out there in the market. Most web designers have a standard set of browsers that they will check your website in but you may, however, need your site to work in others, including iPhones, Blackberry and old versions of web browsers. (The need for any non-standard browser choices should have been picked up in the specification phase.)

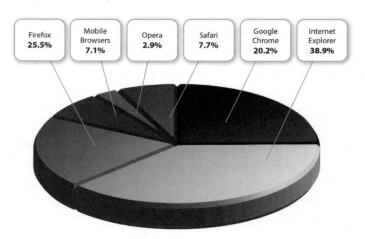

Firefox **25.5%**   Mobile Browsers **7.1%**   Opera **2.9%**   Safari **7.7%**   Google Chrome **20.2%**   Internet Explorer **38.9%**

Fig 8 Current browser market share

Beta Testing

Once the site has been alpha tested it's ready for you to get your hands on it. This will be in the form of a web address to the front-end and a separate one for the CMS (usually the same but ending in /admin or /logon, etc.). It is unlikely that it will be your actual domain name as it's more likely to be a link to your web designers' development server.

However, before you begin the process of testing you'll probably need some training on the system first. It's possible that there will already be documentation (especially if it's an off-the-peg system) but it is more typical to find that training is either face-to-face or over the phone. Whichever way it's done, get some training under your belt as it will accelerate your testing and content entering.

Here are a few of the things you might be checking for:
1. Can I add/edit/delete a page?
2. Can I reorder pages?
3. What happens to the front end if I put too much text in?
4. Do specific functions work (sorting data, wrapping pictures around text, etc.)?
5. Do the video controls work when I upload a movie?
6. Do the forms work and send their data to the right email address/external system?
7. And so on...

As you progress through your testing you'll find that your observations fall into three categories:
1. Bugs (failure of the system to work as intended)
    - Don't expect to pay for these.
2. Interpretation of specification (sometimes, no matter how clear you think you've been, someone interprets what you've said differently)
    - This can be a grey area with respect to charges. You'll probably need to clarify whether you're going to be charged before getting your web designers to make any changes – you may be relying on their goodwill.
3. Change request (even the best laid plans of mice and men can sometimes end up changing)

- If you're making a request outside the parameters of the specification, expect to pay more but do make sure you get a quote in writing first.

Use the table I provided above to enter your results and feedback to your web designers. However, don't dribble your test results to them, wait until you've done all the testing then feedback in one go. They will be able to get all the bugs/issues resolved much faster if it's done in one chunk rather than in dribs and drabs.

Remember that although you may have given yourself time to test, you also need to give your web designers time to fix any bugs.

■ ENTERING CONTENT

A Word of Caution

Firstly, what I've found to be quite prevalent is that customers miss the beta testing phase and start entering their content straightaway. While it is certainly fun to start immediately, I can't emphasise enough the value of beta testing first. Just entering content will not flush out all the issues and bugs and so you run the risk of discovering bugs or misinterpreted functionality long after the project is complete. This risk translates into you having to pay for any updates because they have happened after the site has gone live and, therefore, after you have signed it off.

Secondly, this can also be the point at which the project stops while you gather your content together and that's why I recommend you assign a Content Hero to help.

Content Heroes

The time to start writing the content for your website is the moment it is commissioned. However, what typically happens is that the web designers will deliver the spangly new website devoid of content. This sends their customer into a flat spin as they suddenly realise they've been so focused on how the website looks and what it will do that they haven't organised anything to go in it. At this point many simply take the content from their old website and copy it over – what a waste!

A content hero stops this from happening – it could be you, a colleague of yours, or even an entire department. They are tasked with the sole purpose of making sure that all the content for the site is written ahead of the delivery of the CMS. Content for your site includes:

1. Written text, for example
    a. Sales copy
    b. Product descriptions
    c. Reviews
    d. Resources
    e. News
    f. FAQs
    g. About Us
    h. Policies/Agreements
    i. Testimonials
    j. And so on...
2. Graphics
    a. Product shots from all angles
    b. Hero images (the big graphic across the top)
    c. Pictures that sit in the main text
    d. Icons
    e. Logos
    f. And so on...
3. Video
4. Audio
5. Emails sent out of the website (from someone filling in an enquiry form, for example)
6. Downloads (brochures, price lists, terms and conditions, etc.)

Your content hero needs to make sure that each part of the business is aware of what content it needs to supply. A simple way to organise this is to send around a form similar to the one below. When you get the forms back you enter content from them directly into the CMS. This means you will be focused on making sure the website is working properly and not whether the content is making sense!

If you're really struggling to get the content written consider employing a copywriter to help.

And don't underestimate how long this process will take. And don't forget that content isn't just the copy but also photos, audio, video, PDF documents, and so on.

Page Details	
Page Name	[Page Name]
Page Description	[Page Description]
Content	[Type in your page's content here.]
Graphics	[Type in the filename(s) of the graphic(s) for this page]
Forms	[List the fields for the form] [Put a * next to those which are mandatory] [Who gets the output of the form?] [Etc...]
Additional	
Functionality	[Add in anything that you need the page to do]
Other	

Fig 9 Sample form for consolidating content

Rules for Entering Content Into Your CMS

Along with figuring out how to use your new CMS, you've somehow got to make the content you're entering look good. Unfortunately, this isn't as simple as it sounds. With a little knowledge, however, and some basic rules, you can make your website look polished and professional.

Text

We all love Microsoft Word and its ilk. It gives us non-designers the opportunity to create lovely looking pages using a simple interface. However, when it comes to websites it has spoiled us as we tend to think our websites are going to have a similar level of design flexibility. That is not the case. Webpages are not at all like Word.

The reason why there isn't the same flexibility is because HTML (the programming language which produces a webpage has limitations to what it can do. When you come to enter content into your CMS (using a content editor[10]), you'll probably be surprised at what isn't possible. All the obvious functions (bold,

[10] If you want to take a look at some of the popular content editors used in today's CMSs check out TinyMCE (tinymce.moxiecode.com) and CKEditor (ckeditor.com). Other out-of-the-box CMSs like Wordpress use their own editor which are not dissimilar from the ones above.

italics, underline, etc.) will be there but not the fancy stuff (different numbering options, drop capitals, cross-referencing, etc.).

If your content editor won't do something you need it to, then ask your web designers to create the page for you as it may require an advanced level of HTML that the editor isn't capable of providing.

One final word of warning. *Do not* copy your content directly from Word into your CMS's content editor. When you do this, Word creates a whole heap of HTML code to try and retain the formatting of your text. Unfortunately, this code causes most CMSs to have a fit and often breaks the page entirely. Here's the drill if your content is in Word:

1. Copy the content into Notepad (or another similar text editor)
2. Paste the content from Notepad into your CMS's editor
3. Reformat the text using the tools in your CMS's editor

Graphics

At some point you will want to add graphics to your website. Most CMSs will let you do this. However, there are a few best practice options you'll need to be aware of in order to make good use of this feature:

1. *Do not* copy graphics from the web (see Licence Check, page 69).
2. Resize your graphics to fit the picture dimensions on your website. Image sizes are measured in pixels, not centimetres or inches. A pixel (or 'picture element') is a dot on the screen. Your website probably won't be much larger than 1024 x 768 pixels so the photos you upload will need to be 'sized' according to the space they are intended to occupy. Get a list of picture dimensions from your web designer and resize your graphics to fit. Remember that most cameras take photos at a resolution of more than 3,000 pixels. So there is no point uploading a file of that size into the CMS because it will be too large to display on the screen and take too long to load. Keeping your image size small also keeps the file size small, which means your webpages load faster.

3. Only use graphics that are 72 dpi. This is the standard number of 'dots per inch' on a monitor. If your graphic has a higher dpi it wouldn't be displayed. (Photos from your camera, print graphics and scanned images will often have a much higher dpi.) If you're not sure how to check or change the dpi, ask your web designers.

7. Remember also to maintain the image's aspect ratio: en.wikipedia.org/wiki/Aspect_ratio_(image).

USABILITY STUDY

With all the bugs and issues resolved you've reached the point where it's worth getting some feedback on the website from a small sample of people before you release it to the world at large.

All you need is to get a handful of people together, sit them in front of a computer and ask them a few questions:

1. Start with the questions you asked from the Design Study (page 67), and continue with...
2. Can you find our contact details?
3. What would you click on first?
4. Can you see where our products/services are?
5. What's the first thing you think of when you see this page?
6. Where do you want to click on this page?
7. And so on...

Get your user to talk out aloud what they're thinking and observing. You could even time how long it takes your subjects to complete certain tasks.

The information you get back can be extraordinary especially as you will suddenly discover a whole slew of obvious things you need to tidy up!

GOING LIVE

With all the testing complete you're now into the final phase of your project: getting it live on the World Wide Web. Just before you do, however, there are a few bits and pieces you need to make sure are covered.

Hosting

Hosting describes the technology used to get your website on the Internet. Hosting companies will play 'host' to your website, email addresses, domain names, FTP access and other accoutrements for your website.

The subject of hosting usually crops up towards the end of the project. Some web design companies will provide hosting, others will recommend hosting companies. Alternatively, you may already have a host with whom you are perfectly happy. However, not all hosting companies work to the same specifications and consequently it doesn't automatically follow that the website you had developed for you will work on any host. For example, if your website was written in PHP then it will only run on UNIX servers. If your website was written in ASP then it will only run on Microsoft servers.

There are other considerations also: how much disk space you will require (this could be an important factor if you are planning on hosting your own videos), how much bandwidth they will give you per month (if yours is a very popular site then you may need extra bandwidth to cope), and so forth. Below is a basic list of questions to ask your web developers and prospective hosting company (your web designers should be able to interpret any technical information which comes back from the hosting companies for you).

1. What operating system is required?
2. How much disk space will be needed (now and in the future)?
3. We have/expect to have X number of visitors per month.
    a. How much bandwidth will we need?
    b. How much RAM will the server require?
4. What redundancy/fail-safes are built into the server (RAID, if a hard drive fails; dual power supply, in case one blows up; etc.)
5. What is the backup policy?
    a. Are the backups taken off-site and/or stored in a disaster-proof location?

There are plenty of ultra-cheap hosting businesses out there but my experience is that cheap solutions don't always provide the full array of support: quality technical support, speedy issue resolution, hack-proof servers and sound backing-up procedures can rarely be achieved for a few pounds a month.

Choosing a host is something you should do in conjunction with your web designers as they will be able to judge the needs of your website from a technical perspective.

Search Engine Links and Domain Name Repointing

If you have an existing website the search engines will probably already know about it. They will also have referenced pages on your old site. The likelihood is that these URLs will no longer be the same on your new site. For example, www.jedscompany.co.uk/company-info may now have changed to www.jedscompany.co.uk/about-us. So, if someone were to click on the first link in Google (a reference from your old site) they would be redirected to your new site. However, while the page's content may exist, its location will be different and the new site will simply report that the page is missing (this is known as a 404 error, see page 45). Eventually the problem will resolve itself because the search engines will update themselves to reflect the URLs on your new website, but in the meantime anyone using a search engine to visit your site will probably end up on a page claiming that what they were looking for doesn't exist.

The easy way around this is to provide a list of all the webpages on your website and the corresponding URL of the new site. You'll end up with a table which looks something like this:

Old URL	New URL
www.jedscompany.co.uk/company-info	www.jedscompany.co.uk/about-us
www.jedscompany.co.uk/bronze-service	www.jedscompany.co.uk/services/bronze
www.jedscompany.co.uk/silver-service	www.jedscompany.co.uk/services/silver
Etc…	

Hand this list over to your web developers who will write a special script that points all the old URLs to their new destinations. Now, if anyone clicks on an old URL from a search engine link, the website will know where to redirect them.

If you have hundreds of pages on your website then this may be just too time-consuming to be practical. In that instance you can use wild cards. A wild card (usually denoted with a '*') simply implies that anything can replace it.

Old URL	New URL
www.jedscompany.co.uk/housesforsale/*	www.jedscompany.co.uk/selling-your-home
www.jedscompany.co.uk/housesforrent/*	www.jedscompany.co.uk/renting-a-home
Etc…	

In the example, pages with anything after /housesforsale/ in the URL will be redirected to the single page /selling-your-home.

It's even possible to have different domain names pointing to different parts of your new website. This can be particularly useful if you have a product or service name as your domain name. Here's an example:

Domain Name	Landing Page on New Website
www.fiesta.co.uk	www.ford.com/fiesta
www.mondeo.co.uk	www.ford.com/mondeo
www.focus.co.uk	www.ford.com/focus

Getting the New Site Live

Once you've sorted out the domain names and links the site is ready to go live. Don't forget that if you are using the same host as your previous website you should take a backup of your old website first. Once the new site has been uploaded take a backup of that too. You web designers can do this for you.

If you are hosting with a new company (or this is a new website) then you will need to repoint your domain names at the server where your website is hosted. Now this can get very complicated because any change to your domain name could also affect where your emails are sent to so it's best to seek advice from your web designers directly. They will be able to tell you what needs changing. Better still, if you can give them access to your domain name[11] then they can make the necessary modifications for you.

[11] The company that you bought your domain name from will have provided you with login details to administer the domain name. These are the details that you and your web designers will need.

If you are uploading a new site 'over' your old one then you won't have to mess with your domain names because your new site will simply appear. However, if you are pointing your domain names to a new web host then it will take up to two days for the Internet to catch up with this change and for everyone in the world to have access to your new site. In the interim, they will see the old site as long as you haven't removed it from your old hosting provider before you make the switch.

■ PROJECT MANAGEMENT

As you can see, developing a website is far from simple and this complexity leads to the need for project management.

Your web design company will be responsible for managing their side of your website's build but you are central to that process. Here are some tips to help that go smoothly:

1. Make sure you have a good project management tool. (If you don't have one check out BaseCamp www.basecamphq.com.[12])

2. If you need to get your team together over the Internet, a fantastic free white-boarding tool is Twiddla (www.twiddla.com).

3. State your expectations and deadlines upfront. (Don't assume your web designers will approach the project as you would.)

4. Be ultra-clear about what you want – always check that they understand your point before progressing.

5. Take the time to understand the process of how they intend to build your website.

6. Ask at what points during the development cycle they need your input.

7. Give your feedback quickly. (Remember any delay from your side could push the deadline back.)

8. If you request changes, don't assume they'll be absorbed into the project cost. Make sure you are aware of any extra costs before commencing the work. You don't want any shocks when the invoice arrives.

[12] I'm not one for endorsements but if you don't already have a project management system then this is the one to use. It's fantastic, 'addictively easy-to-use' and perfect for web projects.

9. Be decisive – how many times have you said 'I should have followed my instincts'? Listen to your intuition and make a decision. It's incredibly liberating, speeds up your response times and helps maintain the project's deadlines.

10. Introduce yourself to everyone working on your project.

11. Be available for consultation at any time.

12. Be willing to take advice.

13. Be patient – websites may look simple on the surface but complex technology lurks beneath and that takes time to develop.

14. One more thing… keep a little contingency money in reserve, just in case. (But don't tell anyone about it!)

THE STRATEGY

Building your site will be an intense time so clear your diary and periodically skim over Chapter 1 (Mindset) just to help you stay on track.

Plus, there are two chapters I'd like you to read next if you haven't already finished your website. The first is the next chapter, 'Discover the 7 Principles of Internet Marketing' and the second is Chapter 7, 'Turn Visitors into Customers.' Reading both these chapters will give you some additional fuel you can slot into your website before it's built. This will save you altering it too much later on.

CHAPTER

Discover the 7 Principles of Internet Marketing

▓ INTRODUCTION

Before we dive into the major topic areas for marketing and growing your website, we should take a moment to understand the foundation stones that will make your efforts all the more successful.

In this chapter we're going to discover the (rarely discussed) principles that will make you more effective than the competition and look at some of the common mistakes web owners make.

Think of these as guiding principles which apply at every level of your online marketing.

▓ PRINCIPLE 1: CUSTOMER PROFILING

Before we can begin marketing we really ought to find out whom we are marketing to! Now I appreciate that customer profiling is the kind of thing you find academic marketing books banging on about, and therefore may seem somewhat remote from day-to-day practice. However, it's worth doing, not because it's a marketing exercise but because of the impact it will have on how you write your website's content.

A while ago I did this exercise on the suggestion of online marketing guru, Frank Kern. I sat down and I imagined as hard as I could, summoning all my experience, my ideal customer. Here's what I came up with.

His name is David. He's 35–50 and married, with two kids. He owns a financially successful UK business and has plans to grow it online, but recognises that his website isn't performing as well as he wants it to and needs updating.

He has upwards of £10k to spend and is trying to make a decision about which web designer to appoint. He is bright but not technical and realistic about how quickly his website can return on its investment.

In one of those bizarre moments of coincidence I rolled up to a sales meeting with the managing director of a big company. His name was David, he was 49, married with two kids, ran a financially successful business, etc. Frank Kern also tells exactly the same story. This is more than just coincidence or luck. When you actively visualise a person rather than an anonymous customer, not only do you clearly define your target market but you also end up using language which is more personally engaging to them.

Let's explore this. Every communication you have via your website will be read by only one person at a time. If, when you are writing, you are able to visualise this person, your writing will naturally be more tuned to the reader. The more you are able to tune into their needs and feelings the stronger the relationship will be between your website and your visitors. Stronger relationships produce more sales. (We'll talk more on this subject in Chapter 7.)

When you are defining your ideal customer (rather than your average buyer) consider these attributes:

1. Name
2. Gender
3. Age
4. Appearance
5. Occupation/Salary
6. Other identifying traits (married, past failures/ successes, likes/dislikes, is there one common identifier which binds your market together?)
7. Emotional needs (to feel secure about the business, freedom from stress, etc.)
8. Core desires (to earn enough to sell the business, get rid of one aspect of their job, have more time with the family, etc.)

Once you know who they are you will know how to communicate with them. Make them your pin-up in your office and every time you think about marketing, begin by thinking about them.

■ PRINCIPLE 2: THE MANY PILLARS OF MARKETING

Imagine the Parthenon in Greece with the roof being your business and the pillars that support it being the marketing activities you use to generate business. Here's what many businesses look like:

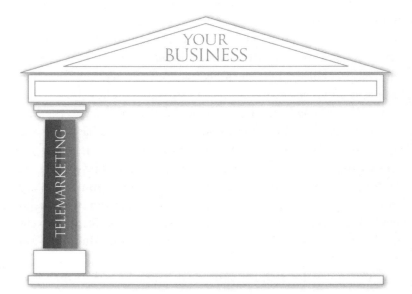

Fig 1 The single-column Parthenon. This diagram is sometimes known as the 'diving board' (if you turn it 90 degrees) from which your business could take a dive!

They usually rely on one or two different marketing approaches (or pillars). The problem here is that it leaves the business exposed. If market changes undermine these methods, their revenue-generating abilities can quickly diminish.

An example would be telemarketing. Recently the Telephone Preference Service has been introduced to limit the ability of companies to cold-call consumers. But other restrictions could also cause trouble: increased telephone costs, complaints, declining conversion rates and so forth. Another example is word-of-mouth; many businesses have grown and even flourished through word-of-mouth recommendations. However, without a structured referrals programme in place you are at the mercy of happenstance and, therefore, unable to predict next month's sales figures.

Essentially, any number of circumstances could create difficulties for a company whose sole income stream is reliant on one form of marketing.

A much safer way of maintaining your income stream is to have several pillars of marketing supporting it. For example, telemarketing, advertising, a website, joint ventures, referrals, etc.

Now if anything happens to one or two of the pillars it's not going to kill the business because the remaining marketing activities will support it.[1]

[1] This model was originated by Jay Abraham, one of the preeminent marketing experts of recent times. You can find out more about Jay at abraham.com.

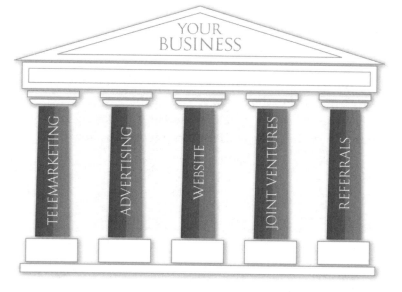

Fig 2 A business receiving multiple revenue streams from several marketing pillars

What this diagram doesn't show is that not all the pillars will be equal – some pillars will be stronger than others. In other words, some marketing activity will be more effective. You would expect to find that the most powerful marketing approach is the one that you've spent most time cultivating. However, in order to run a steady business, you'll need to create, develop and strengthen other approaches too.

In reality this is common sense but it certainly helps to draw out your business's version of the Parthenon. What would yours look like?

Now, there's a flaw in my diagram. Have you spotted it? Look hard... The flaw is in the 'Website' pillar. Here's why.

Most businesses think of their websites as another string to their marketing bow, another pillar in the Parthenon. That is their fatal mistake. The mistake hinges on a simple premise, namely, that just putting a website on the Internet will automatically create visitors, leads, sales and a steady income for your business.

It won't.

Imagine you build a 5-star hotel in the middle of a beautiful forest, complete with spa, gym and amazing restaurant. Now imagine forgetting to build a road to it, or doing any advertising whatsoever. Would it be a huge surprise when it opens to find no one turns up?

Nobody in their right mind would ever do this (except perhaps one or two candidates from *The Apprentice*) and yet it happens on the Internet all the time because people believe that putting a website on the Internet will automatically result in visitors. It doesn't.

If you did nothing to attract visitors to your website, it's a pretty sure bet that you won't get many sales. That's why it is necessary to view your website as needing the same marketing support as your business. Let's use our Parthenon model to show that.

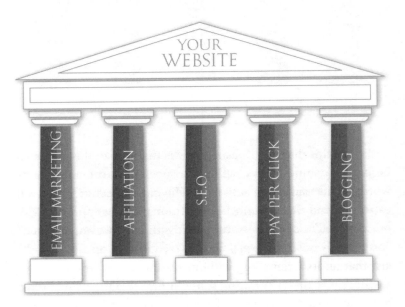

Fig 3 A website being supported by multiple marketing activities

Now our website has become the roof and is being supported by a series of marketing activities: Email Marketing, Affiliation, SEO, Pay-per-Click, etc.

What each of these pillars is doing is generating traffic to your site or building relationships. However, you could equally add conversion-improving techniques like split-testing, improved copy, live chat systems and so on. Any activity which either creates traffic or improves conversions can be seen as supporting your website. Your website can, in turn, truly be seen to support your business.

I guess it will come as no surprise to you that very often, websites are only supported by one marketing pillar (if, indeed they are supported at all). Here's a real-life story to illustrate the difference.

We developed ecommerce websites for two customers. Both customers' sites were the same in terms of functionality and investment, but one turns over more than half a million in sales each year, the other does almost zero. The difference is not the marketplace, the products, the website or the design and technology. The difference is that one is strongly marketed by its owner and the other is not. Our hero in this story began with Google AdWords and then continued to add additional pillars including Yahoo!, Bing, PriceRunner, MoneySupermarket, Ebay, and next the world!

Whether your website is there to support your business or it actually *is* your business, you should make this model the heart of your marketing approach.

PRINCIPLE 3: TESTING

The next marketing principle we should apply is testing.

Consider Cadbury. Long before one of its chocolate bars gets to the shelves it undergoes all kinds of changes. In fact Cadbury has testing laboratories where it produces different variations of the idea and tests them out through dedicated tasting panels. (If you know how I can get myself onto one of those panels please tell me!) Eventually, it will pick a successful chocolate bar on the basis of the results it gets back from the tests. Cadbury didn't just market its Creme Egg without testing it first to see if it was a winner – if Cadbury hadn't tested it first to gauge the market's reaction to it, the company could have thrown millions down the drain. Now let's see how testing applies to marketing.

There is no shortage of marketing ideas. You could get your message out about your product or service in a hundred different ways. For example, direct mail, email, radio, advertising, TV, word-of-mouth, advertorials – the list goes on. However, it's almost impossible to know what kind of return you would get without trying each one out. This could turn out to be very long-winded. The trick to effective marketing, therefore, is to trial an approach which gives you a result for the least amount of effort. The mantra for testing is, 'Test small, learn fast, improve.'

Let's take an example. You have £2,000 you would like to spend on promoting your business. You have a gut feel that direct mail would be the best method. So you spend your money on buying a database, printing a brochure and having the envelopes stuffed and posted. You've spent your £2,000 and now you sit back and wait. Let's say you get a response rate of about 2 per cent (which according to the industry averages for direct mail would be pretty good). Now depending on what you're selling, a 2 per cent response rate may translate into a huge amount of money or a dead loss – either way, it cost you £2,000 to find out. But what if there were a method of marketing which gave you a better response than 2 per cent? Sadly, you wouldn't be able to find out because you've blown your budget. So let's take a different approach.

You've still got your £2,000 to spend but this time you're going to split the money into quarters and test four different marketing approaches simultaneously: direct mail, advertising in a local paper, telemarketing and email. Let's imagine these are the results you get back.

Marketing Approach	Sales Results	Cost	Revenue
Direct Mail	2%	£500	£400
Local Advertising	8%	£500	£1,600
Telemarketing	5%	£500	£1,000
Email	6%	£500	£1,200

Now we can see how much money each marketing approach generated and straightaway you can see that local advertising was four times more effective than direct mail, with email and telemarketing coming a close second and third. It's obvious that direct mail doesn't pass the test, which means you should replace it with a different marketing approach that might do better.

Had you put all of your eggs in one basket with direct mail, you would have invested £2,000 but only generated £1,600. By testing three other approaches simultaneously you've made £4,200. For some companies these kinds of results could be the difference between success and outright failure.

What this illustrates is a very simple principle: it literally pays to test several marketing approaches side by side.

The key approach is to test on a small scale with a budget that will give you a meaningful result.

What concerns many companies (especially with Internet marketing) is that they will lose money testing a particular marketing strategy. My counterargument to this is the gambler's motto: Never bet more than you can afford to lose. In marketing, this is sound advice.

As you can see this rather neatly links in with the Parthenon principle as each successful marketing approach you test is a new pillar supporting your business.

Testing on the Internet

The internet gives us a unique opportunity to test several ideas at the same time. You could test different sales approaches, or different ways of generating traffic, or different sales emails. And you can do all this as part of one overall test (as each test's results feed into another). So testing multiple approaches to generate traffic results in more people seeing your sales pages, which in turn results in more people signing up for your emails. And because you are testing several different sales messages in your emails, it increases your sales.

This means that testing on the Internet is fundamentally different from offline testing. In the offline world, marketing approaches are often separate, and the results of one have little impact on another. For example, the results of your direct mail campaign will have no impact on the results of your local advertising campaign. This is often not the case on the Internet because each marketing element you test can be linked together.

The fact that one improvement in marketing can have a positive knock-on effect upon another is what makes Internet marketing so exciting. The easiest way to understand this is to visualise your marketing as a process in which the *output* of one approach affects the *input* of the next approach.

testing traffic
marketing
approaches

greater
traffic =
more sales

improve
copy on
web site

more
conversions =
more sales

improve
customer
emails

more
emails sent =
more sales

**Fig 4 The flow of
marketing: where one
improvement ripples
down, multiplying its
effects as it goes.**

To demonstrate this more clearly take a look at Fig 4. We begin at the top by testing some new marketing approaches to generate more traffic. As a result we see an increase in visitors to the website. This would in itself increase our sales but we've also been testing writing better copy for our sales pages. Again, this would in itself increase sales. However, the increased traffic plus the improved sales pages have a greater result on our sales than either one would have in isolation.

We continue with our testing and begin to send out emails to our customers. That also improves our sales. But the fact that we've been testing and improving the other marketing approaches further up in the chain means that our email marketing is producing more sales.

Once you begin to see your marketing as an interconnected process, you will see that even the slightest improvement multiplies itself down the chain.

What is shocking is that the more marketing elements there are in your test process, the more money you will make. In other words when you test ten ideas you give yourself nine more opportunities to find a more profitable solution than if you had only tested one. Not only does it make commercial sense but it's also a great boardroom argument against the naysayers who attack new ideas and approaches.

One final thought. You get results from your Internet test in a fraction of the time you would from offline marketing – just consider how fast the response is from email marketing (minutes and hours) as compared to direct mail (days and weeks).

Split-testing

Split-testing has been used by businesses for a long time. In fact advertising copywriters who wanted to improve the effectiveness of their adverts were using this technique more than a hundred years ago. What they recognised was that it was very unlikely that they had written the perfect advert the first time round. So they would run two different adverts and see which one yielded the better result. Then they would drop the failed advert and write another to try and beat the winner. The great thing about this approach is that because you're always aiming to beat the winner, you end up creating a perpetual cycle of improvement.

You can split-test almost every type of marketing. Let's imagine that you've written a free report that you want to give away on your website. So, you ask yourself a question: Do I get more downloads if it's a written report or if it's a podcast? What you are doing is testing to find the most effective way of getting your message over to your reader. Here you are split-testing the report in both formats to see which gets downloaded the most.

Or you might want to test to see if one version of your home page works better than another. You run one home page for a few weeks and then run the other for the same length of time. You compare the results and see which one was more effective.

Here's another idea. Let's say you have 5,000 subscribers to your email list. You are about to send all 5,000 an email inviting them to immediately purchase your latest product. Let's imagine that your first e-mail offers 10 per cent off but you also want to test whether offering £10 off yields a better response. All you need to do is send your first offer to one group of 500 and your second offer to another group of 500. Whichever e-mail performs better is the one you should then send to the remaining 4,000.

If you fancy taking this to a really advanced level, you can continue to do your split-testing by writing another email which tries to outperform the winner of your last test but still only testing 500 at a time. It will certainly take you longer to do but it could easily double your profits. The other great advantage of this technique is that because you know which offer works best, you can now apply that knowledge to all of your other forms of marketing!

There will be instances of where you can't (or don't want to) split-test your entire traffic. For example, you might want to test a provocative headline or a bigger-than-normal discount or a free high-value sample. This is where you might perceive there to be a 'risk' that precedes the results of your test. In this case I would suggest that you still try it but only with 20 per cent of your prospects or traffic to your website. You can use the other 80 per cent as a control (or baseline) for the experiment.

Advanced Split-testing (AB/C Testing)

So what is AB/C testing?

Let's say you're running an advertising campaign and the headline is, 'Ladies Elegant Dresswear Sale.'

You won't know whether this is the most effective headline unless you run a slightly different one and measure the compara-

2 If you change more than
one thing at a time, you won't
be able to identify which of
the things you changed made
the difference.

tive results. The important thing about A/B testing is you only change *one thing at a time.*[2] So your second headline might be, 'Ladies Dresswear Sale Now On.' The problem with this technique is threefold:

1. It assumes your initial idea was good in the first place
2. You can only make improvements by small degrees
3. There will always be a 'ceiling' of success which you cannot improve upon

This brings us to AB/C testing. A good deal of marketing is about creativity, so it makes sense that you test two creative ideas rather than two variations of one idea. However, A/B testing only allows for the latter; therefore, you need to add a second, completely fresh and different idea, C, into the testing mix. For example, '10 per cent off Ladies Dresswear.'

By introducing C, you can test whether it is a fundamental improvement on either A or B. If your C test is more successful than A or B, then you split-test it (i.e. it becomes the new A/B). That would then leave you with the option of creating a new C test. This enables you to test two different ideas at the same time.

By adding C into your split-test system, you can improve your marketing by orders of magnitude rather than increments.[3]

[3] If you would like to look at some more advanced testing software, go to www.google.com/websiteoptimizer and adcomparator.com.

■ PRINCIPLE 4: THE DOUBLING MINDSET

We all face barriers in business – financial, organisational, logistical – but there are none more difficult to overcome than the mental barriers which we create for ourselves. These barriers create limitations, which is why most businesses struggle to imagine how they might increase their online profits by just 10–15 per cent. The idea that they can double their profits in record time seems just too far-fetched to be believable.

In the first chapter I discussed how your mindset can fundamentally affect your success. Now I would like to show you one of the most essential mental steps towards success in online entrepreneurship: the Doubling Mindset.

There is a widespread belief, held to be absolutely true, that the results you get are directly proportional to the effort that you put in. In other words, one unit of effort equals one unit of reward. And it all seems so reasonable: the greater the effort, the greater the reward. We even see this rule hold true in real life.

Fig 5 The classical belief that 1 unit of effort results in 1 unit of reward

If you want to run a mile in four minutes instead of eight you are going to have to run twice as fast. If you want to get your PhD done in two years and not four you're going to have to work twice as hard. If you want to double your bank balance you're also going to have to work twice as hard. Right?

Wrong. That's one example where the rule breaks down.

In fact, this where what looks like common sense turns out to be complete nonsense. The idea that one unit of effort equals one unit of results in business is ludicrous and potentially very damaging to your future success. Millionaires can't work any harder than anybody else yet they generate huge results. In fact, many of them don't work as hard as they could and yet still create dramatic effects in their businesses.

So, what's the fundamental difference between them and a regular business? Well, oddly, not much.

Every business has the ability to take one unit of effort and multiply it into more than one unit of results. A simple example would be Elvis Presley's 'Jailhouse Rock' – he sang it once but it's been sold millions of times over.

So, sitting in between the work you put in and the results you get out is a process which multiplies the effects of your effort. The really successful businesses and entrepreneurs have mastered that process and spend their time maximising every opportunity for improving it.

Fig 6 The Doubling Mindset, where 1 unit of effort is multiplied by a process that results in multiple units of reward

Richard Branson's business has many multiplier engines which create outstanding results, where one unit of his effort is equivalent to thousands of units of output. The same applies for Warren Buffett, Bill Gates and Felix Dennis.

You too have a multiplier engine in your business. In fact, you've got lots of these engines all hard at work, creating the profits that you generate. That means you have multiple opportunities to create truly excellent results. All you need to do is recognise where the multiplier engines are and maximise their effects.

Examples of multiplier engines in your business include outsourcing your workload to employees/freelancers; developing a product which can be sold many times[4]; a printed brochure (written once, read many times)[5]; a photocopier; and so on. And marketing itself is a multiplier, as every pound you invest is designed to yield many more in return.

What I find genuinely astonishing is how many businesses ignore perhaps the most powerful and fundamentally business-changing engine they have at their disposal – their website.

Within your website are numerous multiplier engines all ready to be optimised. A simple example would be any sales page. You write it once but it is seen multiple times and generates money for you multiple times. If you improve your sales page (through split-testing, writing more compelling copy, etc.) then you are optimising the engine and increasing the number of multiple units of 'result' it can generate.

[4] Consultants often find this difficult because they can only sell their advice to one company at a time. If they write a book, however, they can sell the advice many times. Publishing the book is the multiplier.

[5] The opposite of the sales brochure is the sales meeting: the former can be sent many times but the latter only conducted once!

Fig 7 How a sales page, written once, creates many units of reward

The more of these engines you activate the more you expect to see results in terms of increases by tens and hundreds of per cent. And that represents a fundamental difference in thinking from those who are content to place limits on their achievement because they simply don't believe that they can double their profitability.

Now let's use this thinking to practical effect and look at how we can double your online business.

PRINCIPLE 5: THE INTERNET EQUATION

Do you remember balancing equations at school? At age 14 it seemed boring and pointless – but it's about to get a lot more exciting.

Let's take a look at the Internet Equation – the only equation you ever need to worry about in your online life.

Fig 8 The Internet Equation

Traffic

This is another way of saying, 'People who visit your website.' It's pretty obvious that you would want as many people to visit as possible, although a very important qualification is that you only want visitors who are interested in your products and services. (There's no point attracting millions all looking for the latest fashion accessory for dogs if you're an IT company!)

Conversions

A conversion could be the number of sales from your ecommerce store, the number of times a contact form is filled in about one of your services, a download of your latest software, and so forth. It could take a number of different forms but it has to be something which leads to your ultimate goal.

Now you may have spotted that traffic happens *off* your website whereas conversions happen *on* your website. This means that, broadly speaking, you generate traffic from other websites and offline marketing whereas you generate conversions exclusively on your website. The remainder of this book is dedicated to helping you maximise the amount of relevant traffic to your website while simultaneously maximising the number of conversions from that traffic.

Success

Online success means different things to different people.

If you run a purely commercial business then the definition of success could boil down to how much profit you make.[6] If you are a charitable organisation you might define success as getting enough donations to carry out the next critical piece of work. If you work in the public sector, success may mean meeting government targets. Whatever online success means to you as an organisation, it has to be measurable. By this I mean you must be able

6 For simplicity I will assume that you are a commercial organisation. However, all of the principles I discuss can also be applied to non-commercial sectors.

to put some numbers against it. In the commercial sector that's easy because any measurements you take are ultimately about how much profit you make. If you work outside the commercial arena it may not be as clear cut; however, it must still be objective and numerical.

If you are running an ecommerce store, success is simply the number of online sales you make. If not then in all likelihood you will need to track your sales offline in the real world. We do this in our business. We have a list of enquiries, where they came from (which website, email, etc.), what stage they are at in the sales cycle and whether they become a customer. This means we know exactly how many enquiries we get from our website that result in sales. You may need to do something similar for your business in order to calculate success for you.

One more thing to keep in mind. Various pages or parts of your website are 'success points.' For example, on an ecommerce store the product page would be a success point, as would the 'Confirm Order' button. Your enquiry form is another success point. Essentially, success points are where the user takes an action which contributes to your online success. By focusing on improving these, you will automatically increase your success as these are the key elements on your site that will generate revenue – in other words, they are mini multiplier engines.

Here's a tip: Write down the hierarchy of your website and mark off those pages which are success points. Whenever you are working on your marketing, testing different approaches or simply being creative, start with these pages first.

PRINCIPLE 6: THE SUCCESS PYRAMID

Online success can mean different things but you arrive at it from just two places:

1.   Getting lots of relevant, qualified traffic to your website, and then
2.   Converting the highest possible number into leads, sales or success points.

There is no point having a fantastic website if no one is visiting it. Equally, there is no point attracting lots of well-targeted traffic to an appalling website. The reality of today's Internet is that you need great traffic *and* a great website – you need to balance your online equation.

There is a simple system which underpins the revenue-generating capabilities of every single website on the Internet. Let's take a look at how it works.

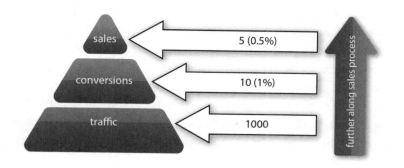

Fig 9 The Success Pyramid showing current sales

Let's start at the bottom of the pyramid and work up. Imagine that you have 1,000 visitors to your website every month. Of those visitors a certain number will leave their contact details. You could think of these as leads. In our example, 10 people have submitted an enquiry form. Let's also imagine that you've got a pretty good sales team and so you are able to convert 50 per cent of those leads. So 1,000 people visit the site, 10 people identify themselves as serious prospects, and 5 are converted into customers. Or, 1 in 200 become customers.[7]

To get a sense of scale it's better to convert these numbers into percentages. This means that 1 per cent of visitors to the website leave their contact details. (You might think that this is an extremely low number but our own experience and other research support the fact that this is about the average across the Internet.) As you can see, this means that we are only converting 0.5 per cent of the visitors that reach our website into cash.

I think that most of us would be jumping up and down if we knew that our website performed this badly. However – and I'm going to let you into a secret here – if you ask the vast majority of web owners what their percentage conversion is, I can almost guarantee they wouldn't have a clue. And not knowing gets more scary when we start looking at it from the commercial angle. Let's do just that, now.

Owning a website costs you some money on a monthly basis. This could be from hosting, your web designer's fees, employee costs and so forth. It could also come from you paying for traf-

[7] Even for ecommerce sites, where a sale and conversion would seem to be the same thing, it can be separated as some people will only get as far as the basket (the ecommerce equivalent of a lead) or they may leave their contact details requesting a telephone sales call instead of immediately buying online.

fic to come to your site (Google AdWords, Yahoo!, Bing, Search Engine Optimisation, etc.). Whatever monthly figure this works out to be is known as your *total cost of ownership*.

Let's go back to our example and imagine that every month you spend £500 on generating traffic and maintaining the website. Let's also imagine that every time you make a sale you earn £100, so 5 sales x £100 nets you £500. This means that in the example above you're spending £500 to earn £500 – you broke even, just! This is not great.

Now most business owners will focus on increasing the amount of traffic to their website – what I call a 'brute-force attack' to increase revenue. You can think of this as simply turning up the volume. Let's see what this does to the numbers.

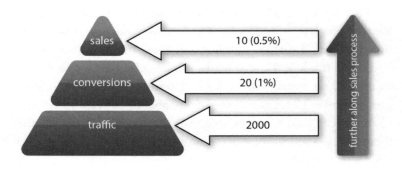

Fig 10 The Success Pyramid showing a doubling of traffic

Well, obviously doubling the traffic results in doubling the sales. But what has this done to the financial side?

Imagine that of the £500 you spend each month on the website £300 is spent generating traffic. This means that your monthly costs have gone up from £500 to £800. (You're spending another £300 on attracting twice as many visitors).

Your spending may have gone up but, thankfully, so have your sales. You made 10 sales at £100 each but your cost of acquiring those customers was £800. The good news is you've jumped into profit by £200 but the bad news is that doubling your traffic has not doubled your profitability.

Now here's where it gets exciting, because this is the part that almost every web owner misses. The way to double your profitability is to double the number of conversions you make on the site. You've got 1,000 people visiting your site every month, so doesn't it feel wrong that only 1 per cent of them are actually interested in what you have to offer? It feels wrong because it *is* wrong. If you had to make 100 telephone calls before you acquired a customer then you're either calling the wrong people or you need to brush up on your sales technique. Either way you'd do whatever it took to make sure that every phone call counted.

Let's take a real-world example to illuminate the point further. You own a shop. You spend all that time finding the right place, furnishing it, buying the right stock. The big day comes, you fling open the doors, 100 people rush in and 99 run back out again. How would you feel? Mortified? Depressed? The bizarre thing is that this happens all the time on websites (remember 1 per cent conversion of traffic is the Internet average) and yet everyone seems to get on with their day jobs without a murmur.

Looking at it from this perspective, doesn't it seem that the natural place we should begin is not turning up the volume of traffic to the website but making the website more efficient at converting the traffic it's already getting? There are hundreds of techniques for doing this and Chapters 6, 7 and 9 of this book are specifically devoted to them. But for now, let's say you make a few changes to the website and after a month of trying different strategies you double the number of conversions. What does this do to the numbers?

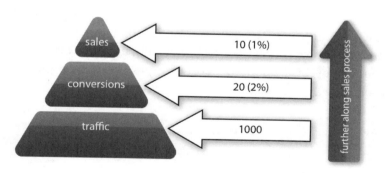

Fig 11 The Success Pyramid showing a doubling of conversions

You're still getting 1,000 people to the website each month but now through some crafty strategies you have doubled the number of enquiries from 10 to 20 and the number of sales from 5 to 10. How does that stack up financially?

Well, you're still spending £500 a month but now you're making £1,000 in sales (10 sales x £100), leaving you £500 in profit. But you don't stop there. No resting on laurels for you! You push on, testing new approaches, applying different techniques and using advanced marketing strategies. By the end of next month, you've done it again.

Now you are making 20 sales from 1,000 visitors. Your turnover is £2,000 but your costs are still £500, leaving you with £1,500 profit. I bet you're enjoying the math now!

You could keep going, each month attempting to double the number of conversions you make from the site. (Remember, you're still only converting 4 per cent of visitors to the site. To me, that still feels a low number.) I believe that if you implement all the strategies I'm going to show you, you could raise that number to 10 per cent, 15 per cent, and beyond. What's important to realise is that it's a never-ending cycle. You have to keep improving and keep testing new approaches in order to maintain and increase the number of conversions from your website. As you can see, boosting conversions is, initially, a far more powerful multiplier engine than boosting traffic.

Here's the icing on the cake. Now you've got some money in the bank, you can afford to spend some cash on increasing the traffic to the website. This means that you are now developing a two-pronged attack. You are finally balancing that Internet Equation. Get this right and you will leave your competitors bewildered.

Here's how that pans out: you now attract 2,000 visitors to the site, get 80 conversions and 40 sales. (It's only costing you £300 more to double your traffic.) Commercially, here's how you stand: your turnover is £4,000, your cost of acquisition is £800 and your profits are £3,200. Nice!

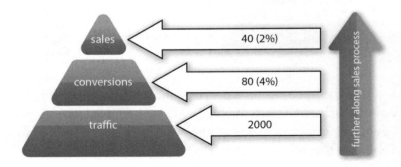

Fig 12 The Success Pyramid showing a doubling of both traffic and conversions

[8] If your business isn't online yet or you don't have the figures, begin by estimating them.

Okay the numbers we've been playing with are illustrative – now you need to draw your own pyramid and populate it with the real numbers from your business.[8] (Don't panic if the results send shivers down your spine, I'm going to make sure that you have all the tools necessary to apply this strategy to your business.)

PRINCIPLE 7: THE REAL CUSTOMER VALUE

While we're in a mathematical frame of mind, I would like to show you a very important way of looking at the value your customer brings to your business – one that could completely alter the way you look at the success of your website. It's called 'lifetime customer value.'

Essentially, it is a very simple but absolutely critical number you need to work out. Many businesses (including online businesses) tend to see the value of their customer as only being the first thing they bought from them (i.e. the value of the first sale). However, in most businesses – and I'm guessing yours is the same – a customer will come back to buy from you more than once. This means that the total value that your customer brings to your business is actually far greater than the first sale. To work this out you need three basic pieces of information: your average sale value; the average number of times your customers buy from you per year; and the average number of years they remain a customer.

Here's an example table to demonstrate this:

Customer Lifetime Value	
Average order value	£250
Average number of repeat orders per year	4
Customer yearly value	£1,000
Average client lifetime with business	5 years
Total lifetime value	£5,000

Let's imagine that an average customer spends £250 per order but purchases 4 times during an average year; this results in a customer yearly value of £1,000. Now imagine that the average customer stays with the business for five years. This means the average lifelong customer's value is £5,000 (5 times their yearly value).

Most businesses don't bother to calculate this and so they end up thinking that their customer is only worth £250. In reality they're worth 20 times that. Doesn't that completely change the way you view every customer? It may be worth taking a few out to dinner! But apart from making us want to approach our existing customers differently, it also hugely influences the amount of money we might be prepared to spend on acquiring that customer.

Let's say that your average customer begins by spending £10 with you but it costs you £10 to acquire them. At first glance it might look like your online business was set for failure. However, because you know that your average customer comes back to you, let's say, 10 times, your customer lifetime value is really £100. This means for every £1 you spend on your online marketing, you are generating £10 in return. (Knowing this also affects how you think about your success pyramid.)

So, I'm sure you can see that once you have this powerful piece of information, it changes the way in which you think about how you go about marketing. Curiously many businesses haven't identified their customer's lifetime value and consequently will remove themselves from certain marketing activities far too quickly, thinking they're not getting a return – and that's fine because it leaves more room in the market for you!

Using Customer Value to Help Work Out Your Online Investment

Now we can take this one step further and tie this in with your website. Let's imagine that you've spent £5,000 on building your website. You'll also need to invest some money in online marketing (pay-per-click advertising, SEO, email marketing, etc.) to put some fuel in your website's tank. I would recommend you spend at least 50 per cent of your website's investment on marketing; this ensures that you don't spend your last penny on building the website only to discover you can't afford to market it.

Now let's plug in our average sale value (£250), the number of repeat sales (4), and your customer's average yearly value (£1,000). So, every customer the website generates is worth £1,000 per year.

If you make 5 sales per month, you earn £1,250, giving you a yearly turnover of £15,000, less your original investment of £7,500, leaving you with a return on your investment of £7,500.

But the *real* value is found when you add in your average customer yearly value, which is actually £1,000 (and not £250). Now you can see that the real yearly return your website is delivering is £60,000, leaving you with an average yearly return on investment of £52,500 – substantially more than if you had not factored in multiple purchases by your customers.

Return on Investment	
Website investment	£5,000
Marketing investment (50% of website value)	£2,500
Total investment	**£7,500**
Average sale value	£250
Average number of repeat sales	4
Average customer yearly value	£1,000
If website makes 5 sales/month	£1,250
If website makes 60 sales/year	£15,000
Return on investment (sales less investment)	**£7,500**
But add in…	
Customer lifetime value	£1,000
Lifetime revenue (60 x £1,000)	£60,000
Yearly return on investment (sales less investment)	**£52,500**

▪ *THE STRATEGY*

In the following chapters you'll have access to some powerful techniques for increasing sales and traffic. However, as we discovered in the first chapter, creating success isn't achieved by blindly following a to-do list. Many of the processes I'll show you are at their most effective when the principles that govern them are in place and fully understood.

So, as you read through the remaining chapters and start applying the knowledge to your business keep in mind these seven principles. If a process isn't working correctly, go back to this chapter (and also Chapter 1) and see if the problem could be resolved by applying one or more of these governing principles.

Let's turn that around. When you see a process in your online business which is doing remarkably well, take a moment to analyse why. See which of the principles are helping it work harder and use that knowledge to magnify your success in other areas.

CHAPTER

Get Instant Traffic to Your Website

■ INTRODUCTION

Once your site is built the next most important action is to get visitors to it. In this chapter, I want to show you one of the most powerful online marketing techniques in the world. It is a tool which will attract hundreds if not thousands of customers to your website 24 hours a day 7 days a week and it is called pay-per-click, or PPC for short.

For the smart marketers like you using pay-per-click systems can be a simple way of putting money in your pocket. Eventually, for every pound you invest in pay-per-click, you should know that you are going to get two pounds, five pounds, a hundred pounds in return. Now, if you think that getting a £100 return on a £1 investment is a bit far-fetched then it's time to get really excited because it is one of the very few online marketing systems where you begin to measure your return in the hundreds of per cent. And if all this sounds too good to be true, well, welcome to the world of the Internet marketer, because that is the kind of success you can achieve.

In this chapter I'm going to show you what pay-per-click is, why it is critical to your future business success and how the system works in practice. Plus I'm going to show you exactly how to set up and structure the system. And finally I'm going to give you some of the most advanced techniques for developing and running hugely successful campaigns.

So, let's dive into the remarkable and profitable world of pay-per-click advertising.

There are three ways to get traffic to your website.

The first is through what is called *direct traffic*. This is when someone types in your website's domain name directly into their browser.

Fig 1 An example of direct traffic

The second is when someone clicks on a link to your website from another website (or email, etc.) – this is called *referred traffic*. (If you're feeling a bit technical, that's known as a backlink or inbound link, and we'll be talking a lot about such links in Chapter 8, on Search Engine Optimisation.)

External links

- Official website ☒
- Corporate homepage ☒
- Official blog ☒
- Google ☒ channel on YouTube
- Google ☒ at CrunchBase
- Google Research ☒
- Google website from November 11, 1998 ☒ at the Internet Archive

Fig 2 An example of referred traffic coming from links off a Wikipedia page

The third method is by being listed on a search engine, and somewhat unsurprisingly, this is called *search traffic*.

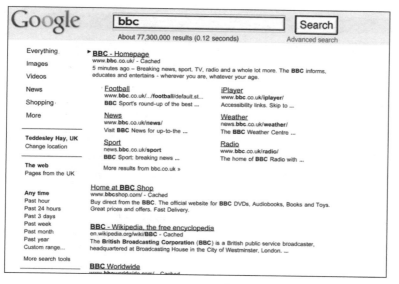

Fig 3 An example of a SERP (Search Engine Results Page) from which search traffic is derived

Very often you will find that direct and referred traffic is the natural result of being well-known, having good SEO and strong offline marketing. To give you an example of this I can pretty much guarantee that Tesco's website gets a higher ratio of direct traffic to search engine traffic than my website and probably yours, too. The reason for this is dead simple: most people would take an educated guess that Tesco's web address is www.tesco.co.uk without having to search for it using a search engine.

However you can't rely on direct traffic alone – you need search traffic too. What most business owners like you are interested in is how to get listed on the search engines. After all, more than 200 million searches are done on Google every day and so it stands to reason that there will be large numbers of people searching for the type of products and services you have to offer.

But there is a snag: getting listed on the search engines isn't the problem – that tends to happen automatically because the search engines trawl the Internet looking for new webpages and changes to existing ones. In all probability you are going to get listed on the major search engines without even trying (unless you're doing something very weird on your website).

The problem is getting listed on the first page.

Let me give you an example of this. Let's say I'm looking for a Sony LCD TV. If I punch 'sony lcd tv' into Google, I get this results page.[1]

[1] These are called SERPS – Search Engine Results Pages.

Fig 4 A standard Google Search Engine Results Page (SERP)

If you look under my search query you'll notice that Google has very kindly told me how many webpages it found which had some relevance to the keywords I typed in. So, I can see that about twenty seven million webpages are relevant and competing to be on this first results page. Despite the huge number of webpages all claiming some relevance to my keyword, Google goes to great lengths to make sure that only those websites which are the *most* relevant to my search are at the top. And, as you know, the further you get away from page 1 the less relevant the results are. In fact, research has shown that only about 24 per cent of people click to page 2 or beyond,[2] telling us that people's perception is that the results shown in page 2 and beyond are simply not as relevant or important as those on page 1. Anything appearing on page 2 would only be seen by the minority of people who are searching.

Now back to our Sony LCD TV example. In order for you to get a decent volume of traffic you would need to appear on the first results page. To put that differently, you would have to outperform 27 million webpages to get there. Now it may sound like an almost impossible task, but when you understand how search engines like Google rank websites, it is quite achievable using specific techniques. These are collectively known as Search Engine Optimisation (SEO).

However, one of the big drawbacks in doing any search engine optimisation to your website is that it can typically take between six and 12 months before you start seeing the results of that effort. Frankly there's no way you should have to wait for that length of time before your website starts getting traffic and before you start making money from it. So, if search engine optimisation isn't going to get you instant traffic because it takes too long to get a decent ranking, what can you do to generate enquiries from the search engines in the meantime?

Well, before I explain that, I just want to address why I'm only going to discuss Google and not Yahoo!, Bing, Ask and so on. It's simply because Google is the most-used search engine in both the UK and the US.[3] In the UK it commands almost 90 per cent of all searches, and nearly 72 per cent in the US.[4] However, after you've completed this chapter and mastered getting traffic from Google, you can move on to the other search engines and dominate them too. Meanwhile, let's start with the one that's going to have the biggest impact, and practise the 80/20 rule.

[2] From Estat and @Position, combining 30 million page views.

[3] One billion people use Google each week!

[4] Figures from www.hitwise.com

Let's begin by having a look at another search results page. This time I typed 'garden furniture.'

Fig 5 Screenshot showing where PPC adverts are located on the SERP

Down the left-hand side of the page (and dimmed-out in my screenshot) are what are referred to as the *organic listings*. These are webpages which Google itself has naturally ranked as relevant to the keywords that I typed in. They are, if you like, free listings. If we look to the right of the page, we see a column of boxes which contains adverts.

What you'll notice is that each box represents a different advertiser, and that they all conform to the same layout, which incidentally, doesn't look that dissimilar from that of the natural listings. (In fact I'm sure that's a deliberate act on Google's part because they know that people don't really see the difference.) Right at the top of the column you'll notice that Google, very subtly, titles this column as 'Ads.'

You can sometimes find ads at the top of the natural listings as well (as in my screenshot). These don't always appear as it depends on how popular the keyword is and how many advertisers are competing against it. If it's a very popular keyword with lots of advertisers then Google shunts the top three adverts over to the top left-hand side so there is more advertising space on the page.

The system which puts these adverts on the search results page is known as Google AdWords.

HOW DOES GOOGLE ADWORDS WORK?

Essentially the AdWords system is what allows advertisers to pay to appear in the search results (and on the first page of a particular SERP for a specific keyword or phrase) and, very crudely speaking, the more you pay the higher your position. This is, therefore, your ticket to getting seen even if your website is nowhere to be found in the organic listings.

Let's see how it works.

1. As an advertiser, you specify keywords and key phrases which you think your prospects are likely to type in.
2. You enter those keywords into Google's pay-per-click system called AdWords, and you write a short advert which is triggered whenever one of your keywords is typed in. This is called 'just-in-time marketing' – users see your ad just when they want to take action (make a purchase, get more information, etc.).
3. If somebody likes the look of your advert, they click on it. That takes them to a page on your website. It's then up to your website to turn them from a prospect into a customer.

And the system is called 'pay-per-click' because you only ever pay Google when someone clicks on your advert. (And if they've clicked on your ad, they're visiting your website, and if they're visiting your website, there's a good chance they're going to become customers.)

The amount that you pay for each click is determined by a number of factors, including the popularity of the keyword, how many advertisers are competing against that keyword, and how popular your advert is.

Let's quickly deal with a question that often gets asked at this point: What's to stop your competitors from clicking on your advert and wasting your money?

Google takes huge precautions to make sure this doesn't happen. Any invalid click actually loses them money. Here's why: If Google's advertisers don't make money from their advertising system, Google's core business – which is based on AdWords – will suffer. However, the fact they are a billion-dollar company proves their advertising mechanism does work, which in turn proves that the system they have in place to detect and stop invalid clicks is highly effective. (In fact they've invested millions – both human and machine – to ensure it does not happen.)

There is another view, namely, if you're making a great return on your PPC investment, who cares if there are a few clicks from your competitors which Google doesn't spot? I know that sounds flippant but I mean it to help you focus on the end goal which is your return and not to worry about a system which may be not be 100 per cent perfect. (For example if 0.5 per cent of your clicks come from your competitors, that doesn't invalidate the 99.5 per cent of clicks that come from potential customers!)

Getting the Right Traffic

[5] A report by Marketing Sherpa discovered that 80 per cent of all the clicks to PPC adverts were derived from 20 per cent of all Internet users. There's our 80/20 rule again!

One key facet to Google AdWords is that you can attract highly focused and qualified traffic to your site.[5] This is because you pick keywords that your customers will be typing in to find your products and services. In other words, your choice of keyword *defines* your choice of visitor.

It can also deliver this traffic almost instantly, because if you suddenly think up a new keyword which attracts more potential business to your site, then as soon as you add it into your AdWords campaign your advert will start appearing against it. In fact, any change you make in your advertising campaign such as changing the wording on an advert, adding new keywords, changing the amount you want to pay for each click and so on is immediately 'actioned' in the system and so you get to see the results straight away. This speed allows you to test different approaches and get a response far faster than any other mass marketing method.

Let's follow up on that thinking for a moment because it's worth comparing Google AdWords against traditional advertising methods, like advertising in your evening paper. You might pay £500 for a half-page advert that goes out to a circulation of 20,000 people. It is likely that of those 20,000 people only a really small number would be interested in what you are selling right now. This means you've still had to pay for the 19,950 who saw your ad but weren't interested at that moment. That's a huge amount of wastage and it's a wastage you don't pay for when you use Google AdWords: If you have attracted 20,000 people to an advert on AdWords you can guarantee it's because they've entered a keyword or phrase that relates to your business.

Although your primary interest in PPC is probably around generating leads and sales, it is a remarkably versatile marketing mechanism. Here are some of the other uses you might consider:

1. Building an email database
2. Distributing publications
3. Driving downloads
4. Educating buyers
5. Gathering market data
6. Increasing online registrations
7. Promoting special events
8. Testing marketing messages

SETTING UP YOUR ACCOUNT

Google regularly updates how you create an AdWords account and by the time I've written this, they'll probably have changed it again. So, rather than me giving you an out-of-date method here's a link directly from Google which steps you through creating your very own AdWords account: adwords.google.com/support/aw/bin/answer.py?hl=en-uk&answer=142822.

Plus there is a short video on account creation here: https://googleemea.connectsolutions.com/p40122033.

There are four steps to running a successful Google AdWords campaign:

1. Getting the right keywords together
2. Writing compelling adverts which attract lots of clicks
3. Having landing pages on your website which compel your visitor to act
4. Analysing the results to optimise and maximise the return you make on the system

■ *SELECTING PROFITABLE KEYWORDS*

Introduction

Keywords are at the very heart of your Google AdWords campaign. Getting this part right will give you access to the mind of your buyer – a sort of Google telepathy. Keywords are what people type into Google when they are looking for something they want. If that keyword is in your AdWords campaign, your ad will appear and when clicked on will take your visitor to your website. So, let's go through the exact steps you need to take in order to create money-making keywords.

Most people just want to jump right in and start thinking up keywords. Now, you can do this but it's likely to become fairly unstructured, and as your keywords expand into the hundreds (as they will) it becomes harder to keep track of what's going on. Half the battle here is being organised. The other half is being able to distinguish between those keywords that make money and those which waste money.

In a moment I'm going to show you how you can create in a structured way hundreds of keywords which potential customers will type in. But before I do there are a couple of questions which are worth keeping in mind as you go through the process.

1.   *What types of questions will your customers ask as they search the Internet?*

On a daily basis your customers give themselves away by typing in keywords and key phrases in order to find your product or service. The trick is knowing what those keywords are in advance. If we had a machine that tapped straight into our customers' minds so that we knew exactly what they were thinking, then we would have the perfect Google AdWords campaign (and be billionaires). But, if you don't have one of those machines, the easiest way to read your customers' minds is to ask your existing customers how they would track down your products and services. This is one of the simplest and best ways of determining relevant keywords.

2.   *What is your customer trying to accomplish?*

Let's use an example. Imagine you sell vitamins. A lot of people will search for specific vitamins and they'll probably type in keywords like 'vitamin C', 'vitamin D', 'multivitamin' and so on. But there's also going to be a group of people who are interested in vitamins from the healthy living angle. They may type in 'food supplements', 'sports supplements', 'natural health', etc.

So, you also want to be asking your customers what they are trying to achieve by using your products and services, listen to the language they use, note it down and use it in your keyword research.

Remember also that your prospect may 'zone-in' on your products, moving from generic to highly specific keywords. For example, someone searching for a skiing holiday may start with the generic 'skiing holiday' but end up with 'sheraton hotel salzburg'. This shows that you will probably need to think in a wider context about your products and services if you are to engage people at all ends of the sales funnel.

Using the above example I've indicated the searches a browser may make below:

keyword(s)	browser's state of mind	what to do with them when they get to your web site
skiing holiday	just browsing	engage them with email marketing
skiing Austria	more focussed, but not committed to buying	as above, but focus on Austria as a resort
skiing hotels Salzburg	quite focussed, high quality lead	make them a clear offer and demonstrate your unique selling points
Sheraton hotel Salzburg	they are nearly at the point they will buy	repeat the above, but with more focus on the booking action

Fig 6 How people sometimes 'spiral into specificity' during their search process

Root Keywords

Now let's get into the actual mechanics of putting our keyword list together.

Let's imagine for the duration of the chapter that you and I are selling suitcases and luggage, as it's a good everyday example for us to use.

The first place to start is with single words that describe what we sell. Here are a few openers:

1. luggage
2. suitcase
3. holdall
4. backpack
5. bag

These are what we call 'root keywords.'

A great way of finding new root keywords is using an online thesaurus. Now we could just grab any old text-based thesaurus but hey, this is the Internet and it ought to be a lot more fun than that. Go to www.visuwords.com, a visual thesaurus that enables you to see the relationships between words.

If you type in one of the root keywords, 'suitcase,' you'll see some interesting suggestions: 'weekender,' 'gripsack,' 'carpetbag,' and also 'luggage.'

If you double-click on 'luggage,' you'll see some other core words: 'trunk,' 'satchel,' 'hatbox' and 'bag.' Double-clicking on 'bag' will reveal a few more. All we're doing at the moment is trying to think up as many single root keywords that relate to what we sell as possible.

Okay, so now we've got our root keywords why not just stop there? Why not have our advert triggered only by these keywords?

Well there are two incredibly important reasons why you need to keep going with your keyword research and not be tempted just to stop at this point.

Firstly, the majority of advertisers using Google AdWords bid on only the most basic or root keywords. They don't invest the time in what we are about to do and as a result you find that the advertiser competition for root keywords is huge.

Now remember that the more competition there is, the higher the bid price for a keyword. I did a quick check on the approxi-

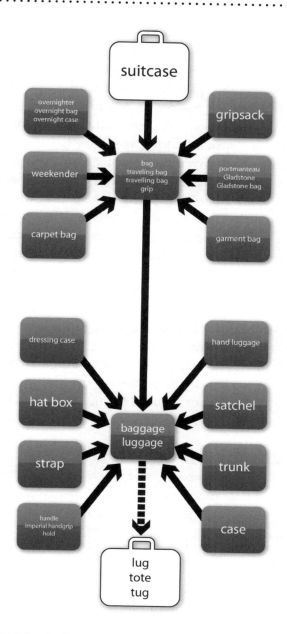

Fig 7 A visual representation of related keywords

mate top bid for the keyword 'luggage' and it was about £1.35. This means that any advertiser who is in the top three positions (i.e. at the top of the page) could be paying *at least* £1.35 for every click on their advert. Compare that with the key phrase 'buy luggage online,' which was only 80p (41 per cent less).

In other words, because fewer advertisers are bidding on the key phrase 'buy luggage online,' the average cost per click is lower. And the reason why there are fewer advertisers is because there aren't many people who are prepared to find cheaper profit-making keywords (except your good self).

Interestingly, this example leads me straight on to the second point: Which of these two people do you think is more likely to buy from you right now? The person who typed in 'luggage'? Or the person who typed in 'buy luggage online'?

Well, I think you'd go with the second. And the reason is they have used keywords which actively express the fact that they are looking to make a purchase, whereas the person who typed in 'luggage' could be interested in all kinds of different things. For example, they might be looking for reviews of luggage or luggage restrictions on flights, or a character called The Luggage from a Terry Pratchett novel.

If we think up as many targeted keywords as possible to put into our campaign,[6] not only is this going to reduce the overall average cost per click but it is also going to help us zero in on customers who are ready to buy.

Incidentally, I find this bit one of the most exciting parts of the whole system because there are some dynamite profit-making keywords just waiting to be found by you, and all you have to do is think them up.

[6] You can have up to 50,000 keywords in your campaign so, for all practical purposes, there isn't really a limit you need to worry about.

Building on Root Keywords

Now that we have our root keywords we can create key phrases which contain our root keywords.

For example 'luggage' could expand into:
1. travel luggage
2. kid's luggage
3. hand luggage
4. discount luggage
5. designer luggage and so on

Fortunately, there are some excellent tools on the Internet that will do most of the 'expanding' for you. The first one is a free tool provided by WordTracker: freekeywords.wordtracker.com.

We can now see the top 100 keywords that people type into the Internet that contain the word 'luggage.' Here are the top few:

Do more with our full Keywords tool. **Try a risk free trial for 7 days!** **Why take the trial?**

luggage   [Search]

☐ include adult words

Keyword (100)	Searches (17,638)	Competition (IAAT)	KEI	KEI3
1 luggage	1,756			
2 samsonite luggage	605			
3 delta luggage fee	580			
4 airline luggage fees	547			
5 carry on luggage rules	459			
6 luggage tags	403			
7 kids luggage	387			
8 motorcycle luggage	373			
9 luggage sets	371			
10 luggage fees	368			

« Previous 1 2 3 4 5 6 7 8 9 10 Next »

You can see why everybody bids on the keyword 'luggage' – it's getting 1,756 searches a day. However, we also know that is costly and not really zoning in on our target market.

As we look down the list we see the numbers getting smaller but the keywords getting more specific. For example, 'samsonite luggage' gets 605 daily searches; so if you sell Samsonite luggage, somebody is far more likely to buy from you if that's what they've typed in to Google than if they just typed in 'luggage.'

The same principle applies to somebody who is looking for 'kids luggage.'[7] If you sell children's luggage then that's the kind of person you want to be attracting to your website. What we are looking for here are keywords that are relevant to what we supply. In other words, we are trying to stick together what somebody wants with what we sell using their keyword choice as the glue.

The next step is to copy the table from WordTracker into a spreadsheet so we can begin to organise the keywords and key phrases.

Let's first rule out those that aren't relevant to what we're selling. Here are the first 20:

Fig 8 Results from WordTracker's free keyword tool

[7] Notice how the apostrophe is missing meaning that most people don't bother with it when searching. However, there will be a few who do (pedantic me being one) so they represent a second keyword 'kid's luggage.'

Keyword	Daily search volume	Relevance
luggage	1,756	
samsonite luggage	605	OK
delta luggage fee	580	Looking for flight restrictions
airline luggage fees	547	Looking for flight restrictions
carry on luggage rules	459	Looking for flight restrictions
luggage tags	403	Not looking for specific luggage
kids luggage	387	OK
motorcycle luggage	373	Don't sell
luggage sets	371	OK
luggage fees	368	Looking for flight restrictions
carry on luggage	329	OK
delta airlines luggage restrictions	321	Looking for flight restrictions
delta luggage	301	Looking for flight restrictions
delsey luggage	296	OK
airline luggage restrictions	278	Looking for flight restrictions
luggage scales	246	Don't sell
airline luggage weight	244	Looking for flight restrictions
heys luggage	239	OK
discount luggage	236	OK
amelia earhart luggage	235	Don't sell

You can see from the list that we've taken out 35 per cent of the keywords because they're not applicable. We're either not selling that brand-name, or people are looking for luggage restrictions on a flight, or they're looking for something we don't sell.

Our list of inappropriate keywords is just as important as those that are because we can put these into Google AdWords as negative keywords (we'll come to them in detail later). Negatives stop our advert from being displayed if someone types in one of these keywords and are a great way of ruling out people who aren't customers and, therefore, stopping wasted clicks from people who aren't going to buy.

Next I'm going to group all the relevant keywords together by the category that they fall into. (You'll find that you're left with a bunch of keywords which don't fall into any particular category –

I've just put them under the general category for now.)

Here's my new list (I've extended the keyword list from my original 20 just for demonstration purposes):

Keyword	Category (Ad Group)
luggage producers	?
luggage tags	Accessories
personalised luggage tags	Accessories
luggage straps	Accessories
luggage wheels	Accessories
samsonite luggage	Brand
travelpro luggage	Brand
atlantic luggage	Brand
delsey luggage	Brand
tumi luggage	Brand
roxy luggage	Brand
carry on luggage	Flying
airline luggage	Flying
motorcycle luggage	General
leather luggage	General
travel luggage	General
luggage and handbags	General
kids luggage	General
lightweight luggage	General
wheeled luggage	General
rolling luggage	General
polka dot luggage	General
luggage school	General
international traveller luggage	General
luggage	High Traffic
designer luggage	Price - High
executive luggage	Price - High
discount luggage	Price - Low
cheap luggage	Price - Low
luggage sets	Sets
polka dot luggage sets	Sets

Sometimes you'll find there's a keyword or key phrase you are unsure about. The one in this example, for me, was 'luggage producers.' It could be that this key phrase is more likely to be typed in by people in the industry. Could it be wholesalers looking for luggage manufacturers? When you get stuck like this the easiest solution is to Google it and see if the results you get back are relevant or not.

Now you might be wondering why we're bothering to group them – why not just throw all the keywords we find into our AdWords campaign and see what happens? The main reason is that Google will reward you by reducing the cost of each click if your campaign is well organised. Organised means that relevant keywords are grouped together – Google loves relevance.

Now the keywords we've added so far are only from Word-Tracker, but there are many others, Google's own being one.

If you haven't set up your AdWords account yet then you

Fig 9 The AdWords Keyword Tool

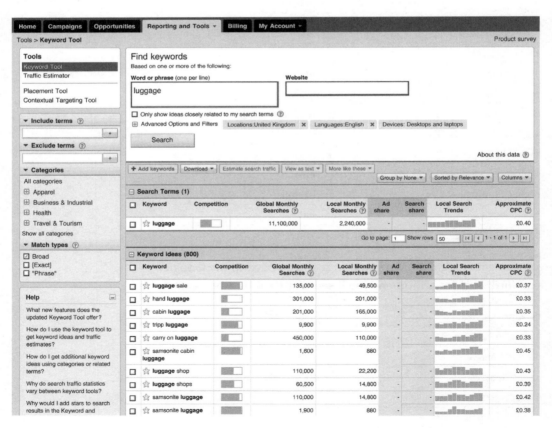

can use the 'external' version of their Keyword Tool (https://adwords.google.com/select/KeywordToolExternal) or log into your AdWords account, click on 'Reporting and Tools' and select Keyword Tool.

Fig 9 is a screenshot from the tool using our luggage example. You can change what region the results are tailored to (as you can see Google has picked up the fact that I'm in the UK).

Some of these include laptop bags, Samsonite, travel accessories, messenger bags, bags, suitcase, tumi, laptop backpack, laptop cases, handbags, backpacks, american tourister, sports bags, lesportsac, suitcases and travel bags, briefcase, computer bags, jansport, ebags and satchel, etc. (Synonyms are great at rapidly expanding your keyword list and giving you lots more ideas.)

The Keyword Tool also tells us how much advertiser competition there is for that keyword and indicates the total number of times that keyword is searched for, along with the average cost per click for advertisers.

We can export this list to our spreadsheet using the 'Download' button (under the Search button) and do the same exercise as we did with WordTracker.

Other Keyword Sources

Here are some other important sources for keywords well worth considering.

The first is to review your website because you probably use keywords in your text which are already very relevant to your products and services. Therefore, they are likely to be the kind of words that your prospects and customers type in. You could also check out your competitors' and suppliers' websites.

Instead of reading the website there is a quick way in which you can get Google to help you out. If you go back to the Google Keyword Tool for a moment you'll see that there is a box called 'Website' Simply enter the web address and click 'Search.'

You can also source keywords from offline sources: brochures, adverts, product literature, Yellow Pages. You can ask your prospects, clients and friends what they'd type in. Review the ads in your local newspaper, advertiser, etc. All these sources will give you fresh keyword ideas.

Below are some more sources of keywords you should use.

Misspellings

Everybody mistypes a keyword occasionally and yet Google will consider that to be your intended search despite offering the correct spelling. However, what you will discover is that far fewer advertisers consider using misspellings and so the competition for those keywords is much reduced, which in turn drops the bid price. A great tool for automatically generating misspellings can be found at tools.seobook.com/spelling/keywords-typos.cgi.

Geographic Keywords

Lots of searches are conducted by people who append a location to their search. Interestingly, few advertisers take the trouble to add these into their AdWords campaign, leaving an opportunity for you. An obvious example, and one you've probably done your-self, is adding 'UK' at the end of your search.

The reason they are so effective is that if someone types in a specific geographic location it means that they are looking for the product or service in that area, and that makes them a highly qualified prospect. Consider using the following geographic types of keyword:

1. Place names
   - 'book sellers gatwick airport'
   - 'things to do near buckingham palace'
2. Counties
   - 'fitness clubs warwickshire'
   - 'days out in oxfordshire'
3. Cities and towns
   - 'solicitors paris'
   - 'estate agents new york'
4. Boroughs
   - 'restaurants westminster'
   - 'taxis yardley'
5. Compass points
   - 'museums north london'
   - 'audi west midlands'
6. Countries
   - 'sony dealership uk'
   - 'holidays australia'

You can use Google to find lists for all the towns, cities, counties and boroughs in the UK.

Creative Keyword Variations

Here are four more ways to create successful keyword variations.

1: Plurals [8]

If you are using phrase match or exact match in your keywords then plurals won't automatically appear as they do with broad matched keywords.

> Let's take a simple example. This could be one of your exact match keywords: [leather suitcase], which means that somebody who typed in 'leather suitcases' won't see your advert. Easy to solve, simply add a new keyword: [leather suitcases].

> So, consider plurals for your various match types. (Don't forget to pluralise your negative phrase and exact match keywords too.)

[8] If you are not familiar with keyword match types then please take a glance at Advanced Keyword Techniques on page 132 before reading this tip.)

2: Hyphens

Occasionally, people type in words which can sometimes be hyphenated. For example,

- air-conditioning
- all-inclusive holiday
- first-class

Take a look at your keywords and see if there are any examples which could be rewritten to include a hyphen.

3: Two-Word Splits

This is the exact opposite of the above. If you are already using a hyphen in your keywords consider, removing it to create two separate words. For example:

- air conditioning
- all inclusive holiday
- first class

4: Concatenations

This is another variation on the last two examples. Sometimes people will combine two words to form one (i.e. they omit the space). For example:

- antivirus
- firstclass
- takeaway
- houseboat

Adding the Keywords into Your AdWords

Next we need to get these keywords into your Google AdWords account, so log in and you'll be presented with a screen similar to this:

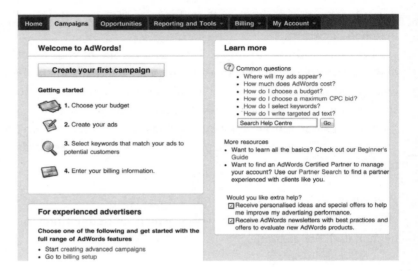

Fig 10 The opening screen to your AdWords account

If you click on the Campaigns tab and 'Create your first campaign,' you'll get a screen much like Fig 11 (right).

In order to get the best out of your first campaign, I'm going to suggest some default settings.

General: Call your campaign something meaningful.

Locations and languages: If you're new to AdWords, I recommend that you only run your campaign in your native language and country.[9] (Unless you are already operating multi-nationally I suggest first winning over your home market before taking on the world.)

Networks and devices: Select 'Let me choose...' and deselect 'Display Network.' We're only going to show ads on Google itself and not on other sites. The Display or Content Network, as it is sometimes known, puts your ads on other people's websites and not just Google's. There's quite an art (indeed a whole book's worth) to getting a Display Network running well, but for now we're going to concentrate on Google because we can exercise more control over it and it provides us with a better testing ground for our keywords.

[9] You can limit your ads to any geographic area: country, county, postcode, etc. You can even draw an area on a map! However, beware, I have found AdWords not to be entirely accurate with this tool. Some of our customers ended up receiving enquiries from their advertising hundreds of miles outside their specified area! That said, it's worth testing especially if your business only pitches to customers within a specific geographical area.

Select campaign settings   Create ad and keywords

Select campaign settings

You're ready to create your first campaign!
Try focusing on one product or service to start. You can edit these settings or expand your account whenever you like. To get help as you go along, hover over the question mark icons on this page.

Load settings ⑦   [Campaign Type ▼]

General

Campaign name   [Campaign #1]

Locations and languages

Locations ⑦   In what geographical locations do you want your ads to be displayed?
⦿ Bundle: **All countries and territories**
○ Bundle: **United States**; **Canada**
○ Country: **United States**
Select one or more other locations

Languages ⑦   What languages do your customers speak?
English Edit

⊞ Advanced location options

Networks and devices

Networks ⑦   ⦿ All available sites (Recommended for new advertisers)
○ Let me choose...

Devices ⑦   ⦿ All available devices (Recommended for new advertisers)
○ Let me choose...

Bidding and budget

Bidding option ⑦   Basic options | Advanced options
⦿ Manual bidding for clicks
○ Automatic bidding to try to maximise clicks for your target budget
☐ CPC bid limit ⑦ £ [   ]

Budget ⑦   £ [   ] per day (Format: 25.00)
Actual daily spend may vary. ⑦

⊞ Delivery method (advanced)

Ad extensions

You can use this optional feature to include relevant business information with your ads. Take a tour.

Location ⑦   ☐ Extend my ads with location information
Sitelinks ⑦   ☐ Extend my ads with links to sections on my site
Call ⑦   ☐ Extend my ads with a phone number

Advanced settings

⊟ Schedule: Start date, end date, ad scheduling
Start date   [15 Oct 2011]

End date   ⦿ None
○ [   ]

Ad scheduling ⑦   **Display ads all days and hours**
Automatic bidding campaigns may not use ad scheduling ⑦

⊟ Ad delivery: Ad rotation, frequency capping
Ad rotation ⑦   ⦿ Optimise for clicks: Show ads expected to provide more clicks
○ Optimise for conversions: Show ads expected to provide more conversions
Unavailable because conversion tracking isn't set up. Setup conversion tracking.
○ Rotate: Show ads more evenly

Frequency capping ⑦   ⦿ No cap on impressions
Display Network only   ○ [   ] Impressions [per day ▼] [per ad group ▼]

⊞ Demographic bidding

[Save and continue] [Cancel new campaign]

Fig 11 The AdWords campaign settings page where you define how your campaign will behave

Bidding and budget: Select 'Manual bidding for clicks,' which means that you control how much you spend on each keyword (instead of AdWords doing it for you). Then select how much you want to spend per day. This helps you keep a ceiling on your advertising spend so it doesn't run away with itself. You can spend as little or as much as you like. The simple rule is to only spend what you feel you can easily afford – don't bet the farm! However, the more you spend, the more clicks you receive and the faster you get data about what's working and what's not. This is a judgement call but I recommend you pick a figure you are comfortable spending.

Ad extensions: These offer a means to make your ad more visible and are fairly self-explanatory. However a detailed description of their usage can be found at adwords.google.com/support/aw/bin/answer.py?hl=en&answer=141826.

Advanced settings:

Schedule (Start date, end date, ad scheduling): You should consider only running your adverts at times when your target market is most likely to be looking for your product or service. If you are a business-to-business company, then you'll probably want your adverts between 8 a.m. and 6 p.m. and not at weekends. If, however, you are running a travel company you may prefer evenings, weekends and weekday lunchtimes. Choose times which are appropriate to both you and your prospects.

Ad delivery (Ad rotation, frequency capping): Choose 'Rotate: Show ads more evenly.' This ensures that Google doesn't try to pick the best-performing advert but instead leaves it to you to determine. This is very important for split-testing purposes because each advert needs equal 'air-time.' If one is being shown more often than another it will skew the results of your split-test. (Later on we'll see how we can use Google Analytics to help us define that time with laser precision.)

Click 'Save and continue' and write yourself your first advert. You can also add in your Maximum Cost per Click, which as Google succinctly puts it is 'the highest price you're willing to pay when someone clicks your ad.' However, *don't* add your keywords yet. Click on 'Save and continue to billing.'

Once you've completed that last phase you can click on 'Campaigns' and you'll see a page not dissimilar to Fig 12.

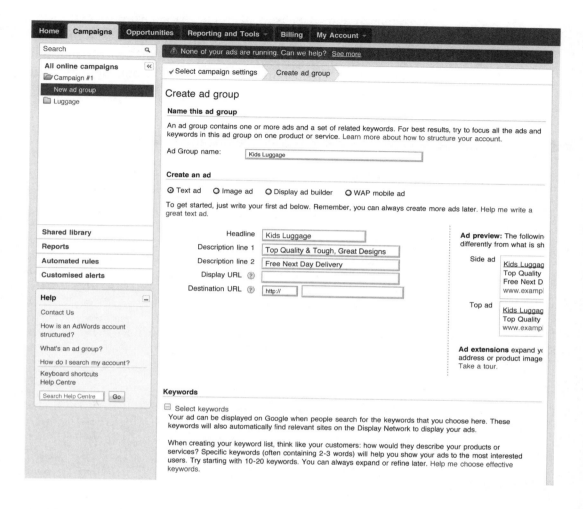

Fig 12 **Entering your first advert into AdWords**

Next you'll need to add your keywords, but we want them organised into the categories we defined for them. We can do this by creating Ad Groups within each campaign. Think of an Ad Group as a category of related keywords. Each Ad Group has its own collection of keywords and adverts which enables you to create a strong relationship between the keywords and the adverts. Put simply if the keywords are all about 'kids luggage' then the advert should be about 'kids luggage' – once again, Google loves relevance. Remember we organised our spreadsheet into groups of related keywords? Well, those groups are the Ad Groups you create in AdWords.

The importance of this approach will become ever clearer as you work with AdWords, but for now click on 'Create a new campaign' and select 'New ad group,' give it a name that's relevant to the keyword category, and copy the keywords from your spreadsheet into AdWords. Keep repeating the process until you end up with screen similar to this one. (I've only done two Ad Groups so you get the idea.)

Fig 13 The keyword statistics screen

Let's take a closer look at the columns of information AdWords initially displays for us:

Keyword, **Campaign** and **Ad Group** should be self-explanatory by now.

Status: This provides you with information about the keyword's condition (eligible, disapproved, paused, deleted, etc.) In the example here you can see that one of my keywords is below the first page bid which means it won't appear on the first page unless I increase my bid for it.

Max CPC (Maximum Cost per Click): How much you are prepared to pay for each keyword. Until your campaign is running and you are collecting data, you probably won't be able to make any judgements about how much you should bid on each keyword. So unless AdWords is telling you that your bid is below the amount you need to pay to be on the first page, you can leave the bids at their default value.

However, if you want to be more scientific than leaving this for Google to determine, use the 'Traffic Estimator' under 'Reporting and Tools.' It will give you some traffic, cost and ad-positioning expectations for each keyword depending on how much you want to pay for each click. It's not exact, so think of it only as a rough guide and not a precise tool.

Clicks: How many clicks your keyword has received (i.e. how many times someone has clicked on your advert having searched using this keyword).

Impr. (Impressions): These is the number of times your advert has been displayed for this keyword. Note, this is not the same as 'seen' because the advert may have appeared beneath the scroll-line[10] of the screen.

CTR (Click-Through Rate): The number of times your keyword has triggered a click on your adverts expressed as a percentage.

Avg CPC (Average Cost per Click): The average cost of each click on your ads.

Cost: How much each keyword has cost in clicks so far.

Avg. Pos. (Average Position): The typical position your advert will be placed at on the screen.

You can repeat the procedure of creating new Ad Groups for each of the keyword groupings in your spreadsheet. Once you've completed that step you can move on to thinking up a new root keyword (we initially focused on 'luggage'; next could be 'suitcase') and then repeat the above procedure again. At this stage I would suggest to limit yourself to no more than four or five campaigns each with no more than ten Ad Groups. That will give you a few hundred keywords to manage and maintain and that's probably enough for now.

However, you don't need to limit yourself by creating Ad Groups which are based on keywords derived from a thesaurus. You can create Ad Groups that are based around more lateral thinking. For example:

[10] The scroll-line is the point at which your window (or monitor) cuts off the rest of the screen. In classical marketing this is sometimes known as the 'fold' referring to the natural fold in newspapers. If possible you want to be above the scroll-line as your ad will be instantly seen.

- domain names
- customer types
- personality types
- your most important products
- promotional offers
- place names
- events you are running

Just thinking along those lines will spark you off into creating a whole new set of keywords.

Remember that each of these keywords has the potential to create a healthy return on investment for you. Equally, some keywords will sap your funds without generating profits and you'll need to find those and quickly remove them from your campaign.

Right now, you won't know which is which so you'll need to run your campaign for long enough so that you start to see some results. You'll probably see some patterns emerging quite quickly which will tell you the keywords or phrases that are dynamite.

Advanced Keyword Techniques

Here's an interesting marketing truth: the more you can define and target your ideal customers, the more likely they are to buy from you. For example, if your perfect customer is female, aged between 24 and 35, on a middle income, who drives, and lives in Surrey, then you have clearly identified your potential buyer (or market) for your product or service. The more accurately you can define your target market, the more likely you are to increase your sales.

So the more you know about your customer, the more focused your marketing. Of course the more specific you are about your customer the narrower and smaller your market becomes. The opposite is also true: the less specific you are about your customer the larger the market.

This principle applies to your AdWords campaign too, except that the way in which we narrow down our customers is not by specifying their age or newspaper preference but instead by the keywords that they type in. We can use a system called keyword matching to do this in our AdWords account.

Let's use our example to illustrate how keyword matching works.

You can enter keywords into AdWords in four different ways:

1. luggage – broad match
2. 'luggage' – phrase match (put " around your keyword)
3. [luggage] – exact match (put [ ] around your keyword)
4. -luggage – negative match (put a - in front of your keyword)

Broad Match

A broad match is when someone uses your keyword or key phrase in *any* part of their search query, which then triggers your advert.

Let's take the key phrase 'business luggage' as an example. Your advert would be triggered if somebody typed any of the following into Google:

- **business luggage**
- cheap **business luggage**
- **business luggage** deals
- lost **business luggage**
- **business** class **luggage** (notice that the keywords are 'split' by another word)
- **luggage** for **business** trips (split and the wrong way around)

Essentially, as long as your keyword or key phrase appears in the user's search query your advert will appear.

This is a 'covering all the bases' type of approach. In other words, you don't have to think up every search phrase that is typed into Google which contains the words 'business' and 'luggage.' The natural result is that broad match keywords generate a lot of traffic.

You may have spotted a disadvantage here. Someone searching for 'lost business luggage' is clearly more interested in finding their luggage than buying some more and, therefore, not our target market at all. Yet our advert is going to appear all the same. That means it could attract unwanted clicks and cost us money. You may also find that broad match keywords become more expensive because it's harder to maintain relevance between the keyword, your advert and your landing pages for widely varying search terms. (More on that later when we discuss Quality Scores, page 149)

Despite these drawbacks broad match keywords can be highly effective and productive. The trick is to watch them like a hawk and make sure you are getting a good return on your investment.

Note that broad match automatically includes misspellings, plurals and relevant synonyms.

Phrase Match

The next type of matching option, phrase match, is similar to broad match except your keyword or phrase has to appear in the order that you have specified.

Let's take our example again but this time we put the keyword in quotation marks to tell AdWords that it is a phrase match keyword: 'business luggage.'

Now, your advert will only be triggered if somebody types into Google:

- cheap **business luggage**
- **business luggage** deals
- lost **business luggage**

But not:

- luggage for business trips
- business travel luggage

This approach gives you greater specificity and often a higher conversion rate as a result because you are excluding some irrelevant searches. However, it could still produce untargeted traffic as 'lost business luggage' will still get through.

A great example of where phrase match can be useful would be for place names and is especially useful if you are a local business advertising in your area, for example 'window cleaner Manchester.'

Exact Match

Using exact match, our advert will only be triggered if somebody types our keyword or phrase in the correct order *and nothing more.*

This time you put square brackets around your keywords to define your exact match.

[business luggage]

This is clearly the greatest level of keyword accuracy you can achieve. In a sense it means you are getting the highest level of relevancy because what the user types in is a direct match with what you want them to type in.

The downside of this is that fewer people will search using these exact keywords and phrases. However, the traffic you do attract will be highly targeted.

Typically, broad matches will give you the most traffic, then phrase matches and finally exact matches. In other words, the more specific you are about what you want people to type in, the fewer of them will do so. This match type gives you the ability to precisely define your target market.

Negative Match

There is one final match type to consider, the negative match. Here we can stop our advert being triggered if someone types in a specific keyword or phrase.

Imagine if you sold photo software, you probably wouldn't want people to click on your advert who typed in the key-phrase 'free photo software'. Equally, you might not want people looking for jobs or careers in software. If you sell expensive handbags, you probably wouldn't want your advert appearing if somebody typed in the phrase 'cheap handbags'.

So there are examples where you actively want your adverts not to be seen by certain groups of people.

In order to enter a negative keyword into AdWords, simply put a minus sign in front of it. For example you might not want people who are looking for employment from you to click on your advert. In that case you might use the following keywords:

- -job
- -jobs
- -salary
- -career
- -careers
- -cv
- -resume

You can even use negative phrase (-'cat thief') and negative exact matches (-[cat thief]). Don't forget that you should include both singular and plural negative keywords if you use phrase and exact matches. You can put negative keywords in both Ad Groups and Campaigns.[11]

[11] Campaign negative keywords apply to all of the Ad Groups in the campaign.

If you use negative keywords carefully there is absolutely no downside to them because all you will be doing is filtering out clicks from people who are not your customers.

I've listed out some of the common negative keywords you may want to add into your campaigns and Ad Groups in Appendix IV (page 345).

One final note about search types. It's best if you separate them into their own Ad Groups because if you lump them together Google will 'cherry pick' the keywords it believes are most appropriate. This is because your broad match includes phrase and exact match keyword searches. In other words, AdWords applies a kind of fuzzy logic to its choice of keyword if you mix your keyword types up.

To illustrate this let's imagine an Ad Group with the following keywords:

chicken feed
[chicken feed]
'chicken feed'

In order to properly assess how each phrase and exact keyword is performing you need to separate it from the broad match otherwise the broad match will 'steal' from the other two and so skew your results. You can do this by setting up a new Ad Group and applying the keywords [chicken feed] and 'chicken feed' as negatives but only for the broad match Ad Group. AdWords will now only pick your exact and phrase match keywords from your new Ad Group and not mix them up with your broad match keyword.

Plus it gives you real clarity as to which match type is working at a glance simply by looking at the overview of each Ad Group. This helps clean up your AdWords laboratory and clarify the results you are getting.

WRITING COMPELLING ADVERTS

If keywords are the blood of your campaign then your adverts are the beating heart.

Writing a good advert is an art. Writing a good advert using AdWords gives you a science on which to base the art.

You have a total of 95 characters to convey your message: 25 in the headline and 35 in lines 2 and 3. There are also 35 characters for a display URL but you can't use this for ad copy. For something so small it's surprising what you can do with it as well as how much subtlety you can apply to it.

Buy **Business Luggage** - Stylish, Hardwearing **Luggage**
Ranges at M&S.
www.marksandspencer.com/luggage
marksandspencer.com is rated ★★★★☆ 201 reviews
Order Online Today!

Fig 14 A typical Google AdWords advert

Fundamentally, Google wants you to deliver relevant content to your visitor – if you can do that then Google will reward you by lowering your cost per click. This means that your advert is the promise to your visitor that the resulting webpage must fulfil.

The easiest way to describe the how-to of advert writing is through a series of tactics which you can employ. Each of these 10 strategies can be used independently or in conjunction with another.

Tactic 1: Structure Your Advert

Let's start with a basic structure for your advert. This is a proven method for getting good results from the outset. (You can experiment with the other approaches after you've tested this one.)

- Title: Repeat the keyword/key phrase the visitor typed in
- Description 1: Describe the benefit
- Description 2: Call to Action
- URL: Ideally, put the keyword/key phrase at the end of your domain name

Here's an example for you:

Title	Business Luggage
Description 1	Tough Luggage, 5-Year Guarantee
Description 2	Free Next-Day Delivery Here…
URL	www.jedscompany.co.uk/business-luggage

To begin writing a good ad ask yourself the following:

1. What is the most important benefit of your product/ service?
2. What feature is most relevant to your customer (easy to order, next-day delivery, etc.)?
3. What can you give them once they click on your advert (free delivery, free download, 5-minute training course, etc.)?

Use the answers you get to get your creative juices flowing. Now let's consider a few ad writing tactics that will help them get clicked on.

Tactic 2: Use the Keyword/Key Phrase as Your Headline

This immediately resolves the question of what the opening line should be on your ad. If the browser typed in 'diy furniture' they have those specific keywords in their mind. This means that they are looking for those keywords on the page. If your advert headline simply says 'DIY Furniture' then you are mirroring exactly what the browser is expecting to see and consequently drawing their eye to your advert. The other advantage is that Google will **embolden** all the words in your advert that match the keywords the browser has typed in, thus adding even greater visual appeal to your advert. In fact, wherever in your advert the keywords are repeated they will be in bold and that includes the URL line.

On this last point I have experimented with actual domain names that include the keyword in them. For example: web-design-birmingham.co.uk for the keywords 'web design' and 'birmingham.' These domain names yielded a 50–70 per cent greater click-through rate. This stands to reason really because the more keywords in bold in your advert, the higher the chance your advert will be noticed above others. However, this takes the thinking one step further because people will perceive your advert to be more relevant if they think that your website is dedicated to the keywords they've typed in. Hence a domain name like www.dog-training.co.uk will do well for keywords relating to dog training (especially if the website is about dog training too!).

Tactic 3: Make Your Advert Only Sell the Click

A common mistake is to try and make the advert copy sell your product or service. A far more effective mechanism is to write copy that inspires the user to click. (In reality, that is the sole purpose of the advert: to get traffic to your website, not to try and close the sale.) The best way to illustrate this is through an example so consider the relative strengths of these two ad lines:

Get the latest fashions
Friendly service

Get 20 Free fashion tips
Look fantastic this summer!

The second one is, of course, more compelling not only because is it offering something for free but because it addresses the real reason why people buy clothes: they want to look good!

Remember, selling the click means creating a compelling reason why the browser should visit your website. It is the website's job to make the sale. (The circus parade isn't the show, it's just getting you interested!)

Tactic 4: Split-test Your Adverts

This idea is deceptively simple but incredibly powerful. You run two adverts simultaneously with different copy and see which performs better. This enables you to see which advert gets more click-throughs or conversions. Once you have a clear winner you modify the copy of the failing advert to try and beat its counterpart. Don't forget to only change one thing at a time!

You may want to review the previous chapter, Advanced Split-testing (AB/C Testing), page 93.

This often reveals that the subtlest of changes make enormous differences. For example, try running two adverts with exactly the same copy but one using capitalised words. (A trick to remember here is to make sure Google rotates the adverts evenly and doesn't try and to show one more than another because it thinks it's better – you're the best judge of what's working for you, not Google. Remember we set this up when we were creating the campaign.)

Tactic 5: Write Action-Based Ads

The purpose of all marketing is to elicit a response. In order to get this response advertisers use a tactic known as a 'call to action.' It is simply telling the reader exactly what they need to do next. (This is best placed on description line 2.) Here are a few examples:

- Book today/now
- Browse our e-store
- Buy now
- Call 24/7
- Call now[12]
- Get a:
  - Free consultation
  - Free delivery
  - Free demo
  - Free download
  - Free quote
  - Free report

[12] Using 'Today' and 'Now' creates a strong compulsion to act in your prospect's mind. Anything which indicates a sense of immediacy – 'Sale Ends Today' – will help attract the click.

- Get the report
- Order today
- See for yourself
- Start now
- Take the test

This list omits the most obvious, namely, 'Click Here.' Google disallows this because it works superbly well at attracting attention, perhaps much better than any other online call to action. But if every AdWords advertiser were using those words the SERPs would be festooned with adverts all saying 'CLICK HERE.' In Google's eyes (and most people's too) this would decrease the overall quality of the 'Google experience.' However, you can use a similar phrase to good effect, without breaking Google's rules. Simply use the single word 'Here.' For example:

- Get a Great Holiday Here.
- For Sat Navs, Start Here

Another call to action tactic is to use an ellipsis ('…') at the end of your call to action. For example:

- Check out our free download…
- Enter our competition and win…

You can also use verbs to instill a sense of speed and action into the opening lines of your adverts. For example,

- Buy
- Check Out
- Choose From
- Discover
- Download
- Watch
- Learn

Tactic 6: Don't Follow the Crowd

Before you advertise on a specific keyword consider what other advertisers are doing. Simply Google the keywords and take a look at the adverts and what they're saying. I recently Googled 'luggage' and the top five adverts all claimed to have sales on and so none stood out. If I wanted to advertise there I would be tempted to use ad copy like:

No Luggage Sale Here!
We Don't Need a Luggage Sale To
Give You the Best Price – Order Now...

OK, so it's a bit tongue-in-cheek but you get the idea: look at what the adverts are saying and see if breaking the mould increases your click-through rate. If your competitors have lots of text in their adverts, use as little text as possible. If everyone else's site is screaming for the order why not try a reverse tactic and send new incoming clicks to an 'about us' type page from which they could then click through to your products/services pages? If everyone is saying how great their company is why not run an ad offering some help in choosing between suppliers in your industry?

Tactic 7: Put the Price in the Advert

Although keywords target your prospect by describing their need there can still be a lot of variation. For example, someone typing in 'luggage bags with wheels' may be happy to pay £100 or more, others might not want to pay more than £30. Even though the keyword has 'defined' the overall market the people that inhabit it are very different. So, if you only supply expensive luggage you won't want people who are looking for cheap luggage clicking on your advert. A simple way to avoid these unnecessary clicks is to put the price in the advert, thus differentiating yourself from the competition and focusing on your buyer. This tactic can work extremely well for high-priced products and services.

Conversely you can put the price in the advert if you know you are offering a lower price than your competition or if none of the competition mentions price. Remember that the goal is to get your visitor to click on your ad and that by presenting a fair price you resolve the biggest issue on most buyers' minds, namely, how much will it cost. Most of your competitors will be too scared to put a price up there for fear that it will put people off which is ironic because what puts people off more is not knowing the price. Remember also that people don't want to waste time researching. If you can help them by 'cutting to the chase' by indicating your preferred customer, you will increase the quality of your visitor.

Tactic 8: Use Dynamic Keyword Insertion

This is a great labour-saving feature and one which you can use to make your headlines mirror the exact keywords the browser typed in (and also makes your headline appear in bold). Simply type in the following into the Title of your advert.

{KeyWord:default keyword}

Whatever the browser typed in will now be mirrored in the headline of your advert. However, if what they typed in exceeds the 25 character limit then whatever you typed in as the 'default keyword' will appear. For example,

{KeyWord:Kids Luggage}

will either display whatever keywords were used in the search or 'Kids Luggage' if the search term exceeded 25 characters.

There are three different ways of using this feature which result in different capitalisations:

1. {Keyword:kids luggage} will appear as kids luggage
2. {Keyword:Kids luggage} will appear as Kids luggage
3. {KeyWord:Kids Luggage} will appear as Kids Luggage

This is a powerful tool but care should be applied because if the browser types in complete rubbish, that too will appear in the title. If you'd like to learn more take a look at Google's help page at adwords.google.com/support/aw/bin/answer.py? hl=en&answer=74996.

Tactic 9: Ask A Question

Sometimes the best way to attract the click is to pique your prospect's curiosity with a simple question:

1. Did You Know that [Keyword] Could [Benefit]?
    *   Did You Know that Lutein Could Save Your Sight?
    *   Did You Know that our Help Could Double Your Business?
2. Confused About [Keyword]?

3. Want to [solution to problem]?
    - Want to Earn More Money from Your Website?
    - Want to Get Fit?
4. Question [Problem]?
    - Do You Hate Debt?
    - Do You Hate Spiders?
    - Suffering IBS for Years?
    - Bored of the 9–5?
5. Here's a variation on the theme by answering a question: How to [solution to problem]
    - How to Keep the Kids Entertained
    - How to Grow Huge Tomatoes

Tactic 10: 21 More Ideas for Compelling Adverts

Here are a bunch of ideas you can test to improve the performance of your adverts:

Language and Layout

1. Capitalise the First Letters in Your Ads. However don't capitalise the small words such as 'a,' 'an,' 'in,' 'on,' 'and,' etc.
2. Get rid of the small words if you can. By doing so you keep your message short and punchy.
3. Don't repeat punctuation (!!), be grammatical and, as Perry Marshall puts it, be 'concise, relevant and accurate.'
4. Use '–' instead of commas for a bit more impact.
5. Use '&' instead of 'and.'
6. Use market abbreviations (assuming that your market understands them), e.g. 'SEO' instead of 'Search Engine Optimisation,' or 'B2B' instead of 'Business to Business.'

Miscellaneous Approaches

1. Use quotes, testimonials and endorsements. For example:
    - 'The Best Read for 2011' – The Times
    - 'Fast, Efficient Service' – Dr John Smith
    - Voted Best Company 2012, PC Shopper

2. Use price guarantees (if you have one): 'Lowest Prices Guaranteed or Double Your Money Back'
3. Use 'Free'
4. Use 'New'
5. Use 'Secrets': 'Unlock the Secrets of Websites', 'Discover the Simple Secret to Hypnosis'
6. Use 'Exposed': 'Google AdWords Exposed'
7. Use 'You Need to': 'You Need to Read This Before Buying a Car'
8. 'Changes Your Life' works better than 'Change Your Life' because the word 'change' implies you have to do something yourself to make it happen. However, 'changes' implies that it will do it for you. You can apply this to many other words. For example: 'Builds You a Better Home', 'Grows Bigger Plants'.
9. Offer simple instructions: '5 Steps to a Flat Tummy', 'How to Win at Poker'

Good Practice

1. Don't use exaggerated claims or language. Keep your ad honest and realistic. (Nobody really believes 'Loose 20 lbs in 5 days').
2. Use the keyword three times (if you can). In the title, descriptions and finally in the ad URL.
3. Use facts and figures: '25% of People Agree', 'Raise Your Profits by 15%', 'Our £500 Guarantee'.
4. Even if you are ranked highly in the organic listings you should still run an advert above your listing. This follows the simple premise that the whole is greater than the sum of the parts, or, 1 + 1 = 3! Firstly, you are giving people more than one opportunity to click on you and secondly, you also look like you are more relevant because you're listed several times.
5. Pitch to your specific market directly. 'Child Management for Teachers', 'Theory Tests for Learner Drivers', 'Tips for Mums', 'Websites for Entrepreneurs'.

LANDING PAGES

You've got your keywords organised, your adverts written. Next you want to send the traffic from your adverts to your website.

This is such an important component in both your overall web strategy and your AdWords campaign that I've written a chapter dedicated to maximising the returns from your webpages (see Chapter 7, Turn Visitors into Customers). However, for the purposes of your campaign (and getting it going) remember to direct your prospects to the most relevant page on your website for the search term they have entered. Don't direct all your traffic to the home page! Although this may seem very obvious, such mistakes are often made.

Remember you want to make it as easy as possible for your visitor to become a customer, either through leaving their details or buying directly: if you have a page that is relevant to the keyword and advert then point your advert to it; otherwise write the page from scratch.

Your starting point is to get the right traffic to the right page – you can refine the whole process later on.

CONVERSIONS AND ANALYSING RESULTS

In any AdWords campaign we want to achieve 3 things:
1. A high Conversion Rate
2. A high Click-Through Rate
3. A low Cost-per-Click

The rest is just statistics. (In fact the above three statistics are the 20 per cent of statistics which, if you concentrate your efforts on, will yield 80 per cent of your campaign's improvements.)

Whenever you come to analysing your campaigns – which you should do regularly – you need to focus on these three key targets.

Setting Up Conversion Tracking

In order to make AdWords truly fly, you must track the number of conversions you make from each keyword and advert. In other words, you must know how many sales resulted from your advertising efforts so you can focus your advertising spending.

The first thing to identify is what a conversion means to you. For example, if you are an ecommerce site it will be when someone sees the 'Thank You' page after a purchase. If you are selling a service or you are not ecommerce-based, a conversion might be the 'Thank You' page after they've filled in a lead-generating form. You can, in fact, measure any page on your website as being a conversion. You simply have to tell AdWords which page it is on your website. However, you'd normally choose a page that's seen after your visitor has taken a specific action.

Fig 15 How conversions are tracked

Now you've picked your pages you can enter them into the AdWords system. Select the 'Reporting & Tools' tab and then the cunningly titled 'Conversions' link. Then select a New Conversion, give it a name and finally select what type of conversion it is: Other | Purchase/Sale | Sign-up | Lead | View of a key page.

Next, AdWords asks you to enter some information about the page that you are tracking, including how much revenue you think each conversion is worth. (This is where you can either add a specific value, your average order value, your best guess, or leave it blank.)

The final screen is where you are given some code to add into the conversion page on your website. Hand this code over to your web designers and which pages to add it to (i.e. the name of the conversion page). Once this step is complete AdWords will start tracking the success of your campaign.

So, to recap, someone types in a keyword, clicks on your ad and gets taken to your website. They buy your product or leave their contact details and hey presto, a conversion is tracked. What you see in your AdWords campaign are two additional columns: 'Conv. (1-per-click)' and 'Cost/Conv. (1-per-click).' The first tells you how many conversions have been generated by that keyword and the latter tells you how much each conversion costs you.

Analysing Keyword Performance

This is where it gets serious! Let's take a look at a sample campaign's results.[13]

[13] Results from an actual campaign. Please note that this was for a high-ticket item service and the figures here should not be considered to be indicative of all AdWords campaigns.

Key-word	Max. CPC	Quality Score	Clicks	Imps	CTR	Avg CPC	Cost	Avg Position	Conv. per Click	Cost per Conv.
1	£2.18	7/10	274	12642	2.17%	£2.01	£550.14	4.73	29	£18.97
2	£2.35	6/10	239	14541	1.64%	£2.02	£483.33	3.52	26	£18.59
3	£2.85	7/10	195	7044	2.77%	£2.55	£498.13	3.86	42	£11.86
4	£2.85	7/10	134	3134	4.28%	£2.60	£348.79	4.94	29	£12.03
5	£2.00	7/10	126	7564	1.67%	£1.69	£213.16	4.64	11	£19.38
6	£2.40	7/10	87	4434	1.96%	£2.01	£175.30	2.94	5	£35.06
7	£2.00	7/10	78	2356	3.31%	£1.42	£110.76	3.19	3	£36.92
8	£2.45	7/10	59	1464	4.03%	£2.21	£130.57	6.87	5	£26.11
9	£2.95	7/10	44	1246	3.53%	£2.62	£115.06	3.53	6	£19.18
10	£2.00	7/10	42	743	5.65%	£1.58	£66.37	3.01	4	£16.59
11	£1.80	6/10	39	3432	1.14%	£1.68	£65.36	3.25	4	£16.34
12	£3.00	7/10	32	471	6.79%	£2.18	£69.68	2.61	7	£9.95
13	£2.70	7/10	26	991	2.62%	£2.40	£62.38	5.4	1	£62.38
14	£2.99	7/10	24	815	2.94%	£2.77	£66.38	2.53	0	£0
15	£2.90	7/10	14	771	1.82%	£2.61	£36.53	3.84	2	£18.26

Cost per Conversion and Conversions

The first thing we're interested in is the Cost per Conversion (the rightmost column). This indicates how much the keyword costs to generate one sale.[14] From our table you can see that keyword 3 is costing only £11.86 whereas keyword 13 is costing £62.38. You can also see that keyword 13 is getting few clicks and has converted less than 3 per cent of its clicks. This is a keyword ripe for culling. (However, before you delete any keyword in your Ad Groups, do make sure that it has received at least 20 clicks. That way you've given it enough of a chance to determine its value.)

Next we're interested in the number of conversions. The more conversions we see a keyword generate the more relevant that keyword/advert and landing page is to our buyers. Conversely, fewer conversions indicates that the keyword is less relevant to our prospects (or that the advert and the landing page are not relevant to the keyword). A classic example of this last point is to

[14] For the purpose of simplifying my example I'm going to assume that a conversion equates to a sale. However, if you are a lead-generating site, a conversion may be the acquisition of a lead as the result of someone filling out your enquiry form.

have a keyword like 'Sony LCD TVs' with an ad title of 'LCD TVs' and a landing page which doesn't mention either 'Sony' or 'LCD TVs'! And this happens a lot in AdWords campaigns so beware – if you see low conversion rates then something is wrong with the advert and/or the landing page. If you have a low click-through rate then your advert may not be compelling enough.

An easy way to assess the conversion rate is by converting it to a percentage:

$$\frac{\text{Number of conversions}}{\text{Number of clicks}} \times 100\%$$

You will quickly see that some keywords will be doing well and others poorly. There will also be a bunch in the middle that are just 'Ok.' Leave these until they start to do better or worse.

Keywords like 6, 7 and 8 have good number of clicks (87, 78 and 59 respectively) but fail to convert well (5, 3 and 5 respectively), which is why they have rather high conversion costs. Now this is where knowing your profit margin and your customer lifetime value really comes into its own, because you can use these figures to calculate whether it's worthwhile continuing with such a high cost per conversion or if you are better off deleting the keywords and saving your money. Essentially, you never want to run keywords that cost more than they make in return.

Whatever an acceptable cost of sale is for you, it certainly pays to focus on the keywords that are doing well. In the example above these are keywords 3, 4 and 12. All have low cost of conversions. These are worth removing from this Ad Group and into their own where more focused ads can be written for them. (You would ideally want them to go to their own landing page too.) This is a process called 'peel and stick.' You peel out the high performers and stick them in their own group with their own advert and their own landing page. By creating a new and more 'relevant' Ad Group you will dramatically increase their effectiveness. Keywords 3 and 4 deserve this particular treatment as they have the highest number of conversions.

You can also 'peel and stick' the bad keywords into a group of their own. This immediately does two things:

1.   Gives underperforming keywords a chance to improve (because you're creating relevant adverts and landing pages for them)

2. Improves the overall quality of the original Ad Group by removing the dross.

Quality Score

The Quality Score (QS) is perhaps one of the most important metrics in your entire campaign. It relates to the 'quality of user experience' you give from keyword to advert to landing page. The stronger the relationship between the three, the higher your quality score will be. Below is the breakdown of the factors making up the QS and as you can see the major factor in determining your Quality Score is your Click-Though Rate (CTR, see page 150). CTR accounts for 65 per cent of your quality score, according to Google's chief economist, Hal Varian.

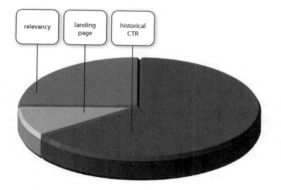

Fig 16 How Google determines your Quality Score

QS is marked out of 10 and you should be aiming for scores of 8 or above.[15]

If your QS starts to fall, this is an indication that there is a problem with your advert and/or landing page. As it falls Google will force you to increase your Cost per Click in order to maintain your advert's position. This is their way of weeding out poor advertisers by pricing them out of the market.

In order to keep your QS high, concentrate your efforts on improving your CTR. You should also make sure that your landing page is relevant, has good, clear navigation and isn't trying to dupe your visitor. On this last point, known as transparency, it's worth remembering that honesty is the best policy. So, for example, if your advert offers reviews of the top 20 shampoos but only promotes one, Google will detect this and lower your Quality Score.

[15] You can see the Quality Score for each keyword by showing the Quality Score column in your AdWords campaign. Plus if you're looking for an insight into the factors Google considers when assessing your landing page take a look at adwords.google.com/support/aw/bin/answer.py?hl=en-uk&answer=46675

Incidentally, if your Quality Score drops below 4 you may find that no matter what you do you cannot get it any higher. The reason for this is because Google has 'failed' your landing page. In this situation you must contact Google directly and ask them to re-evaluate your landing page. Currently this has to be done by a person and is not automated (hence the reason for contacting Google).

If you are struggling to keep your Quality Score up then consider refocusing your landing pages onto (or indeed, into) a blog. It's widely reported that Google loves blogs because they deliver:

1. Relevance to the topic
2. Lots of information which is regularly updated (so you must add and change the blog on a regular basis, i.e. at least every 20 days)
3. A sense of impartiality

Click-Through Rate

Click-Through Rate is Google's measure of how relevant and compelling your advert is in relation to search term which was typed in. The more relevant people find your advert, the higher your Click-Through Rate will be. (This is one reason why we spend so much time ensuring that the keywords from the search term are repeated in the advert.) You could think of CTR as votes for your advert (and in particular, a vote of relevancy). Google likes to see a minimum CTR of 1 per cent, although you should be aiming for much higher than that.

Even so, it should not be the final arbiter in your decision-making. For example take a look at keyword 3. The CTR is less than half that of keyword 10. To make matters worse, the cost per click (CPC) is almost £1 more! But when you calculate the conversion percentage, keyword 3 has a 22 per cent conversion rate (42/195) whereas keyword 10 only has a 10 per cent conversion rate (4/42). Despite having a lower CTR and costing more, keyword 3 is still a better performing keyword.

Use CTR as a guide to the relevance of your keyword and advert. The higher the Click-Through Rate the greater the relevance between keyword and advert.

A simple way to improve your CTR is to split-test your adverts. If you have poor-performing adverts then the CTR for your keywords will reflect that. However, the higher the CTR the better Google will perceive your keywords to be – your quality score will rise and your cost per click will drop – so this is an important metric to watch.

Cost Per Click and Advert Positioning

Think of Cost Per Click (CPC) as a game. The game is to reduce it as much as possible while still maintaining (or increasing) your conversions. Google will automatically reduce your CPC as your Quality Score for each keyword improves. To begin with, you should pay enough to get on the first page and ideally into the top three positions. (In other words, you'll initially be paying more than your competitors.) Once there you can gradually reduce your CPC by a few pence. Every so often drop your CPC and assess what happens. Do your conversions drop off? Do you get fewer clicks but more conversions? Does your ad position crash? If you see the performance dropping off, increase the CPC again, review your ads, update the landing page, etc. However, very often you'll find that you can reduce the CPC while maintaining good performance (especially if your CTR and QS are high).

The trick here is to test, test, test!

Take care not to get involved in bidding wars. It is very tempting, especially when your campaign is going well, to pitch your advert at first position on the page. However, research identifies that while you will typically receive anything between three and seven times more clicks from being in first position, the conversion rate does not appreciably increase. One of the reasons for this may be the 'click-happy browser.' Often browsers will only take a few seconds in deciding where to click, so if your advert is in pole position they are more likely to click on it. This is typically because most people click on the 'search' button which is nearest to the top advert so the least amount of mouse movement takes them to the first ad. It does not, however, mean that they are 'committed.' The typical browsing behaviour of a committed user (i.e. someone who has a genuine need) will be more thorough. They will take the time to read adverts in positions 2, 3 and 4 so they can weigh up options. Thus, your advert is best served in one of these positions or even lower down the field. Again, test your ad positioning to find the 'lost cost, high conversion' sweet spot.

There is another school of thought on this point and this is to simply let those who do want to engage in bidding wars get on with it. If your competitors want to slug it out for pole position, let them. The reality is that you will increase your CTR and conversions by implementing my strategies to a far greater degree than by attempting to bludgeon your way to the top at all cost.

As an aside, Google provides the facility to manage your CPC for you. However, while this might be a time-saving option, experience shows it does not produce the best results. Ultimately, there is no substitute for your own judgement.

General Analysis Help

As you begin to analyse your AdWords campaign you'll need to start making some decisions about your keywords: which to delete, pause, run with, move to other Ad Groups, etc., and it can all get a bit confusing. So here are some pointers to help you decide how to handle your keywords.

If you find that the CPC is getting too high then take a look at your QS to make sure you haven't got an issue developing. Also consider using a different matching type (exact match or phrase match). Also try to think up other keywords which use this keyword as its root.

If you are getting very few impressions for an exact match keyword try using either phrase or broad matching types. (If you're already using these and still getting few impressions the keyword is not worth keeping unless you can prove its ROI). If it has not received any impressions for two months then it's time to delete it.

If a keyword looks like it's getting a good number of impressions, expand upon it.

1. Create more keywords using it as a root
2. Swap the keywords around and use exact/phrase matching
    - 'hairdressers washington' becomes 'washington hairdressers'
3. Add in new match types
4. 'Peel and Stick' it into its own Ad Group

You may want to consider using a poorly performing keyword as a negative.

Finally don't delete a poorly performing keyword until you've considered:

1. rearranging the order of the words
2. reverting to broad match
3. trying exact/phrase match
4. assessing it as a negative
5. changing its bid price
6. reviewing the landing page it is linked to (could that be the cause of the problem?)
7. typing it into Google to see what websites and adverts are being displayed

However, *do* delete it if there are zero clicks and more than 100 impressions (it's killing your Quality Score to keep it!).

You may find this helpful: Google has developed an offline tool you can use to manage your account called the AdWords Editor. It can be a real labour saver and is well worth a look (www. google.com/intl/en/adwordseditor).

Analysing Advert Performance

Along with analysing keyword performance you will also need to assess how your adverts are doing. Clicking on the 'Ads' tab will reveal the performance of each of your adverts. Drill into a specific Ad Group and take a look.

In the example below we are split-testing three different adverts. Adverts 1 and 2 are similar (perhaps the only difference is a change in headline) whereas advert 3 is a completely different approach. You may recall this AB/C split-testing tactic from the previous chapter.

Advert	Clicks	Impr.	CTR	Avg CPC	Cost	Avg. Pos.	Conv. per click	Cost per Conv.
Ad 1	359	11,752	3.05%	£2.35	£842.17	4.3	55	£15.31
Ad 2	194	17,969	1.08%	£1.24	£241.45	6.6	3	£80.48
Ad 3	257	10,920	2.35%	£2.07	£531.96	4.7	39	£13.64

Again we focusing on the cost per conversion, which highlights the big difference between ads 1 and 2. Evidently we need to stop running the second ad as it is costing more than £80 per conversion.

However, it looks as though our new idea (advert 3) is doing better than both. In the above example I would be tempted to get rid of adverts 1 and 2 and split-test a variation on advert 3. I would also be inclined to try fresh idea against my now top-performing advert.

As I mentioned earlier CTR is an important factor in maintaining a high Quality Score in your AdWords campaign. So, always keep a careful eye on this metric as low CTRs will lower your Quality Score

A great tool on the Internet to assess the performance of two competing adverts is Split Tester (www.splittester.com). Simply punch in the data from each of your adverts and this website will tell you which advert is performing better. It will even tell you if you don't have enough data for a conclusion to be drawn (this is known as statistical significance).

Another great online tool for assessing how well your adverts are performing is Super Split Tester (www.supersplittester.com). This is different because it calculates the profit per 1,000 impressions using your conversion data. Again you just punch the numbers in and it will then pick the winning advert and tell you how much money you will make from both.

▪ *TRACKING OFFLINE CONVERSIONS*

For many, a conversion on Google will only be halfway to the sale. If like me you need to track the sale in the 'real world' then here are some pointers to help you.

Let's imagine that a Google conversion takes you to the point that someone has left their contact details with you via a form on your website. Firstly, get in touch straightaway and ask them what they typed in to find you (it's a long shot whether they'll remember but it's worth trying). Then make sure that you keep track of whether they become a customer or not using whatever system you like. We keep a simple spreadsheet of all our enquiries and match them up to who has become a customer. From these results you can assess how many new customers you are acquiring through AdWords. You'll already know their order value so adding them up is a relatively simple process. Once you know how many you are converting less the cost of AdWords, you've identified your ROI (Return on Investment).

Not everyone, however, will leave their contact details; some will simply phone you up there and then. This can present a problem because unless everyone who picks up the telephone to a prospect asks, 'How did you find out about us?' you may be receiving calls as a result of your AdWords campaign but never realising it. The easy way around this is to purchase a telephone number which is only used on your website.[16] That way when you get the itemised bill you can marry the numbers with your new customers.

Here's one more thought on the subject of conversions and the offline world. If you've tested an effective marketing message through your adverts and landing pages it stands to reason that it would work on other forms of advertising. So, if you've got a great headline that always gets the click, it will probably grab people's attention if you send it as a letter or report title, exhibition banner, newspaper advert, etc.

[16] It is possible to customise a telephone system to have a separate telephone number for each of the keywords you use. That way, you can assess the ROI of each keyword that prospects call. This is an ultra-advanced tactic but great if you're running a call centre.

Key Questions to Help Your Analysis

To help you get a sense of what you should be looking out for in your AdWords campaign, ask yourself the following questions:

1. What are your top-performing keywords?
2. What are your top-performing ads?
3. Which keywords lead to the most sales and why?
4. Which ads lead to the most sales and why?
5. Now ask the same four questions again but looking for the lowest performers.

■ THE ULTIMATE GOOGLE STRATEGY

If you've got this far and your head is starting to spin, don't worry, because anyone who's ever used Google AdWords has been here. The trick is not to lose focus of a very simple rule: the keyword must be relevant to the advert which must be relevant to the landing page. All you need to do is make sure that your campaign links these elements together. This is because Google are very keen on ensuring that the results the user gets from typing in the keywords are highly relevant. (Imagine if you were looking for a local hairdresser and adverts for car mechanics appeared!) So, putting it bluntly, if the keywords typed in are 'free PC repair advice' then your ad should say ' free PC repair advice' and the page they are directed to should contain the free PC repair advice! This sounds simple but it can get complex. The problem occurs with the more keywords that you have. Very often there will be some 'drift' away from the core content of the landing page and even though you may immediately see the relationship, your prospect may not. For example, if you sell BMWs you may also want to attract new customers to service their cars. If your advert takes the browser to the home page there may be no reference to the service department. Google will then penalise your advert by pushing it down the rankings, forcing you to increase your bid price. The solution is very simple: always direct the browser to the part of your website which bears most relevance to the keyword that they have typed in.

Remember that AdWords requires constant testing, analysis and adjustment, all of which sounds like an almighty pain, but I promise you if you get it right you will relish every second you spend on it.

WHY YOU SHOULD USE ADWORDS BEFORE SEO

Usually, when a website is finished, the first thing the business owner thinks of is getting the site as high as they can on the search engines. And so they should: getting listed is vital if you want to take advantage of free traffic from the likes of Google.

However, the majority think the way to do that is through optimising their website so that the search engines will naturally rank them more highly. This is a process called Search Engine Optimisation, and we'll deal with that in Chapter 8. However, in order to do any Search Engine Optimisation you need to know what keywords your website needs to be optimised against. So, let's say you sell pet supplies. You might want your website to appear in the search engine listings when someone types in keywords like 'pet supplies', 'pet toys', 'aquarium tanks', etc.

The average-sized website can only be optimised for only a handful of keywords so you can't go wild and think up every keyword that might relate to your business as you can with AdWords. And herein lies the trap most web owners fall into: they go for the keywords that they think will yield them the highest amount of traffic to their website. The confusion here is that not all traffic is great traffic. It doesn't follow that the more traffic you have, the more sales you make. Opting for high-traffic keywords means that you are also attracting traffic which has no interest in your product.

Let's take the key phrase 'pet supplies'. At first glance it would seem the obvious choice for a pet supplies company. However, this keyword would also attract traffic from people who use the key phrase for other purposes, for example:

- pet supplies wholesalers
- free pet supplies
- pet supplies medicines
- cheap pet supplies
- local pet supplies
- exotic pet supplies
- holistic pet supplies and so on.

None of these may relate to what they sell.

However, there are certain keywords that, when people type into the search engines, will be tightly focused on the products and services that you supply on your website. In fact, there will be specific keywords that result in sales and you will see those when you analyse your conversions in AdWords.

Below is a real-life case study of a company selling an anti-virus product called Sophos. It reveals some fascinating information about any suppositions one may have about which keywords result in sales.

There are three ways people could type the primary keywords into a web browser:

1. sophos antivirus
2. sophos anti-virus
3. sophos anti virus

But which of the three should be Search Engine Optimised for the website? The results were extraordinary.

Fig 17 is a screenshot from the campaign. What you can see here are two keywords which are almost identical: 'sophos anti-virus' and 'sophos antivirus'. If you didn't know any better you would probably SEO both of these keywords for your website. However, when you look at the AdWords campaign we can see that at first glance the 'sophos anti-virus' keyword is doing incredibly well – it's only attracting less than one-third the traffic of its rival 'sophos antivirus' and yet it is generating more interest (5.93% CTR vs 2.19% CTR). But let's take a look at the last two columns. Our 'winning' keyword 'sophos anti-virus' didn't

Keyword	Max. CPC	Clicks	Imps	CTR	Avg CPC	Conv. rate	Cost per Conv.
sophus	£0.50	677	4129	16.39%	£0.12	9.72%	£0.85
sofos	£0.05	602	4819	12.49%	£0.06	0.49%	£13.30
sophos anti virus	£2.00	348	5691	6.11%	£1.31	10.53%	£10.25
sophos anti-virus	£1.70	108	1819	5.93%	£0.98	0.00%	£0.00
sophos antivirus	£2.50	102	4640	2.19%	£0.54	7.69%	£11.90
buy sophos	£0.35	70	665	10.52%	£0.13	0.00%	£0.00
sophos antivirus software	£0.50	20	358	5.58%	£0.50	0.00%	£0.00

Fig 17 SEO: 'sophos anti-virus' versus 'sophos anti virus'

Keyword	Max. CPC	Clicks	Imps	CTR	Avg CPC	Conv. rate	Cost per Conv.
sophus	£0.50	677	4129	16.39%	£0.12	9.72%	£0.85
sofos	£0.05	602	4819	12.49%	£0.06	0.49%	£13.30
sophos anti virus	£2.00	348	5691	6.11%	£1.31	10.53%	£10.25
sophos anti-virus	£1.70	108	1819	5.93%	£0.98	0.00%	£0.00
sophos antivirus	£2.50	102	4640	2.19%	£0.54	7.69%	£11.90
buy sophos	£0.35	70	665	10.52%	£0.13	0.00%	£0.00
sophos antivirus software	£0.50	20	358	5.58%	£0.50	0.00%	£0.00

Fig 18 SEO: 'sophos anti virus' versus 'sophos antivirus'

convert into a single sale! Whereas our 'losing' keyword 'sophos antivirus' converted nearly 8 per cent of its traffic. So, it's pretty clear which keyword you would SEO for your website.

Or is it? Now let's compare our new winner 'sophos antivirus' with another variation, 'sophos anti virus' (Fig 18). Firstly, both keywords are getting conversions so we know they're both making money, but you can immediately see that the keyword 'sophos anti virus' is getting more than three times as many clicks as 'sophos antivirus.' Put differently, the keyword 'sophos antivirus' when shown resulted in 2.19 per cent of people visiting the website, whereas the keyword 'sophos anti virus' resulted in 6.11 per cent of people visiting the website. Plus, 'sophos anti virus' was converting more of its traffic into sales: 10.53 per cent as opposed to 7.69 per cent, and as a result was costing less to make the sale!

So, the ultimate winner – and the keyword we SEO for – would be 'sophos anti virus.'

But here's the surprise. We also ran a misspelling of the word Sophos, 'sophus' (Fig 19). What we found was truly astonishing.

Keyword	Max. CPC	Clicks	Imps	CTR	Avg CPC	Conv. rate	Cost per Conv.
sophus	£0.50	677	4129	16.39%	£0.12	9.72%	£0.85
						BEST CHOICE	
sofos	£0.05	602	4819	12.49%	£0.06	0.49%	£13.30
sophos anti virus	£2.00	348	5691	6.11%	£1.31	10.53%	£10.25
						LOGICAL CHOICE	
sophos anti-virus	£1.70	108	1819	5.93%	£0.98	0.00%	£0.00
sophos antivirus	£2.50	102	4640	2.19%	£0.54	7.69%	£11.90
buy sophos	£0.35	70	665	10.52%	£0.13	0.00%	£0.00
sophos antivirus software	£0.50	20	358	5.58%	£0.50	0.00%	£0.00

Fig 19 SEO: 'sophos' versus 'sophus' – a misspelling

It generated more clicks than the three primary keywords put together! *And* it had the second highest conversion rate, with nearly 10 per cent of its traffic turning into a sale. However, the true value lay in the final column which tells you how much each conversion (in this case, sale) cost. What you see straightaway is that each sale generated by the keywords 'sophos antivirus' and 'sophos anti virus' cost, on average, £11.08, whereas our misspelled keyword, 'sophus', cost only £0.85! In other words it was more than 13 times more cost-efficient than the other keywords. We now have a second, utterly unpredicted, and highly valuable keyword to add to our Search Engine Optimisation list.

What this exercise really underlines is that you simply cannot second-guess which keywords are the ones that make you money. Choosing purely on the basis of the amount of traffic each keyword generates does not guarantee financial success.

The Google AdWords system gives you the ability to make decisions based on knowledge and understanding rather than guesswork. It uncovers a wealth of information about your keywords which allow you to begin gold-digging.

In the end, it means you can tell your SEO company exactly which keywords will generate profits – and that's why you should invest in AdWords before investing in SEO.

■ THE STRATEGY

Typically, the average Google AdWords campaign starts with a sense of real excitement. Then comes the realisation that there's more to it than meets the eye. Many see their CPC spiral upwards, causing them to suspend their advertising or quit altogether. This is, of course, wonderful as it leaves more space in the market for intelligent marketers like you.

Oddly, I've met many web owners over the years who watch their CPC rise with a sense of resignation as though they were powerless to do anything about it. This is ridiculous. If the CPC is rising it's because there's a problem in the account itself and not just because Google wants to make more money.

Google seems to be in the habit of rewarding intelligent use of AdWords: the more you refine your campaign following Google's principles, the lower your CPC will be. But be careless, break the rules or fail to analyse your results and your CPC will creep up.

AdWords is a marvellous system because it gives you access to instant traffic, targeted markets, an unprecedented level of reporting and analysis and all, near enough, in real time! Use the system well, analyse regularly, tune and re-tune your landing pages and you'll be standing at the Google AdWords cash machine for many years to come.

6

CHAPTER

Build Lasting Relationships with Your Customers

▦ INTRODUCTION

Email has revolutionised the way we communicate. Yet strangely most businesses see email as merely a means to make their general communications more efficient and in doing so overlook its marketing benefits. This opportunity is exciting because if you do email marketing well you will create such trust between you and your recipients that they will actively look forward to receiving your communications and in doing so become highly motivated customers.

In a survey of 3,186 marketers by MarketingSherpa in 2008, some 64 per cent said that email marketing provided a good ROI or was their strongest tactic – which put it as the No. 1 proven strategy, far ahead of Search Engine Optimisation (SEO), pay-per-click, public relations, direct mail, online and print advertising.

Imagine sending thousands of emails to pre-qualified recipients who feel that you are personally addressing their needs and concerns. What would that do to the profits of your business for the years ahead?

Plus there's one other thing that makes this a really exciting proposition: I can almost guarantee that your competitors won't be doing it and as a result they will be leaving more opportunities on the table for you to take.

But before I begin I want to acknowledge one of the major barriers most businesses mistakenly use as a reason not to try email marketing: the worry they would be accused of spamming.

Spam is a very specific form of email. Firstly, it is unsolicited

– in other words, you are not expecting to receive it. Secondly, it is from an undisclosed or hidden source. And thirdly, it is trying to sell you something which you probably don't want. Oh yes, and it's illegal!

Email marketing, on the other hand, couldn't be further from spam. Firstly, you will only be sending emails to people who have signed up to receive them – this is known as 'opting in' – and so they will be expecting to receive them. Secondly, they'll know who you are. And thirdly, they will have registered a specific interest in your product or service. Good email marketing is not spamming and spamming is not good email marketing.

Now that we've laid the spam question to rest let's take a look at some of the key advantages of email marketing.

1. It costs next to nothing to get your message out to a wide range of potential customers.[1] Especially if you compare it against conventional marketing media such as newspapers, direct mail and so on.

2. It can be incredibly targeted. If somebody has opted in to your list it's because they are interested in what you have to offer. The natural effect of this is that you end up with a list of high-quality prospects.

3. It has the advantage of being instant, which means that within a few seconds of sending your email your prospect can be reading and acting on your message. Again, compare that with traditional marketing methods where you may have to wait weeks, months or, in the case of Yellow Pages, up to an entire year before your message gets seen.

4. It's incredibly easy to track, so you can work out exactly how effective your message has been. Just remember that the reason why we track the effectiveness of our marketing is to constantly improve it.

5. Email has proven to be a highly effective way of generating sales. DoubleClick's recent email consumer study discovered that 70 per cent of online shoppers had made a purchase because of receiving an email inviting them to buy. The relevance of email even works offline, in the real world. The same study reported that 59 per cent of email recipients had bought in a retail

[1] For example, email marketing service AWeber charges $29 per month for up to 2,500 subscribers, and iContact charges $29 per month for up to 2,500 subscribers.

store directly as a result of receiving an email from that business. So not only is it able to attract customers to your website but customers into your physical store (if you have one).

6. By building your database of prospects' email addresses you are really building a community of people who are predisposed to your products or services which you can email at any point to generate sales. For example, if business is a little slow at a particular time, you can drop your database an email and lift your sales there and then. A good email list can be a goldmine with very deep seams.

7. And finally, unlike other forms of direct communication such as telemarketing, an email will usually always get through to the intended person (assuming you follow the steps I'll outline later on in this chapter).

One final point, I do not recommend that you buy a database of email addresses. While this may be the quick way to kick-start your email campaign, it has some significant drawbacks. Principally these are around the quality of the database you are emailing. With a 'pre-built' database, you are emailing people who *may* be interested in your products or services but haven't specifically said so. Think of this as being similar to watching an advert on TV: the advert has been chosen to relate to the audience but each individual hasn't requested to see that advert. This means that there is a significant level of wastage as a result. This approach is known as *interruption marketing* because the viewer is not expecting to see your message – it just appears in front of them. Billboards, radio advertising and even shop signs are forms of interruption marketing.

Now consider a database of email addresses from people who have requested information from you. Firstly, this is a highly targeted group of people; secondly they are actively expecting your message. This is known as *permission marketing*[2] and is far more likely to deliver paying customers than the interruption method. Think about it, who would you rather pitch to: a room full of passersby dragged in from the street or people who believe you can help them? (It's worth noting that the act of someone opting in to you email marketing is actually a clear buying signal!)

[2] Seth Godin wrote one of the foundation stones for the permission-based marketing revolution called 'Permission Marketing: Turning Strangers into Friends and Friends into Customers'. If you would like to get the detail behind the thinking, buy his book.

The next question is, if you've got to build the database of people yourself, how do you do it? Well, what follows is the strategy for email marketing success.

YOUR EMAIL STRATEGY

Email marketing comprises four key elements:

1. **Knowing Your List** – Actually, it's not a list, it's a person but we'll come to that in a moment.
2. **Building a List** – Get traffic[3] to a landing page[4] that allows them to opt-in to your emails.
3. **Building Your Relationship** – Regularly send high value emails to your subscribers.
4. **Winning the Sale** – Send your subscribers to a webpage which adds value and ultimately sells your products or services.

In this chapter we'll go as far as a 'Building Your Relationship' with your reader, and then in Chapter 7 we'll discover how to use copy and landing page conversion tactics to 'win the sale.'

Below is a diagram of the process of email success:

[3] Google AdWords is one method but you could also attract emails in the offline world too. For example, if you were a dentist you could give leaflets to patients advising them of a webpage which they could visit and sign up for some information on how to keep young teeth healthy.

[4] A landing page is a webpage which your visitor lands directly on without first viewing any other page on your website.

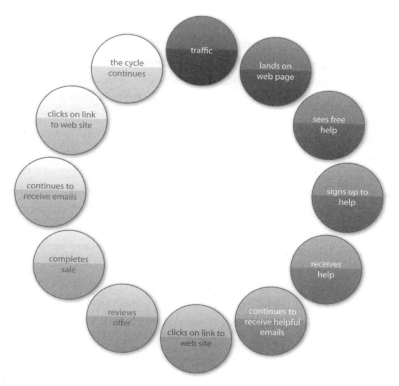

Fig 1 The cycle of email marketing

■ *KNOWING YOUR LIST*

Many companies see their emails as being sent to a 'list,' a database if you will, without any acknowledgement that there is a human being at the other end. Every email delivered is to a person and that person has hopes, dreams, desires, problems, loves and hates, just like you and me. In email marketing it pays to think of your list as people and not numbers. Every email is a personal communication between you and them. If your email makes people feel that you are talking exclusively to them it will cement the relationship.

Now's the time for you to look back at the first of our 7 Principles of Online Marketing and do your Customer Profiling. Write up your customer and pin him/her to your desk so every time you think about sending an email out, you're sending it to *them* and not your 'list.'

Most email systems allow you to create more than one list, giving you the ability to build email campaigns targeted at specific 'groups' of recipients. For example, you could create one list for customers and one for prospects.

You may want to subdivide your email marketing campaign down even further. It might be that each list/group could be separated into the various products or services that you supply. Or maybe you want to divide them by demographic (age, sex, income, etc.) or even psychographic classifications (interests, lifestyle, behaviour, and so on). What happens as you divide your audience up is that your emails become more and more specific. The upside to this is that the more targeted your emails, the more relevant they will be and the higher the likelihood of sales. The downside is that your audience gets smaller and smaller and you have to write more emails. Of course, the reverse happens if you don't segment them – your emails are less specific but reach a wider audience.

My advice to you if you are starting out is to cast a wide net and see what happens. In other words, attract as many people on to your email list as possible by discussing general topics. You can subdivide your list later on down the line. Also, if you notice an obvious division in your list from the emails you get back you may want to 'peel' those people off and invite them to join a more specific email list you are running.

If you're still struggling to know where to begin then I suggest starting a campaign aimed at your existing customers. For the most part they will be happy to receive your emails as they will probably be expecting to receive some form of communication from you anyway plus people who already know you are usually very happy to give feedback on your campaign.

BUILDING A LIST

You website will be the primary means to build your list. In other words you will be using your website to gather email addresses from people who are actively interested in what you have to offer. But how do you get them to give up their email address in the first place? Easy, you simply prove your value to them by being helpful!

Proving Your Value

Let's dive into to one of the biggest (and largely unknown) concepts on the Internet. I haven't mentioned this until now because email marketing is a great example of where to use it but once you 'get it' you'll see its applicability to almost every part of your online life.

> *First Law of Value: People are primarily surfing for information and not to be sold to.*

If you think about your own approach to browsing, you'll probably find that you go online largely to answer a question. You might be interested in finding a new supplier, researching a better working practice, looking up an industry article – it could be anything, but most of the time it relates to gathering information and getting help. However, because you are in a 'research' mode you're probably not in the mood to get your money out, at least not yet.

Flip this around and imagine how we react in the real world. If you walk into a shop and the sales assistant immediately pounces on you asking if they can be of help, most people's standard response is to say 'No thanks, just looking.' The reason we react like this is that we're not ready to get into a sales conversation. We'd rather have a look round, find the thing we're interested in and maybe then start talking about it.

This is also very often the case online – before you start trying to make a sale you need to help people understand that you are the right company they should be working with. The way to do that is to offer them lots of information and free help. Wouldn't that be the way you would want to be approached if you were the customer? Trying to rush people into a sale is more likely to get them to click away from your website than engage with it.

We buy once we've got all the information and advice we need. As potential suppliers to your prospects it makes sense to engage them at the beginning of the relationship – the point they are looking for information – instead of trying to crow-bar your way in at the end of the sales process. The natural consequence of providing unpressurised help and support is that people will want to buy from you because you are not trying to manipulate them into a sale.

So, if people are primarily interested in information and advice first, what can you do to help them?

Enter our second law of the Internet:

Second Law of Value: Help your prospect for free first, sell to them second.

It's the word 'free' which usually throws business people into a state of panic. Giving stuff away for free may seem mad but there are some incredibly powerful reasons why you should do this:

1. It helps your prospect overcome their problem and answers their questions.
2. It demonstrates your skills and proves your value upfront before you invoice them.
3. It establishes your relationship on a good footing from the get go (who doesn't love free stuff?).
4. It reassures the recipient of your credibility.

It's worth expanding the last point above because trust is a very important part of the whole business relationship. We tend to want to deal with businesses with whom we have already established a relationship. A significant component of that relationship is the trust we place in them to do a good job and the trust they place in us that we will pay for the good job. Whenever we start a new business relationship there is always a level of hesitancy as all parties try to understand each other, their value, and the job at hand. By providing information that unlocks that understanding, you demonstrate to your prospect your skill, helpfulness and ultimately your value – all in one go.

Although it may 'feel' like you're giving something away for free, in reality you're not. Any equitable business transaction is principally an exchange of value. Typically we exchange the value of our goods and services for the value of the money we receive. So even though it looks like we're giving something for free, we are asking for them to part with their email address. Therefore, it's logical to offer them something of value in exchange for the value of their email address.

Now this is such a liberating experience because it means you don't have to feel as though you need to find the perfect form of words to convince people that they want to use your service. You don't have to worry about trying to prise the sale out of them. Instead, all you're doing is helping them make the best buying decision they can by giving them great information. Remember the reason why people are surfing the web in the first place is because they're looking for information, not looking to be sold to.

What Can You Give Away?

So, what is it that you can give away? Well, your expertise for starters. I bet if we sat down for 20 minutes you could come up with at least five things that I never knew about your business, market sector, product or service. And if you could write that up into genuinely useful information then you already have the outline of an article or report which you can give away in exchange for an email address. If you're still stuck for ideas here are a few:

- Your top tips on...
- Case studies
- Your opinion on [your industry, economic trends, best practice]
- What's new/hot
- How to...
- Reviews
- Resource links on the Internet
- Tell a story
- Interview your client/supplier/yourself
- X-day training series
- Debunk the myth of...
- Run a survey
- Offer some interesting statistics
- White papers

- Something humorous (for example, a story, anecdote, etc.)
- Customer/company success stories
- Dates in the industry
- Quiz or competition
- Ask for a contribution/comment
- FAQs (for example, handling the classic objections to buying your service/product)
- Breaking news
- Tools calculators, worksheets, templates, checklists)
- Q&A

So when you are thinking about the content of your email think in terms of giving rather than selling. Think of it as helping, advising and informing. So, your sign-up landing pages and emails are between 80 per cent and 100 per cent genuine interesting information, and 20 per cent or less marketing and sales.

How Do You Do It?

Once you've decided what you are going to give away you'll need to do the following:

Choose an Email Marketing Software

There are several online services that can manage your email marketing for you. You don't have to use Microsoft Outlook or Hotmail or something of that nature to perform this task (and to be honest it's best if you don't). The software that exists to do this is quite mature, quick to set up and easy to use. It allows you to compose your emails, manage your database and handle all the unsubscribe and record management issues.

Some of the key players in the market are:

1. AWeber – www.aweber.com
2. MailChimp – www.mailchimp.com
3. Constant Contact – www.constantcontact.com
4. iContact – www.icontact.com

They are, in essence, one-stop solutions for your email marketing. Some even can help you create landing pages for people to sign up to.

Get Your Web Designers On the Case

Once you've decided who's going to manage your emails you'll need to tell your web designers about it. It shouldn't be too difficult to add your email marketing into your existing site although the ideal would be to build it in from the beginning of your web project. They will need to know:

1. The technical details about integrating the email system into your website (ask someone at the email software company to provide you with this)
2. Which pages need altering
3. The copy and content to be added
4. Which list (if you've set-up more than one) in the email software to link to the sign-up form

You may want your CMS to control the content so you can update your landing page in the future. If so make sure your web designers know about this. You may also want them to add the following functionality into your CMS to enable you to manage the sign-up part of your landing pages more effectively, including the ability to:

1. Change the copy
2. Add new graphics
3. Move the form on the page
4. Subscribe people to a different target list

It may cost you a little more to get your CMS updated in the short term, but the flexibility it gives you will more than pay off in the long term.

Legal Stuff

The prevalence of spam has led to legislation to prevent it. The Americans developed an entire legal framework called Can-Spam (www.ftc.gov/bcp/edu/microsites/spam/rules.htm) whereas in the UK we've largely relied on the Data Protection Act to cover it (www.ico.gov.uk/for_organisations/data_protection.aspx).

Essentially there are two different approaches depending on who you are asking to opt in if you operate in the UK.[5]

[5] Look to your own country's legislation to clarify your position.

Business to Consumer

If you are a business emailing an individual consumer or member of the public:

1. You must be able to prove that the individual opted in to your email marketing (Most of the online email marketing systems will record this information for you)
2. You must provide an Unsubscribe (Again most systems will do this for you)
3. You must state who you are and provide a valid contact address

Business to Business

If you are emailing a business then technically the Business-to-Consumer rules do not apply to you as businesses are seen as needing less protection. However, my advice is to maintain the same level of integrity with your business customers as you would with individuals.

Some good practice guidelines

I recommend that you are completely transparent when requesting email addresses on your sign-up page. So, make it easy to understand what is on offer, state how you will use their email address (i.e. exclusively for your business, or passed on to third parties, etc.), provide a clear link to your privacy policy and state they can unsubscribe at any time.

You should also provide a valid address and contact details in your email along with an unsubscribe facility.

For further information take a look at Business Link's excellent online resource (alturl.com/d6og5 and www.ico.gov.uk/for_organisations/privacy_and_electronic_communications.aspx) and also www.ico.gov.uk/upload/documents/library/data_protection/practical_application/electronic_mail_marketing_12_06.pdf

The Sign-Up Page

The purpose of your sign-up page is to demonstrate what you are going to give away in exchange for your visitor's email address. Let's take a look at an example of a landing page. Here's one that demonstrates a simple way of attracting the email – with '10 Great Reasons to Visit North Devon':

Fig 2 Landing page with an incentive to sign up

And here's another. Notice how the incentive to sign-up takes you to another page. This is so the visitor can see more about what they will get in exchange for their email address and gives the company more opportunity to express the value of what they're giving away.

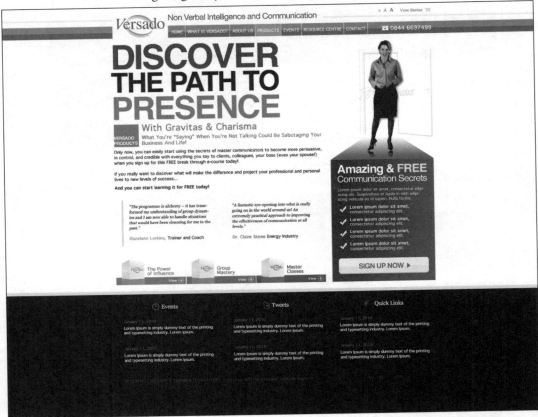

Fig 3 Landing page with an incentive to sign up

In successive chapters we'll take an in-depth look at improving your landing pages and writing compelling sales copy but for now these examples are intended to give you an idea what a sign-up landing page actually looks like.

Name Squeeze Pages

Name squeeze pages are landing pages which try to force the visitor to give up their email address by offering no alternative option – either sign-up or leave. It's an interesting principle and takes the idea to the extreme. It focuses exclusively on describing what's on offer in exchange for the opt-in. Typically, these pages have no navigation and are just one webpage. Here's an example of one:

Fig 4 A name squeeze page

I'm not a big fan of this approach – not least because Google hates it. They don't see this as representing a good user experience because it doesn't demonstrate any depth of information – it's not a website, it's just a stand-alone webpage. (If you are running an AdWords campaign which links to such pages beware of your Quality Score taking a tumble!)

Google (and I think most people, for that matter) prefer pages which are part of a main website, link to other relevant parts of the site, give away something of use and also offer a sign-up. Use name squeeze pages sparingly, if at all.

The Double Opt-In vs Single Opt-In Debate

When someone signs up to your email list their subscription can be handled in one of two ways:

1. Double opt-in: After your visitor has signed up they will receive an email requesting that they confirm their subscription by clicking on a link.
2. Single opt-in: No confirmation email is sent and the user simply begins to receive your emails.

Firstly, let me say that I don't have a preference one way or the other except to note that a double opt-in is regarded as 'good practice'. Those against it suggest that it is an unnecessary cost to the overhead of acquiring the email address since it requires the subscriber to take an extra step which they may be resistant to do. People may not click on the confirmation link because they don't see the email, forget what they've subscribed to (and then possibly confuse it with spam), delete it accidentally, have second thoughts about signing up and so on. Consequently, you've paid to get the user to fill in the sign-up form but because they failed to click on the confirmation email they failed to become a subscriber.

Those on the opposite side of the fence support the double opt-in because it can produce a more focused list of buyers. In fact, MarketingSherpa discovered that only 68 per cent of users enter a valid email address anyway, meaning that without the double opt-in process just under one third of your database would be undeliverable. A study by AWeber also identified double opt-ins as reducing unsubscribes and complaints and thereby increasing the quality of the mailing list.

The argument will continue to rage. However, testing both approaches is very simple as most email marketing software provides the facility to switch it on and off at will.

When They Sign Up, Surprise Them

When somebody signs-up to receive your emails you will typically take them to a page which tells them that their sign-up was successful. However, very few businesses use these pages to their fullest effect. For example:

> Congratulations!
>
> You have successfully signed-up to my mailing list!
>
> As a 'thank you' I would like to give you this very special report:
>
> Simply, click here to view **The Amazing Report I have Written For You!**
>
> I will send you your first email right now so please check your inbox.

You could also use your sign-up page to list the key benefits of your business, its products and services, case studies, testimonials or even offer a podcast for download.

The great thing about this technique is that you're not having to under-promise in order to over-deliver; you are simply over-delivering, and people love extra, unexpected value.

BUILDING AN ONLINE RELATIONSHIP: GETTING STARTED

We've reached the point where someone has:

1. Landed on your sign-up page
2. Signed up
3. Had their details recorded by your email marketing software
4. Received their first email[6]

Should we stop there? After all we've captured their email address and sent them an email. Job done. Well it would, of course, be fantastic if everyone we emailed instantly loved us and sent money, but they're probably not going to do that after just one email contact. (It's rare for you to make a cold call out of the blue and be taking money at the end of it. Most of us only part with our hard-earned cash when we're happy with the relationship we have with our supplier – and that's something which takes time to develop.) In fact, I have seen time and time again examples of businesses that have sent out one communication to their customers or prospects and then been surprised at the poor response rate. Most people want to rush in and go for the kill as quickly as possible, but for the majority of us, that's not how we buy – which is why one-shot communications have such a poor response rate.

Let me give you some statistics to support this. These are generalised marketplace averages but they give you a feel for how people's behaviour patterns break down:[7]

[6] As soon as they have signed up for the information it should immediately appear in their inbox. This is critical – if it doesn't happen immediately then not only are you not meeting their expectations but when it does arrive it could easily be lost in the noise of their inbox.

[7] This is called the Diffusion of Innovations Model and refers to the degree to which people accept innovation and new ideas – when you pitch your business to a prospect you are the 'new idea'. If you'd like to read a bit more about this subject and you're feeling in an academic mood, check out www.ou.edu/deptcomm/dodjcc/groups/99A2/theories.htm.

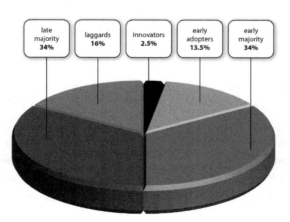

Fig 5 How quickly people respond to sales messages

late majority 34% | laggards 16% | innovators 2.5% | early adopters 13.5% | early majority 34%

It begins with the Innovators, at 2.5 per cent, who typically react to new offers almost immediately, without giving it too much thought. They will be the first to buy and coincidentally their share is around the same percentage you get back from a single-shot direct mail campaign that's performing really well. Coincidence?

Next are the Early Adopters, who are also fairly impulsive and respond soon after the Innovators but take a little more time about their decision.

However, as you can see, Early and Late Majority form the bulk and need more persuasion before buying. They are more cautious and like to shop around before coming to a buying decision and probably are a bit like you and me.

And finally we have the Laggards, who only take action after everybody else. These are the people whose door you'll be banging on for a long time before they decide to buy from you.

In summary, the Innovators and Early Adopters will buy from you early on with only a little persuasion, and the Laggards will take ages; but it's plain to see that you are going to get most of your sales by appealing to the majority, who make up 67 per cent of the market.

For example, there are very few people who will wake up one day with the intention to buy a car, walk into the showroom and just buy one. Most of us like to go round the showrooms, read the brochures, get on the Internet, do some research, maybe read the car magazines, ask our friends, go for a test-drive, and do this over a period of time. That's because, critical to our choice is the concept of commitment. Most who buy are committed to that choice for some time. So, it's pretty unlikely that someone who is about to buy a car will do so from the first website they find!

It also pays to examine your own browsing habits and identify what compels you to buy from one particular website over another. Generally we find that the more complex or expensive the purchase, the more reassurance we require. Just consider the difference between buying a DVD online and a DVD player. Naturally, you are going to spend more time researching the DVD player and not just the product but the company supplying it. This reveals an interesting fact you can use to your advantage when developing your website: the more money your customer is going to spend, the more time they will invest in the selection process.

So if you need to convince a sceptical market of just how good your business is, it is going to be pretty unlikely that you can do that in one email. The key to convincing the majority is maintaining a continuity of communication,[8] which is just a posh way of saying keep emailing them high-value, free information.

Now, of course all the statistics I have given you doesn't mean that the averages will hold up – you may have more Innovators in your market, or more Laggards, or a smaller majority. The trick is not to give up. Keep emailing them great information. Keep showing them just how much expertise is in your business and how much ability your company has. Eventually your persistence will pay off and your sales will steadily rise.

[8] On average it takes at least seven communications to move a prospect into a position where they are likely to buy from you. This was the finding of Jay Conrad Levinson – one of the fathers of modern marketing. He later revised that figure to 21, suggesting that each communication needs to be reiterated three times before people get the meaning in the message.

How Often Should You Send Your Emails?

Obviously, there's no single answer to that but here are a few things for you to consider.

Take a look at the average length of time it takes for a prospect to become a client and use that as a guide. For example, if it takes approximately one month for a prospect to become a customer then you might want to send out your emails once or twice weekly. If your sales cycle is longer then you would spread your emails out accordingly.

You could also use your product or service life-cycle as a guide to your email frequency.

However, my gut feeling is that sending anything less than once every three to four weeks will have a much reduced effect because people will simply forget who you are especially if you are having to compete for reading time in the average noisy inbox.

You may want to consider reducing the frequency of your emails once you're past the point of the average sales cycle because the lead is beginning to 'cool off'. However, you should certainly never stop because in sales 'no' never means 'no'; it simply means 'not now'!

You can also ask your clients how often they would like you to communicate with them. It's best to ask after you've sent a few emails so they've already got a sense of the material you're sending.

Once you decide how frequently you are going to be communicating with your customers and prospects you have then made a commitment to maintain that communication. In other words if you say in your first introductory email that you will be emailing them every two weeks you have made a promise you must keep. In fact, stating how regularly you're going to send these emails has a two-fold advantage:

1. It makes your recipient aware of the frequency and, thus, manages their expectations.
2. It commits you to putting the time aside to writing the emails (or to getting somebody else to write the emails) and so underwrites your campaign's success.

One final point, only send your emails when you've got something of value to say. Don't be tempted to fall into an 'anything will do' policy just because you've got to get your fortnightly email out.

Pre-written Emails vs Instant Emails

When you send your emails you can use one of two methods:

1. Have them prewritten as part of a series or
2. Send them out on a 'write as you go' basis

Pre-written emails can form a series so when each person signs up they begin at email number one and progress sequentially through the series. What this enables you to do is create a kind of running monologue. It means you can break the information down into easily digestible chunks and order that information into a logical flow. This technique is great if you want to give away a free X-day training course, or get across a complex point, or tell a story, etc.

The opposite is to write the emails as and when you've got something to say. (Although I'd still advocate you have some sort of structure and flow to them.) This method can be great if you want to respond to events in the press, product or service launches or indeed anything which has an immediate quality to it.

Of course, why not interweave the two methods and get the best of both worlds. I particularly favour beginning with a series of preset emails and then continuing with more ad-hoc emails.

HTML vs Plain Text Emails

Many businesses send emails that look like a mini webpage from their website.

These are called HTML emails and have the advantage of looking graphical – being able to put your logo in the email, pictures of your product creating an attractive layout, etc. The alternative are those written by your friends and colleagues in just plain text.

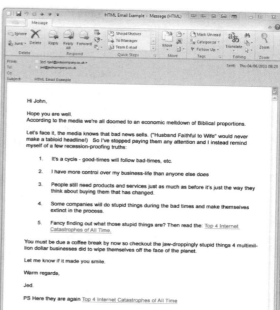

Fig 6 HTML email versus plain text email

I'm sure you will agree there is a big difference between the two. My preference is towards plain text emails because we're more likely to read emails that look like they've come from people we know rather than an anonymous corporation. It's pretty straightforward psychology really: we deal with those things that look more personal first. The problem with HTML emails is that while they look cool and hit all the branding criteria of the sender, they also look like the email equivalent of junk mail.

Let me give you an example of what I mean. Which envelope would you open first – a handwritten envelope or a printed one? Well I bet you would go for the handwritten one because it's more personal. Now which letter which you read first – a letter with no graphics and no logo and which begins with an opening using your first name or a glossy document with lots of pictures and different coloured text in two columns? Well, I'm going to guess again that you would go for the first, more personal, one. This is because we are so used to junk mail looking ever more eye-catching that as soon as we see it our brains automatically assume it's junk and we throw it away. Interestingly, exactly the same thing happens when people read emails. An email which looks like the electronic equivalent of junk mail will be read after one that looks more personalised but plainer.

HTML emails have a few more disadvantages. Firstly, unless you are technical and used to coding in HTML, you'll need to get your web designers to do it for you. Not only does that mean that you will probably have to wait for your email to be completed but it also means that you could lose the ability to send an unscheduled email there and then. Some of the online email marketing services are now beginning to offer HTML templates, which is fine, but because they are templates you run the risk of your email looking like generic junk mail.

Secondly, not every email system displays HTML in the same way. For example, Hotmail displays HTML emails differently from Outlook, which in turn displays them differently from Lotus Notes. This makes it tricky without professional help to build an HTML email that looks good under all circumstances.

Finally, if your recipient has their preview panel set up in a weird way they could end up only seeing a small portion of your email. Making people fumble for the mouse to scroll around your email is going to impair your message.

In terms of communicating information the plain text email is far better because it doesn't matter what shape the preview pane is in, the text will adjust to fill the space. It also means that the reader doesn't have to do anything like resize the window, change the preview size or mess around with scrollbars in order to read the message. This is especially relevant for Blackberry and other mobile device users. If you really need to show people pictures and offer them downloads then the logical place to do that would be on your website. Simply provide a link to the relevant page in your email.

I'm not suggesting that you shouldn't ever send HTML emails. If you think that your audience would react better to them then I would recommend that you give it a go – but send out plain text versions of the emails as well and see which one gets the better response.

BUILDING AN ONLINE RELATIONSHIP: CRAFTING POWERFUL EMAILS

There are five key components to a successful email. Think of them as hurdles you must jump in sequence. You begin by delivering the email which must then be opened. Opening it doesn't mean it is read, however – that's the next hurdle. Finally, you want someone to click through to your website where you can complete the sale, get the lead or do whatever it is you need them to do.

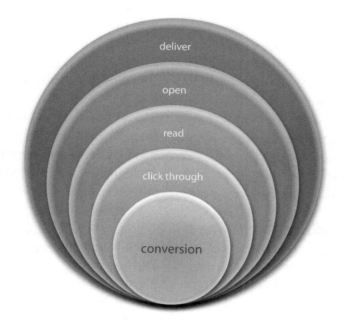

deliver

open

read

click through

conversion

Fig 7 The five key steps to zoning in on email conversions

In the remainder of this chapter we'll focus on getting recipients to the point where they click through to your website.

So essentially it's a process and as with any process each step can be optimised. And as you'll know from my chapter on marketing principles, as you optimise each process the effects magnify themselves further downstream. As you measure each one of these elements think of how you can improve each to increase the final conversion figure. The first four are usually measured by your email marketing company's online software, and the last by website analytics.

The key metric you are ultimately looking for is your ROI. Here's how you might calculate that:

$$\frac{\text{Number of click-throughs}}{\text{Number of emails sent}} \times 100\%$$

So if you sent 1,000 emails and had a click-through of 450, your click-through rate is 45 per cent. Now let's calculate the conversion rate:

$$\frac{\text{Number of sales}}{\text{Number of click-throughs}} \times 100\%$$

Let's say you had 81 sales from the 450 click-throughs, that would give you an 18 per cent conversion rate. Now let's calculate the revenue.

If each of the 81 sales earns you £50, then your email to 1,000 people has netted you £4,050. Or each email you sent earned you £4.05. So, every time you add another email address you are effectively increasing your revenue by £4.05 – and that's only from this one email!

If you are running a Google AdWords campaign to generate traffic to your landing page you can easily see how much each conversion is costing (using conversion tracking). Let's imagine that the cost of acquiring each email address is £1.50; then your profits would be at £2.55 per email address (£4.05 – £1.50). Cool!

Maximising Your Deliverability

In simple terms deliverability refers to the number of people on your list who actually receive your email.

The first guarantee to ensuring your email gets delivered is using a reputable email marketing system. Sending ten thousand emails via Outlook or Hotmail will probably get you blacklisted and upset your ISP no end!

The other factor is the content of your email itself, which could lead to it being classified as spam. As the spam problem continues to grow, more and more businesses are using spam-filtering software to ensure that only relevant emails are delivered to their staff. However, the software is never 100 per cent accurate and occasionally a legitimate email gets caught in the filter.

Spam filters very often work by assessing the contents of the email. They look for specific words or phrases that are more consistent with spam than legitimate email. As each 'spam' word or phrase is identified it gets counted towards an overall spam score. If that score passes a certain threshold the software regards it as spam and takes whatever action it has been programmed to do (delete it, send it to a spam folder, collate it as part of a weekly spam digest, etc.).

The problem is that many perfectly normal words and phrases can contribute to your spam score and, if used often enough, end up causing your emails to be classified as spam. Below I have provided a list of some of the more common spam trigger words[9] and phrases for you to avoid using in your emails[10]:

[9] Many thanks go to Meqoda Daily for the initial list.

[10] Please bear in mind that these words and phrases change on a continual basis so you might want to run your emails through an online spam checker. Many of the online email marketing systems include this feature as part of their package. However, you can also look on Google using the key phrase 'online spam test.'

50% off!	Discount!	Loans
Amazing	Double your income	Lose weight
Amazing stuff	Eliminate debt	Million dollars
Call now!	Free grant money	No investment
Cash bonus	Free installation	Opportunity
Click here	Free investment	Satisfaction guaranteed
Collect	Free leads	Serious cash
Compare	Free preview	You're a winner!
Compare rates	Free!	
Credit	'Hidden'	
Credit bureaus	'Hidden' assets	

The following phrases won't automatically cause your email to be marked as spam; however, they will contribute to an increased scoring that could lead to them being marked as spam.

Act now!	Get paid	Save up to
All natural	Giving it away	Special promotion
All new	Great offer	Time limited
As seen on…	Guarantee	Unsecured debt/credit
Avoid bankruptcy	Guaranteed	Vacation
Buy direct	Join millions	While supplies last
Cash	No cost, no fees	Why pay more?
Casino	Offer	Winner
Consolidate your debt	One time	Work at home
Don't delete	Order now	You've been selected
Easy terms	Please read	

It is also best to avoid quotation marks, $, £ or ! in your subject lines as well as CAPITAL LETTERS. Some spam filters even filter out Freephone numbers in the subject line. Also don't conceal your 'from' address; use a real one like jed@morganwylie.co.uk instead of super-awesome-marketing-guru@morganwylie.co.uk – no matter how true it may be!

A simple way to check to see if your emails are getting through is to send a few to someone in your own company as well as your friends and business colleagues.

If you are having real difficulty with deliverability it may be that you are on a spam blacklist. If you suspect this to be the case the Spamhaus website (www.spamhaus.org) may be able to confirm it and help you get off the list.[11] If you want to maximise your deliverability or if it's becoming a problem you can use third-party services like Return Path (www.returnpath.net)

[11] You will need to type in your host IP address. (If you don't know what this is ask your ISP or IT expert/ manager to help.)

to help. (They also offer a free email reputation check at www. senderscore.org.)

Here's a great resource about the law and spam in the UK: www.wiredsafety.org/gb/law/spam/index.html.

Maximising Your Open Rates: The Subject Line

Now let's take a look at the structure and content of your email and begin with one of the most important and yet, oddly, overlooked parts of an email: the subject line.

Having a great subject line is like having a key that unlocks your reader's time: it can get them sufficiently interested to read your email instead of them hitting the delete key. So, here's what you need to do when you write your subject line: sell the action of opening your email, not its content.

There are various ways in which you can do this.

For example, you could create interest:
- Julie, here's the story...
- Why on Earth do we do that?
- The secrets of...
- 7 things your XYZ won't tell you
- 10 tips for the perfect dinner party

Or you could out right ask somebody to do something:
- Steve, here's what I want you to do

Or you can ask a question:
- What if you could retire today?
- Do you know how to?
- Matt, will you test this?

Or ask for help:
- David, I need your advice

You could also try putting a time limitation into your subject lines. For example, 'Only 5 days to go.' What this does is appeal to a very important part of human psychology called the scarcity mentality – the part of us that doesn't want to miss out on an opportunity. The way to get readers to take action is to tell them they only have a limited time in which to act and that they'll miss out if they don't. For example, 'Kim, it's gone at 5 p.m. tonight.'

The idea is that you write a few short words which are punchy enough to look a little different from the standard emails we get. However, please don't be tempted to write a subject line that doesn't relate to the content of your email. All that will do is confuse the reader and create a negative perception of your business.

Now, most of us get a bit delete-key trigger-happy when we are reading our emails and it would be easy for yours to get accidentally deleted if the title is not immediately recognisable. Here's where the subject line can really help you. If you always name your email in the same way it will be instantly recognised and less likely to be deleted. Here's a couple of examples of what I mean:

- Jed's Marketing Tips – only 1 per cent of people get this right!
- Acme 60 Second Help – 5 ways to leapfrog your competitors.

Each email would begin with the same words ('Jed's Marketing Tips' and 'Acme 60 Second Help' in the examples above), clearly identifying who it's from.

Another way to catch someone's eye is to personalise the subject line. Most email marketing software allows you to put the first name of your recipient in the subject.

- David, Can you help me with this?

Seeing your own name can be a very powerful factor in determining whether you should open the email because it tells you that it's from someone you know. (Less than 5 per cent of emails sent are personalised, plus the research shows that personalising increases your email's open rates.)

A variation on this theme which is particularly useful if you don't have their first name is to use their role instead. For example, 'Vital Information *Business Owners* Need To Know.'

It's also important to know what to avoid in the subject line.

- Hi
- FYI
- FREE
- A blank subject line
- Anything you've ever seen in the subject line of a spam email!

Another factor in your subject line's success is how much of it can be read. People use all kinds of software on their computers and online to review their emails. Unfortunately, there is very little consistency between each of these products. So the simple rule of thumb is to keep your subject line to no more than 6–8 words or less than 50 characters and remember to put the most important words in the subject line first. For example, rather than saying 'Here's Our Special 10% Discount', say, '10% Discount Especially For You.' That way you can guarantee that the most important words will be visible (and read first).

The next step is getting the email opened and the reader to click on what you have to offer! So here are twenty tips to turn your email campaign into an outright success.

Maximising Reads and Click-Through Rates

1: Get the Greeting Right

I know this may sound obvious but always to put a greeting at the beginning of your email. The reason why I mention that is because you wouldn't believe how many emails (mostly HTML) get sent without a simple 'hello.' They launch straight into whatever they're trying to sell. Just by putting the salutation right at the beginning, it tells your reader that you know them and that small personal touch can be the difference between somebody recognising and reading your email and thinking it's junk and deleting it.

Openings with 'Hi' are better than nothing, but 'Dear John' or 'Hi Julie' are even better. Try to avoid greetings like 'Dear Sir/ Madam' because that's about as impersonal as you can possibly get – and it may panic your reader into believing that the tax authorities are pursuing them.

2: Personalisation

When someone fills in your sign-up form, they will very often give you specific details about themselves. It might be their first name, last name, company name and so on. The great thing about modern email marketing systems is that they can take this information and enter it into your email just as you would mail-merge a document. This is how you are able to say 'Dear John' rather than 'Dear Sir.'

So, an excellent way of personalising your email is to use this information throughout. For example, halfway down the email you may want to say 'John, I know your time is limited.' Or, if you captured their company name, 'How much more money do you think ABC Solicitors could save?'

This has a powerful effect because it's rare that we see our name written twice in an email and seeing it for a second time refocuses our attention, making this a great technique to use when you have something important to say.

Two words of caution about this: firstly, don't overuse it, because it starts to look unnatural; and secondly, if your reader didn't type in the information into the sign-up form properly, your email can start to look quite strange. For example, you may have requested that users enter only their first name into the sign-up form but they entered their whole name instead. That means that whenever the system uses their first name rather than 'Dear John' it comes out as 'Dear John Smith' and that somewhat kills off the personalised effect.

An easy way around this is to make sure that you regularly look at your mailing list database and clean up any errors in the data. (If you have a really big database, you may want to get somebody else to do that for you.)

3: The Opening Lines

I don't know what it is about computers but even the most laid-back and patient of people suddenly develop the attention span of a concussed gnat when sat in front of one. What this means is that people usually make the decision whether to carry on reading or not within the first few seconds of opening your email and that means you've got to make your opening punchy and exciting. An effective way to do this is to unravel the most interesting point that you have to make, right upfront alongside a promise of how you can improve the reader's situation. For example:

Dear John,

Did you know that 8 out of 10 people read a headline but only 2 out of 10 people read any further? Here are some powerful tips which will help you convert readers into buyers!

That's an example of a short and punchy opening designed to draw the reader deeper into the email.

Many people use online email services like Gmail or Hotmail, both of which give a mini-preview of the email before we open it. Here's screenshot from my Gmail account showing an email from ace email marketing genius, Frank Kern:

| Frank Kern | **my big ego - and the EVIL J.J.** - OK - I know this is silly but it's kind of a windfall for you :-) Here's the deal - |

Apart from one of Frank's typically amusing and intriguing subject lines, I can see the first few lines of his email. Frank has crafted his opening to pique my interest within a few words. Now compare this to another email:

| **Xmas gift guide and free delivery** - send to friend icon To share this message, click here if you can't view |

As you can see, the opening copy is hardly inspiring – ah, the ever-present dangers of HTML emails!

Just remember these two points: grab your readers' attention and tell them how to improve their situation.

4: Get to the Point

As I just said, when it comes to the Internet, our attention span is pretty poor, which means that if whatever we are reading doesn't stop us in our tracks, we'll move on to something else.

So you've already grabbed the attention of your reader by having a great opening paragraph, but the rest of your email needs to be just as punchy. Make your point quickly; write short sentences and short paragraphs, as large blocks of writing look daunting and are difficult to read.

An easy way to help you do this is to write your email, count how many words you've written and then try and reduce that word count by about 25 per cent. I promise you, you'll be surprised at just how much you can take out without losing the sense of the message.

If it turns out that you've got just too much to communicate, consider splitting your email up into a series and delivering them as separate emails; alternatively, create a page on your website and link people to it from the email.

5: Keep it Simple

Always keep your copy simple and straightforward. I'm not suggesting that you become patronising but you don't want to force your reader to think too hard just because your language is overcomplicated. Often this just obscures the point the writer is trying to make.

The solution to this is easy. Firstly, keep your sentences short, avoid jargon or terminology which might not be understood, and check your readability score. On this last point, you can do it either by asking a few people to see if your email makes sense and/ or use Microsoft Word's grammar checker to analyse your readability score. As a guide you should be aiming for a Flesch Reading Ease score of above 60 (the point at which 'plain English' begins).

Remember, the simpler the language, the faster you get your point across, and if your reader understands everything in your email then they are more likely to take the action that you want them to.

6: Long Copy vs Short Copy

There has long raged a debate in marketing circles about whether it is better to use long or short copy. In the end it seems that the studies seem to be supporting longer copy. This is primarily because long copy answers all the questions a prospect may have upfront and thus overcomes any barriers to the sale.

However, I think it's a very different situation with email. Just imagine you've got 20 emails in your inbox. Eighteen of them are one or two paragraphs long and the remaining two are 8–9 paragraphs long. Which ones would you deal with first? I'm guessing you'd probably deal with the short ones first so you can get them out of the way and file the other two for when you have a bit more time. Unfortunately, most people never get to the point where they have 'a bit more time' and consequently only end up reading those long emails which they absolutely have to.

Another important aspect about emails is scrolling. If your email is so long it scrolls, fewer people will make the effort to scroll to the end of the email. In other words, the majority of people simply won't read beyond the scroll-line, leaving only the first portion of your email read.

By keeping your emails short and punchy you ensure you get your point across, you keep the interest of your reader and you get them quickly to the point where they can take action.

Just one final thought: it might be that there is simply too much information that you want to communicate than you can get over in a few paragraphs. In that situation, you may want to try the 'continued on my website' approach. Find a 'cliff-hanger' in your email and stop there. For example:

- And if you want to discover how I managed to…
- And here's how you do it…
- But it got worse…
- And just when I was about to give up…

By the way, the actual text in your link also has an impact on your click through rates. MarketingSherpa did some extensive research into which phrases produced the best click-through rate from emails to websites. Here are the top three most effective phrases:

1. Click to continue (8.53%)
2. Continue to article (3.3%)
3. Read more (1.8%)

7: Formatting Text Emails

Although there isn't very much that you can do by way of formatting a plain text email, there are a few things you can do to make the email more readable.

Remember that most people scan emails. They do this so they can get a sense of the information before they make a decision to commit to reading it thoroughly. To make it easy for your reader to scan through your email its best to break your paragraphs up into no more than 3–4 sentences.

And don't be worried about one-sentence paragraphs.

These stand out and are great at communicating important information. For example, it would be worth separating out into its own paragraph this sentence…

> Here's where you need to go to take advantage of this one-time offer…

Don't forget you can also use things like bullet points and numbered lists to make your emails easy to read.

If your email ended up having several sections, it's well worth heading them up in capital letters. You could even make your heading stand out like this:

HERE'S HOW IT'S GOING TO HELP YOU

8: Don't Use Attachments

Let's take an example to illustrate this. Imagine you want to send all of your customers your latest price list. The temptation would be to simply attach it to an email and send it out as a PDF document. However, this can have some technical drawbacks and some lost marketing opportunities.

The technical issue is around deliverability. Some email systems block all attachments automatically, or by the type of attachments it is (such as audio or movie files) or if the attachment is over a certain size. So straightaway you could hit barriers that stop your email getting through which means at best it gets through without the attachment or at worst it never gets through at all.

It's also worth remembering that emails with large attachments can take a long time to download plus they can harbour viruses and all kinds of other nasties which you won't want to send on to your customer.

Then let's move on to the missed marketing opportunity. If you send out an attachment you don't really know if anybody's read it so it's untrackable. However, if you place a link in your email to a page on your website where they can download the file, from there you will know exactly how many people wanted to read it because you can count the number of times it has been downloaded. What that tells you is how important that document is to your readership and therefore, whether you should be sending more similar material to them more frequently.

9: Spelling and Grammar

This is such a simple thing and yet if overlooked can be disastrous to your email reputation. If you use Microsoft Word, for example, then you can do this as you go along. However, there are online alternatives like www.spellchecker.net which offers an excellent spell-checker, grammar checker and thesaurus.

10: Call to Action

As you know, giving away great information should be at the very heart of your email campaign. However, you mustn't lose sight of the fact that you also want your readers to do something for you. This means that in your emails, you must have a clear 'call to action.'

For example, let's say your email discusses the merits of two products. This would give you the opportunity to end your email with something like:

> Now you know which product will suit you best, call me today on 0800 980 2580.

Or if you're sending a 'frequently asked questions' email you might want to sign off with:

> Get access to this vital profit boosting information right now at our website: www.jedscompany.co.uk/special-information-for-you.

> If we haven't answered all your questions here, please email us at questions@jedscompany.co.uk

You could even focus the total content of your email entirely on one action you want your reader to take: offering some free consultancy, clicking on a link to a specific webpage, watching a video, downloading a podcast or white paper.

However, only present one action per email. If you offer the reader lots of different choices you are more likely to confuse them into inaction.

11: Use Links to Your Website

For most email marketers, email is simply the means to get the reader to visit the website and then take an appropriate action, so always have a link in your email, if only to your website's home page. You will find though that mostly your emails are on specific subjects for which your website has a dedicated page. In that case, make the link in your email link to that specific page. This just makes the whole process for the reader so much easier and relevant because when they click on the link, the page they see is relevant to what they have just been reading.

Of course, the page you take your reader to depends on the content of your email. For example, if you're giving away free information in your email it is quite natural to take people to a page where they can continue to get more free information. However, if you reach the point in your email sequence where you're ready to make a specific offer, then the webpage you take them to may request further details from them or indeed carry a straightforward offer for them to buy. So you use the link as your call to action. Don't underestimate the power of putting links in your emails – for many email marketers the link is the only reason why they send the email in the first place.

Also it's not just webpages that you could be linking people to. You may want them to gain access to multimedia such as videos or podcasts or download your latest free e-book.

Now, the temptation would be just to put the link at the end of your email. However, you will get more people clicking on a link if you repeat it two to three times across the length of the email. This is a great little technique because if you've written a really compelling email your reader won't need to get to the bottom before they'll want to click on the link. In that situation, having the link peppered throughout the email makes it easy for them to find the link when they need it.

12: Make Exclusive Offers

Here's a different way of viewing the people on your list: they're not prospects or customers, they are members of an exclusive club. It's then up to you to decide what you want to offer this select group of people.

A simple way to do this is to make them an offer that they couldn't normally get from your business. It might be that you want to offer them 10 per cent off or a free gift if they purchase from you today or access to some information that you are not giving to anybody else.

Whatever it may be, there is real power in making people feel valued because they are part of something special and exclusive.

13: Get Into Sales Conversations the Relaxed Way

When it comes to writing an email which sells your business, some people will react to a very direct request for the sale from you. However, others will not. Even so, you can use your emails as a means to begin one-to-one conversations with them. You can ask for their:

- comments
- questions
- advice
- thoughts on a particular industry situation
- reaction your latest press release

Here's an example.

> Subject: Your Thoughts on XYZ
>
> Dear John,
>
> This is Jed. I wrote the 5-day course on 'Choosing the Perfect Web Designer.'
>
> You recently finished my course and I'm just curious: Did it help you? Please be honest.
>
> Warm regards,

14: How To Sign Off

How you end your email is just as important as how you begin it. So here's a simple formula you can use.

Make your last sign-off combine four things: a repetition of the value they've received from the email, the action you want your reader to take, the title of your next email and when they'll get it.

This does several positive things: it reminds them of the benefits you've given in your email, reinforces what you want them to do, puts in their mind the expectation of your next email and when they're going to receive it. The effect of this is that they look forward to your email and aren't surprised when they receive it. (Unexpected emails are more likely to get deleted.)

Here's an example of the formula in action:

> From this email you've got three incredibly useful tools to help your web design project go smoothly. And here they are:
>
> www.jedscompany.co.uk/toolkit
>
> Tomorrow we are going to talk about your planning your new website!
>
> Until then, warm regards,
>
> Jed

I usually end with 'Warm regards.' To me, this seems a bit more personal than 'Best wishes' or 'Yours sincerely' and a bit more formal than 'Cheers' or 'All the best.'

Now there's one final piece to add and that is the 'P.S.' It may surprise you to know but when people receive a letter they tend to read the first paragraph and the P.S. before they read anything else. In email terms this means that your P.S. needs to contain some core information which will benefit the reader. It could be something as simple as restating the benefit or an offer, for example:

> P.S. don't forget this offer is only available until midnight tonight. Click here to...

You could even use the P.S. as a means to promote your email series. After all, it doesn't cost anything to ask your reader to forward the email to a friend who may benefit from it:

> If this email has been forwarded to you, why not sign-up and get the rest of this FREE series at www.jedscompany.co.uk/signup

You could even use your P.S. to mention a brief success story or a link to your website. The important thing to remember is that people read the P.S. so take advantage of an 'always read' part of your email.

15: Link Your Emails

A useful strategy for keeping your readership engaged with your emails is to tell them what they read in the last email. This reminds them of the value of your previous email and that they are not receiving an unsolicited email. Here's a simple example:

> Dear John,
>
> You may remember I last wrote to you about XYZ. Well, today I found something really interesting I thought you ought to know...

If you get really organised you can specify how long it will be before you send the next one.

> [On Thursday / Tomorrow / In 3 Days / Next week] I'll send you some fascinating information I recently stumbled over about XYZ!

16: Use a Signature

This is simply the standard text that appears at the bottom of every one of your emails after your name.

Now, of course it is up to you to choose what you put in your signature but I would recommend at least the following:

1. business name
2. business address
3. telephone number
4. email address
5. web address

You may also want to add one or two sentences which describe the core benefit of using your business or a guarantee you offer or tag line. Use it as a bit of promotional real estate.

Just to give you a quick example of what I mean, if you were a travel agent, rather than saying 'The Number 1 Travel Agent in the West Midlands,' you might say 'Guaranteed to Find You the Best Holiday Deal in the West Midlands.'

17: Offering an Unsubscribe

All your emails must give the recipient the opportunity to unsubscribe at any point. Usually this is done by them clicking on a link at the very bottom of your email (best to keep it out of the way so it doesn't get accidentally clicked – put a few carriage returns between your sign-off and the unsubscribe link). Clicking the link will take them to a page on your website. This is your last chance to remind them of what they'll miss. Here's an example of the kind of copy you might want to put on this page:

> You're about to unsubscribe!
>
> I'm sorry that you've decided to leave us but I do hope you managed to get far enough into the series to find:
>
> 1. The Secrets of Building Successful Websites
>
> 2. The Web Designer's Toolkit for Millionaires
>
> 3. My Special Podcast on 3 Ways to Double Your Business
>
> All you need to do is click on the button below and we'll immediately stop sending you any more emails.
>
> Many thanks and good luck!

You can even put links in the page so your reader can review one last time how good your information is before they finally say good-bye. Never stop them from leaving or make unsubscribing an impossible process but do remind them of your value all the way!

18: Follow Up Fast

Research done by MarketingSherpa indicates that it is vital to follow up within 24 hours of any sales email message. Any later and are you six times less likely to make the conversion.

You could follow up with another email or telephone call or direct mail (if you can get the timing right). But the research is clear – follow-up within 24 hours and you will achieve six times more sales.

19: Split-Test Your Emails

Let's say you have 5,000 subscribers to your email list. You are about to send all 5,000 your latest email inviting them to immediately purchase your latest product.

But wait! You're missing out on the opportunity of increasing your profits!

Let's imagine that your first email offers 10 per cent off. You could also test an alternative offer, like £10 off. At this point you won't know which will work better. All you need to do is send your first offer to one group of 500 and your second offer to another group of 500. Whichever email performs better is the one you then send to the remaining 4,000.

If you fancy taking this to a really advanced level you can continue to do your split-testing by writing another email which tries to outperform the winner of your last test but again, only testing 500 at a time. It will certainly take you longer to do but it could easily double your profits in the process.

20: PDF Your Emails

If you regularly write to your email membership you will quickly find that you have written a great deal of really valuable information about your business. Now, email being what it is, you can't always guarantee that everyone gets all of your emails. (They get caught by spam filters, get accidentally deleted, email systems fail and so on.)

So, collate all your emails into one PDF. Put a link at the bottom of all your subsequent emails to a page on your website where they can download your now pre-written free e-book. It's a simple technique which reuses existing material to create added value for your customer.

■ THE STRATEGY

Email marketing is one of the foundation stones for creating and maintaining productive relationships with your customers. It conveys your expertise, develops your credibility, establishes rapport and ultimately makes people confident about giving you their business. Plus, the content of your emails is applicable to both prospects and customers alike!

The biggest barrier most web owners have is the barrier of belief – they don't believe they can do it, because they're not confident in their ability to write. They may tell you it's because email marketing won't work, or because it's spam or that they don't have time but the real reason is fear – fear undermining their self-belief. Don't let that happen to you. Be confident in your abilities, get used to writing and do it regularly.

Remember: What people read is a major influence in the decisions they take. Make sure they're reading great things about your business and not your competitor's!

CHAPTER 7

Turn Visitors into Customers

INTRODUCTION

Let me take a moment to congratulate you. You've got to the point where qualified traffic is landing on a well-built and organised website. Plus you've got them joining your email list so you can continue to market to them over the weeks, months and years ahead. In essence, you have a system which has a means of generating customers.

The next step is to take that system and optimise it. This means maximising the number of prospects who become customers, and how you achieve that is through testing.[1] Imagine you are looking at a page on your website that might help convince a prospect to become a customer. The question in your mind should be 'What can I do to increase the conversions from this single page?' And how you go about doing this is by asking yourself another question, 'What happens if I change…?'

In this chapter I will be proposing a whole raft of things you can test and change to convert more prospects into customers. However, a word of caution before we begin: there are no magic formulas, secret strategies or strange handshakes which guarantee online success. There are, however, lots of strategies, tips, ideas and techniques which, when you apply them, can significantly improve your profitability. Some, you may feel will not work on your website and if that's the case, reserve your judgement and try them anyway!

WHICH WEBPAGES SHOULD YOU FOCUS ON?

The first thing to note is that we are typically only going to make one change at a time per page but that we can make changes to multiple pages across the website. However, some pages are more important than others (obviously) so first of all, let's review what

[1] If you need to remind yourself how online testing works, take another look at pages 89–96.

should be first on our optimisation list. Here's an example outline of a website:

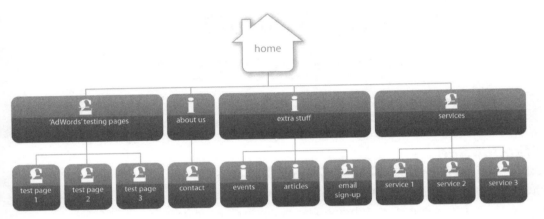

Fig 1 Sample website hierarchy indicating conversion testing pages and 'informational' pages

When you look at your page hierarchy it will become pretty obvious which pages are the money earners and which are browsing/informational/non-sales critical pages. So, you naturally place a priority focus on the pages which are most likely to earn you customers. In our example above I have indicated these pages with a '£' sign.

Your home page is a bit of an oddity because it has to be a jack of all trades: grabbing your visitors' attention, describing the benefits, pointing them to the sales pages of your site, and much more. It's not exclusively informational nor sales-led but nonetheless it should definitely be a focus for your conversion activity.

Remember that your visitors can browse to a page from another page on your website or they can land on a page directly from the search engines. In fact, any page on your website can be considered a 'landing page' because the search engines reference every page on your website (unless you specifically tell them not to) and so, with the right search criteria, any of your pages could be directly accessible from a search engine. Logically, then, if you were to split your sales message up over two webpages on your site, your visitor may only see one of them. So, make sure that each page on your site carries its own complete sales message.

You will notice from the diagram that I've introduced something called 'AdWords testing pages.' Sometimes it's useful to have pages on your website that do not appear in the main navigation as you may want to test variations of a sales page on your visitors coming from specific AdGroups in your AdWords campaigns. For example, if you wanted to sell to people living in London, Beijing and New York you would create three separate landing pages tailored to the interests of each geographic area. These landing pages wouldn't be visible from your website's navigation because you wouldn't want everyone who visits your site to be able to access them. This technique means that some of your testing landing pages will float free of your navigation, giving you the freedom to test ideas without having an impact on your main website.

SPLIT-TESTING YOUR LANDING PAGES

There is one technique which underpins everything that you will learn in this chapter and that is split-testing. We have covered this topic in Chapter 4 so you already know what it is and why we use it. However, we can apply this knowledge in a very specific way to your website.

Let's follow an example to see how this works.

Imagine on your home page you decide to offer a sale. The big headline is 'Great Savings on LCD and Plasma TVs' but you also want to test a different headline, 'Free Delivery on LCD and Plasma TVs', to see which one generates more conversions. (By the way, just the idea of split-testing any page on a website, let alone the home page, would propel you into the top 1 per cent of online businesses.)

The ultra-simple way of testing your two home pages is to run one after the other. You could test 'Great Savings on LCD and Plasma TVs' for a month and then run the 'Free Delivery on LCD

Fig 2 Split-testing a home page idea

2 This is known as 'statistical significance' and you can work out whether you've got enough responses upon which to base a decision by using this mathematical tool. (You'll need to be in a mathematical mood to do this but there are tools online which will work it out for you if you do a web search for 'statistical significance calculator.')

and Plasma TVs' headline for a month. How long each test lasts would be determined by how much traffic you have coming to your website. The more traffic you have, the faster you can determine what's working and what's not. For example, if you get 1,000 visitors to your home page every day then you wouldn't need to wait two months before making a decision as to which of the two headlines is the winner. Equally, if you are only getting 100 visitors a month then you might need to wait longer until you get enough responses for you to make a decision.[2]

Running your home page tests sequentially, however, has a number of shortcomings. Firstly, it means that you have to wait before you get the results (two months in our example) and that you must wait until the test is complete before making a decision – you can't judge each headline's performance as you go. Secondly, if you are just starting out and have limited traffic coming to your website the duration of your tests could get prolonged beyond usefulness. Thirdly, your traffic may have a 'time-bound' nature to it. For example, an extended test wouldn't work if you are running a bank holiday, Christmas or Summer sale, etc. Plus if you are in a service industry like construction, tourism or air-conditioning sales, your traffic may have a seasonal quality to it.

The good news is there is a way to run your tests in *parallel* rather than in sequence. In our example you would create two home pages at the same time. You then use special software which alternates your two home pages to visitors. So, Visitor 1 sees Home Page A, Visitor 2 sees Home Page B, Visitor 3 sees Home Page A, Visitor 4 sees Home Page B, and so on (see Fig 3). The software is clever enough to recognise which visitor saw which home page so if they return to your website they see the same home page they did when they first visited.

This elegant split-testing solution means that you can see how each home page test is performing (in real time) and identify your winner in record time.

There are various online solutions which will do this for you. For example, Hypertracker (www.hypertracker.com) is a commercial solution costing around $20 a month. Alternatively (and indeed inevitably) Google has a solution called the Google Optimiser (www.google.com/websiteoptimizer) which is free. Both require a little bit of technical know-how so you may feel inclined to hand the implementation over to your web designers.

Now that you've got the methodology and the technology to split-test your key pages, you can move onto the many and various tests you can engage in to convert your visitors into customers. However, don't forget that split-testing is an incredibly powerful tool and gives you a significant competitive edge.

Fig 3 How simultaneous webpage split-testing works

Just before you begin, here are two quick practical tips:

1. Always make sure you are split-testing two or more pages. Don't just change one page hoping to see an improvement because you need a 'control' page to compare your results with.

2. Only test one thing at a time. If you test more than one thing simultaneously you won't know which of your changes produced the improvement.

WRITING WINNING COPY

If there is one single thing you can do to radically increase the number of conversions from your website, it is to improve your copy. Copy is any word that appears on your website, including the headline, the main content, the navigation menu, the words on buttons, the text in your footer, the hover text over a hyperlink, and so on.

Why is it so important?

Well, let me just take a second to explain. When most companies develop a new website they pay far more attention to how it looks than what it says. They get carried away with art and design. It's as though they're having their dream car built for them but fixate on the body shape and completely fail to notice that the engine is powered entirely by hamsters. It's a very strange phenomenon. I remember one customer spending three days changing the width of a border around his site. The border's width didn't earn him any extra money and he could have better spent that time improving his copy or even getting the site live three days earlier.

Basically, nobody ever made a sale purely on the basis of how pretty their website looked. In reality people are influenced to buy based on the words they read, so the more compelling your words, the more conversions you will make. (Indeed it could be argued that conversions are the combination of highly relevant visitors meeting a highly compelling offer.)

Unfortunately, it feels like many websites have been written by people who would rather be doing their tax returns than convincing their visitors to buy from them. And if it's not been poorly thought through then it's probably been copied from the previous website or worse still, the brochure they had printed in 2005!

Just to underline the significance of this, let's take a real-world example. Who would you send to your biggest customer to pitch your latest product?

1. One of your professional sales staff who knows your product inside out, understands your customers, knows what they need, knows how to help them, and is articulate?

2. Or the chap who came to fix the photocopier?

Clearly, it's a salesperson. (Equally you wouldn't expect your salesperson to fix the copier!) You find the best person for the job.

Now to return to your website, you don't personally know who is visiting your website, which means you must assume they are about to become your best customer and, therefore, you should do your utmost to impress and influence them. In other words, your website's copy should present you in the best possible light and give your visitors the best chance of understanding your product and service so they can make the right buying decision.

Though most of us are not professional copywriters, that doesn't mean we can't become great copywriters if we apply a few simple strategies. Here are the key things you need to know to help you along.

Copy Strategy 1: Just Begin!

Ok, so you're thinking about improving you website's copy and staring at a blank screen and... nothing. It's perfectly normal to feel some anxiety about not knowing where to start so, like the *Hitchhiker's Guide to the Galaxy* says, 'Don't Panic.' Unless you are a professional writer, it is unlikely that you won't feel a bit daunted by this. What you're feeling is perfectly normal but overcoming this hurdle is without doubt the biggest obstacle most people face. In fact, the majority find it so difficult to overcome this that they get no further and because they don't, they miss out on a huge opportunity to increase their conversions.

Firstly, give yourself a minimum of two hours to start with, find the quietest time of the week and find the quietest period of the day. Hold all your calls or switch on the answer-phone and then start writing.

It doesn't matter if you begin in the middle and work your way out or start at the end and work backwards to the beginning. Remember that this isn't an exam and no one is going to mark you on how well you perform – it doesn't need to be perfect the first time. All you need to do is get the basic ideas down and then refine them later on. The more you write, the more confident you become about writing and the less daunting the whole process becomes.

I find that whenever I write anything, the first attempt is, honestly, pretty rough. It takes me at least a couple of rewrites to get it right. So I recommend getting the broad brushstrokes of what you want to say down and then going through a process of refining until it is exactly how you want it.

Copy Strategy 2: WIIFM

A big problem with many websites' copy is that it's self-centred. You know the kind of thing...

'*We've been established since 1748 ... we tailor our services to our client's needs ... we made widgets for Louis XVIII ... we're the largest ... we're proud of our reputation ... we have 18 offices throughout the UK ... '*

If this were a date, you would have faked a call on your mobile, escaped through the lavatory window or feigned death by lying face down in a bowl of peanuts. However, if you *were* on a date with your website's visitor you'd probably start by showing inter-

est in them *before* you tell them how amazing you are. And that is the difference between writing self-centred copy which switches people off and visitor-centred copy which engages your reader.

The trick to doing this is to ask yourself this question as though you were your visitor:

'What's in it for me?'

The Americans turned this into an expression – 'Tune in to WII-FM' and that's just what you need to do. In other words, flip the conversation around; instead of talking about yourself, talk about them: What is your visitor going to get out of using your website, working with you, having your service or buying your product? What do they get back? (Remember, you are asking them for their money so you want to present a convincing argument as to why they should part with it.)

So here's a useful exercise to help you identify what the WIIFM is in your business. It's called the Pain/Pleasure Pendulum.

Strange though this is, we often make purchases which help us achieve a state of pleasure. In other words, the result of a purchase is a pleasurable experience, be that buying a new television, employing an accountant, going on holiday, renting lovely office space, and so on. It would be very rare to find someone who deliberately made a purchase that causes them pain. In fact, pain is the condition which most people want to move away from when they make a purchase. Each of your customers will have a 'pain' which your product or service takes away.

One of the key elements in successful copywriting is identifying the pain of the prospect and showing them how it turns into pleasure when they become your customer. (Think of it as their problem being overcome by your solution.) Let's take the example of an accountant. What's the pain that people who are needing accountants feel versus the pleasure of using their service?

Pain		Pleasure
Doing the accounts requires effort and knowledge	⇨	Just hand over the accounts and it all gets done
Fear of getting it wrong: penalties, prison (!), etc.	⇨	Guaranteed to be within the law and penalty-free
Dealing with officials	⇨	Don't have to communicate with the authorities
Cost of time	⇨	Frees up your time

Now take your business and look at the 'pain' your customers are in before they use your service and the 'pleasure' they receive by using your product/service afterwards. Once you've done your table as above, you'll have a description of why people will want to use your service.

You can now turn the pleasure of using your business into clear benefits you can express on your website. Below, the 'Why use us' column is the final copy you would use:

Pleasure		Why use us
Just hand over the accounts and it all gets done	⇨	Let us take the stress out of your accounts with our 100% hassle-free service
Guaranteed to be within the law and penalty-free	⇨	Never again worry if you've got your tax return right and on time
No need to communicate with the authorities	⇨	Save yourself the headache of dealing with Inland Revenue
Frees up your time	⇨	Recover days of lost productivity by letting us handle your accounts

You can then promote these as benefits of using your business. Which leads us neatly on to...

Copy Strategy 3: Features vs Benefits

Ask any average business about their product or service and they'll give you a list. Unfortunately, it's more often than not the wrong list. Let's take the example of a car dealership. Ask them about the latest model and here's the kind of information you get:

1. Good fuel economy
2. Big boot
3. ABS brakes
4. 0–60 in 9 seconds

Those are the *features* of the car, but what most people want to know (even if they don't ask) are the *benefits*. Let's review the list again but this time adding in the benefits:

Feature		Benefit
Good fuel economy	⇨	Saves you money on fuel bills
Big boot	⇨	You can take the family on holiday for two weeks with space to spare
ABS brakes	⇨	Keeps you and your family safe
0–60 in 9 seconds	⇨	Makes you look ultra-cool

Here's another example: the fact your car has a GPS is a *feature* but arriving at all your meetings on time and unflustered is the *benefit*.

People may listen to the features but they buy the benefits. So, take a look at your products or services and build a table like the one above. Focus your copy on the benefits and you will unlock your buyer's wallet. Don't forget to use WIIFM and the Pain/Pleasure Pendulum to help you identify your business's benefits.

Copy Strategy 4: Be Conversational

So, what style should you adopt when you are writing your copy? Well the temptation is to write in formal, business-like terms. However, this often comes over as being distant and impersonal which tends to turn people off.

Here's an example of what I mean:

ABC Accountants is a firm of Chartered Accountants and Registered Auditors established in 2005. It has attracted a large number of companies through its reputation, efficiency and customer focus.

In an ever-changing world, ABC Accountants' clients are confident that their affairs are in good hands. This confidence derives from our approach to professional matters and by the results from our recommendations.

Well, it sounds very professional, but hardly friendly, inviting or personal. Now compare it with this from an IT support company:

IT goes wrong – we're not scaremongering, it's just a fact of life.

When it does, we're here to help. Our approach to your IT is simple:

- Get there fast (98% on-site within 4 hours)

- Fix it fast (99% of visits are first-time fixes)

- Report and prevent (our preventive advice will save you money)

Here's our promise to you: if you aren't impressed by our speed and quality of service on our first visit, we will give you your money back!

So, let's start with a simple conversation. If we can help we'll tell you; if we can't, we'll leave it at that.

Call us today…

Now, doesn't that sound more like the type of company you'd want to start a business relationship with? Notice that one of the key reasons it sounds more personal is that they use the word 'you'. In fact, writing in the first and second person automatically makes your writing sound personal. So using 'I', and 'me', 'my', 'you', 'yours', etc. creates a personal connection with your reader.

If you're still unsure about getting the style right, here's a really easy technique to help you: simply, write as you speak.[3] This technique works because in our day-to-day lives we hear more than we read and so we are more tuned in to the language that we use in everyday speech. If you write in the same style you would use to speak then you'll find your copy easier to write and your visitors will find it easier to read.

[3] This may not work if you speak in cockney rhyming slang (though it may make your website more fun to read!).

After you've been writing for a while you'll start to get a sense of your own style and that's when you really begin to enjoy the process. One of our clients, for example, is great at telling stories and he usually has me doubled over laughing. His web copy is successful because although he's very respectful of the reader, he uses humour to get his point across. What he learned was that he was actually far better and more natural writing in that style than trying to write in serious 'business speak'. So, give yourself a bit of time to let your style develop and mature naturally.

Copy Strategy 5: AIDCA

When it comes to writing a webpage from scratch, having a good structure will make all the difference to your reader. Fortunately copywriters have a secret formula they use to do this which goes from the top of your page to the bottom. Here's the structure below with an example for illustrative purposes:

Structure	Example (very basic)
Attention	Make money from your website!
Interest	Did you know that only 1% of visitors become customers?
Desire	Here's how you can convert the other 99%
Commitment	100% satisfaction guaranteed or your money back
Action	Click here to buy the book!

Now let's take a look at the structure in a bit more detail:

1. **Attention**: Grab your visitor's attention with a headline. The headline keeps your visitor on the landing page and keeps them reading.

   - 'How to Win Friends and Influence People'
   - 'Which of these £5–£10 bestsellers do you want – for only £1 each?'
   - 'Discover the Fortune that Lies Hidden in Your Salary'
   - 'Free Book – Tells you 12 Secrets of Better Lawn Care'

   If you're stuck for a headline, focus on the *one major* problem that your visitor needs to solve – it's the one that appears more 'dangerous' than all the rest, for example 'WARNING: Losing Your Home in a Fire is Bad Enough, but What if Your Insurance Didn't Cover You?'

2. **Interest**: Now you've stopped them with your attention-grabbing headline you need to create some interest so they can carry on reading. This is the point at which you use the copy you've written about solving your visitor's problem and where they read how you are going to move them from pain to pleasure. You should also use this area of your webpage to describe the benefits of your business, its products and services.

3. **Desire**: Next you need to tell them why they want what you have to offer. Here you are focusing on satisfying that 'want' often buried in your visitor's subconscious. Ask yourself: what do they want as opposed to what you think they need. If you're a first-time astronaut doing a space-walk you need a space suit but what you want is someone with a camera! One final point. An extraordinarily effective tactic in creating desire is to restrict the availability of what you have to offer, for example, 'Only 3 Days left', 'Only 20 Places Remain', 'Low on Stock', etc. This approach creates a strong feeling of desire by appealing to the 'scarcity mentality' – the feeling that they might miss out on something really great.

4. **Commitment**: This is where you can demonstrate your credibility using testimonials, guarantees, trade, partner and customer logos, association memberships, kite-marks, support options and so on. Present what you can that will give your visitor confidence in buying from you. (There's more on this subject later on in this chapter under Testimonials, page 226, and Guarantees, page 227.)

5. **Action**: This is arguably the most important aspect to the page because it describes what you want your visitor to do next (buy, sign-up, download, etc.). It could be in the form of a button ('Buy Now') or a line of text ('Get in Touch Today') or a form, a hyperlink or email link.

Take a random sales page on your site and see how closely it follows this structure. Add in any missing elements to help strengthen the page's sales proposition.

Copy Strategy 6: John Carlton's 'Here's What I Got...'

The AIDCA structure is not the only one you can use. Frank Kern was given this structure for a sales page by his friend John Carlton and it is about as simple and straightforward as it gets. Here's the format John gave to Frank:

1. Here's What I Got...
2. Here's What [XYZ] Will Do For You...
3. Here's What I Want You to Do Next...

It looks deceptively simple but here's the catch – people try and complicate it believing that nothing that simple can actually work and in doing so, lessen its impact! Frank Kern followed this approach (to the letter, even including the headings as they are) and launched several successful products to the tune of hundreds of thousands of dollars.

The key to the structure is to, as Frank puts it, 'Get to the point and don't be afraid.' Simply be direct and clear.

Copy Strategy 7: Pace Your Reader

Most people surf quite quickly which means that the average length of time they spend on a website can be very short. Some marketers have argued that it takes only a few seconds before a visitor decides to stay and look further or leave and try another website. The reason visitors make such quick decisions is that ingrained into our psychology is the need to move from pain to pleasure (problem to solution) as quickly as possible. There are other factors which influence browsing speed but the bottom line is that the initial search is done at speed. Once you acknowledge this, it can change the way you look at your website.

Imagine you are sprinting down the road at full tilt. Suddenly a passing cat decides to run in front of you, forcing you to come to a crashing halt. Firstly, it takes quite a lot of energy to stop dead and secondly it's a fairly uncomfortable process (especially for the cat if you can't stop). When your visitor is browsing at speed, if they land on your website and are confronted with big paragraphs of text that go on forever or lots of flashy graphics all vying for attention, then you force your visitor to go from fast browsing to very slow 'information absorption' browsing. This is effectively trying to make them to stop dead and, as we discussed, this is an uncomfortable feeling when you're running and also when you're browsing. More often than not your visitors won't expend the energy in slowing down – they will simply bounce off your page because it looks too much like hard work to wade through.

A better way to manage your visitor is to acknowledge that they are browsing at speed and make sure that the landing pages on your website only slow them up enough for them to absorb the key facts. Once you've piqued their interest with a flavoursome headline and bullet-pointed list of benefits, you can then offer them the opportunity of reading more about what your business does.

An easy way to achieve this is to have simple, clear and sparsely populated sales pages (at least above the fold) which get the basics of what you have on offer across to your visitor. You can then provide them with hyperlinks to other more detailed pages (or save the detail for further on down the page).

Now this is a controversial point and not everyone will agree with me because what I'm really saying is that in the first instance, short copy is better than long copy. In fact, in most circumstances research indicates that long copy outperforms short copy. However, in the instance of someone initially landing on your site, gently slowing them down to a pace where they can absorb the long copy is, I believe, a tactic which has substantial merit.

Now take a look at any one of your sales pages and imagine that you have landed on it for the first time. Give yourself no more than 15 seconds and make a snap decision: would you stay or would you go? In other words, does the page articulate enough to your visitor in those 15 seconds to convince them to stay and read more? This is, obviously, quite a subjective test and you're probably not the best person for it because you're too close to your website and your business. Instead, this is a job for a group of test subjects for you to find and quiz.

Copy Strategy 8: Use Bullets and Numbered Lists

Research from the British Computer Society shows that people read slower on screen, with less accuracy, and get tired faster. This is very important for us to know because we need to be sensitive to how people read online in order to get our point across most effectively.

One way in which you can keep people engaged is to use bullets and numbered lists to help break the page up and focus their eye on the key information. Using lists has several advantages:

1. Helps you order your information
2. Keeps your message concise
3. Makes your page scannable so your visitor can find information relevant to them quickly

Now, here's a really advanced tip. We humans can only handle so many 'chunks' of information at a time before we edit them out. The general consensus is that seven (plus or minus two) is the maximum – this is called 'chunking.' The more complex the information, the less we remember. Shorten your lists right down if the information is detailed or lengthen them (up to nine-deep) if it's very basic.

Another little gem is that, oddly, people don't read lists from the top down. In a list of five bullet points, the biggest impact is made by point 1, then 5, then 2, then 4; point 3 is the least likely to be noticed. If you've got a list which has a priority to it, order the points like this:

1. Priority 1
2. Priority 3
3. Priority 5
4. Priority 4
5. Priority 2

Copy Strategy 9: Button Text

Obvious places to find buttons are on forms (sign-up, contact, etc.), on product pages, next to search boxes, and so on. The fact that there is a button on a page already indicates that something will happen when you press it. From your perspective it's probably very important that the button gets clicked on as it will initiate the next step towards your prospect becoming a customer. But the text on the button itself can be used to further sell the need to act.

For example, let's imagine you've got a sign-up box for your email marketing. The button at the bottom of the form might say 'Submit.' Most people implicitly understand what the button will do because the button itself stands out on the page, so why not jazz up the message so they are clicking on a *benefit* and not just an instruction. For example, the button could say:

- Get Your Free Report Now
- Click to Receive Your VIP Newsletter
- Download Your Free Trial Here
- Get Started Now
- Join Us

Now there is a counter-argument that by changing the name of the button to something unexpected you force the visitor to think a little more about their action. I think that as long as it's presenting the benefit of the action then that's fine. However, do make the button visually obvious and the call-to-action text clear.

If you're worried that the button might not look obvious enough, you can always add the text 'Submit' to the front of your wording. So now it might read:

- SUBMIT: Get Your Free Report Now
- SUBMIT: Click to Receive Your VIP Newsletter

■ CONVERSION TACTICS

By now you will have reviewed and improved the copy on your website, making it more compelling, interesting, and focused on your visitor rather than you, which leaves the doors wide open for to you to improve everything else!

Your ability to test and explore some of the options I'm going to present to you will be partly determined by how much control your content management system gives you, the costs your web designers may charge for doing it and the time you have. So you may want to build your own prioritised list of 'stuff to test.'

Remember that the primary aim is to increase the number of conversions from your website, so you need to be sure that you are either measuring them using your split-testing software or keeping track of them in other ways. For example, use Google AdWords or Google Analytics, or count the number of enquiries in your inbox, or get your sales force to ask which page the prospects were on before they called your company. As long as you are measuring, you can assess the success of your changes.

Below are some ideas to help you begin the process of improving your conversions.

Covering the Basics

Let's start with the basics. Here is a list of elements on the page which you should be split-testing:

Headings

Test:

1. Different headings
2. Using sub-headings
3. Changing the
    a. font
    b. colour
    c. size
    d. position
4. Swapping for a picture
5. Using in conjunction with a picture

Graphics

Test:

1. Different types of graphics
    a. photos
    b. diagrams
    c. illustrations
2. Different sizes (small, medium, large, super-large)

3. Different shapes
4. Offering a zooming-in/out facility
5. Providing more than one photo of a product (front, back, side, etc.)
6. 360° panorama photos
7. If appropriate, offer a sense of scale (like putting a pencil next to the item)
8. Pictures which generate an emotional response: funny, zany, serious, ludicrous, etc.
9. Reducing (or removing) the size of your 'hero' image at the top of your page (or adding/increasing the size)
10. No graphics on the page

Copy

Test:

1. Different layouts (1 column, 2 columns, 3 columns, etc., using sidebars and pull-ins. If you're looking for layout ideas pick up any magazine, see how they do it.)
2. Using synopses, pull-ins (information on the edge of the page), 'break-out boxes' (boxes anywhere on the page – you often see these used for quotations)
3. Different font colours and backgrounds (for example, black on white versus yellow on blue)
4. Different font sizes
5. Using bold, block capitals and other types of text effects to strengthen your message (although try to avoid italics as it's often hard to read on screen)
6. Using a highlighter pen effect on important words
7. Different lengths of copy

Hyperlinks

Test:

1. Different wordings (to make them more compelling)
2. Different colours (blue is the standard but as long as there's an underline you could experiment with different-coloured hyperlinks)
3. Roll-over colours (when you move your mouse over a hyperlink and it temporarily changes colour, that's a roll-over)

4. Replacing a hyperlink with a graphic that has more visual impact but is still clickable (especially useful if the hyperlink is a key action on the page, like 'Contact Us' or 'Buy Now')

Buttons

Test:

1. Different
    a. sizes
    b. shapes
    c. colours
2. Different wordings
3. Converting them back to hyperlinks or 'doubling-up' by introducing a hyperlink directly beneath which takes them to the same page as the button
4. Adding a graphic or icon to the button to make it more obvious

Calls to Action

Test:

1. Different positions of your call to action on the page including
    a. sign-up boxes
    b. 'Buy Now' buttons
    c. download buttons
    d. enquiry forms
    e. hyperlinks
2. Changing the wording
3. Combining all the test ideas in this section to improve your calls to action

Contact Details

Now you would assume that every company would make it ultra-easy for any visitor to find out how to contact them. And yet, I've lost count of the number of times I've really struggled to find a telephone number or an appropriate email address so I can give the company my business.

For example, how many times have you seen the 'Contact Us' page under the 'About Us' section? In fact, some are so keen for you not to contact them, they will put their 'Contact Us' link right at the very bottom of their home page next to their Privacy and Legal links. Occasionally, the company is so 'desperate' to have your business they completely omit any contact details from their website.

So, imagine you visited your website for the first time; don't actively search for your contact details, instead imagine that you have been hit with a blunt object and aren't concentrating that well. Now, how easy is it for you to find your company's contact details and take the appropriate action?

Here are some approaches to increase the number of contacts from your website.

Contact Tip 1

Always keep your telephone number visible and prominent on every page. Why every page? Because you can never anticipate when somebody is going to decide to make contact with you. Therefore, by putting a contact point on every page, you make it easy for them to get in touch. (If you make visitors search to get in touch with you, a good number of them will give up trying and go somewhere else. And just in case you're wondering, yes, people really are that easily frustrated – web statistics bear it out.)

By the way, if your telephone number is a picture and not text, make sure you apply an alt-tag which contains the telephone number. (Your CMS or web designers should be able to do this for you.) An alt-tag is just a text description of a graphic and it's very important to the search engines. It would also mean that your telephone number will become searchable – a handy advantage if someone's been left with only your telephone number on their desk.

Contact Tip 2

Use a unique telephone number for your website. This will allow you to track how many telephone enquiries you've had directly from your website. Strangely, few businesses do this and so any form of sales measurement that they are doing falls into a black hole because they can't distinguish what's come from their website and what's come from anywhere else. Remember the analyst's golden rule: You can't improve what you're not measuring.

Contact Tip 3

Keep all your contact details together in one area. Your telephone number, address, relevant email addresses, general enquiry form etc., should all be accessible from one place.

Contact Tip 4

If you are an ecommerce store and you're about to ask someone for their credit card details, give them confidence that you are the real deal by putting your address, telephone number and email address on the product, basket and payment pages, so if your visitor wants to make contact with you, they can easily do so.

Enquiry Forms

For many websites getting someone to fill in their enquiry form is the ultimate goal because that counts as a lead you can follow up on. So, think of your enquiry form as the last step in your website's sales process. It's a little like having done all the selling but now needing your visitor to sign the contract. Getting your enquiry form right helps overcome the last bit of resistance in your visitor's mind to taking that final action. Here are a few techniques you can use to make your enquiry forms convert more of your visitors into active leads.

Enquiry Form Tip 1

Keep your enquiry forms simple. Don't ask your visitor for their dog's name, inside leg measurement and their favourite colour when the most important thing to you is probably just a name, telephone number and email address.

Enquiry Form Tip 2

I'll illustrate this tip with a quick story. We had a customer who had one enquiry form which had seven questions on it. When we looked at his web statistics we noticed that while lots of people were visiting the contact page only about 20 per cent were filling in the form. Something was wrong. When we spoke to him we discovered that he was only really interested in getting basic information (name, email address and telephone number), all the rest were useful but not vital. The solution was to divide the form in two: the top part was titled 'Quick Form' and only contained the three primary questions and the form beneath was titled 'More

Details (Optional)' and contained the rest. Very importantly, there was a 'Submit' button underneath each of the forms. After a few weeks we went back and looked at the results to find that the number of people filling in the form had jumped from 20 per cent to over 50 per cent. That's more than twice as many leads and absolutely no cost to his business. This is a great example of how making minor changes can generate major results. It's also a technique worth testing on your website.

Enquiry Form Tip 3

Check out your web statistics. In the above example we would never have known that a problem existed with his enquiry form unless we had reviewed the web statistics. There were three very important pieces of information that helped us and would help you.

The first is the number of people visiting your contact page. That tells you how many people were interested enough in what you do to think about making contact.

The second is the number of times the 'Thank You' page has been viewed. That tells you how many times the enquiry form was successfully filled then. (Incidentally, check that that number is the same as the number of enquiry emails you got.)

The third is the percentage of people who filled in the enquiry form. That then tells you how effective the form is.

$$\frac{\text{Number of visitors to the Thank You page}}{\text{Number of visitors to the Contact page}} \times 100\%$$

Once you've got this statistic you have a measurement which you can use as a baseline for your improvements.

Enquiry Form Tip 4

Even though your visitors are 90 per cent there, you still need to persuade them to fill in the form, so keep selling the idea that you can help them. For example, the text above your enquiry form might read:

Just pass on your details below and we will be in touch with you in less than 1 hour (PLUS we will also send you a FREE report on XYZ).

Or:

Please fill in the form below and don't forget our product/ service is backed by our XYZ guarantee.

Remember to keep selling the benefits of your business even on the contact page!

Enquiry Form Tip 5

Don't give your visitor the opportunity to click away from the page. Don't offer them any related page links, FAQs, downloads, etc. These could serve as a distraction and entice the visitor away from the one thing you want them to do, which is filling in the enquiry form.

Enquiry Form Tip 6

Here's a simple rule for forms: the more mandatory fields you ask people to fill in, the fewer responses you will get. What's interesting about this little formula is that while the number of responses diminishes, the quality of the leads increases. Conversely if you only have a couple of fields for the visitor to fill in then you are likely to receive more responses, but of lesser quality.

This allows you to throttle back or open up the number of leads you are acquiring, depending on the quality of the leads you are receiving.

Audio and Video

One of the most underused and yet exciting opportunities for your website lies with multimedia. Almost every PC, Mac and laptop has the capability of playing back audio and video. In fact, the streaming of audio and video has become so popular that the Visual Networking Index Forecast predicts that by 2014, some 90 per cent of the Internet's traffic will be video.

And yet multimedia is hardly used on websites to sell products and services. There are two principal barriers as to why businesses don't use multimedia:

1. They think it's too 'technical' to implement
2. They think it needs to look ultra-professional

In reality neither of these apply.

1. All you need is a basic camcorder, some simple video editing software (Adobe Premiere Elements or Sony Vegas, for example) and a YouTube account.

2. Don't worry about producing an unpolished video as how professional the results look has little bearing on whether people buy. Remember, the more 'real' your efforts look, the more honest they appear. (Most people would rather buy a second-hand car from an oily looking mechanic than an oily looking salesman!)

The key here is to experiment, because I can pretty much guarantee that your competitors will be too scared to try. Here are some examples of how you could use video:

1. Demonstrate your product or service
2. Interview a customer
3. Interview a salesperson
4. Show the results of your product or service (or the results of *not* using your product or service)
5. Do a mini presentation
6. Be instructional (www.howcast.com are great at this)
7. Show your team at work
8. Shoot an event, conference, keynote presentation
9. Shoot a 'Day in the Life of...'
10. A tour around your workshop, factory, premises, etc.

The unspoken advantage of video is credibility – it creates a stronger sense of trust between you and your visitor because they don't need to imagine what they're reading, they can actually see it! For example, demonstrating how your quality assurance process really works in your production plant *proves* to your visitor that they will get a quality product.

Use video to help your prospect understand your business, how you can help them and why they should use you.

Here are some simple tips to shooting a good video:

1. Give as much great value in your video as you would in any of your emails
2. Keep your video short and to the point
3. Always end with a call to action
4. If you're going to use a presenter, try to match them to the target market

5. Add your web address and contact details (somewhere) into the video

Adding video to your website couldn't be easier. You can either use your CMS to add video (if it gives you that facility) or upload your video to YouTube, Vimeo, Metacafe, Dailymotion or any other of the major video sites and use the 'Embed' feature on those sites to copy some code into your website. This code embeds the video in your website even though it is played back from whichever site you originally uploaded it to.

Video is still perceived as a high value way of presenting information on the web, so you should always put it as close to the top of the page as is sensible. You could even use it as an incentive to attract sign-ups for your email campaigns – 'Sign up and get 3 Great Videos on XYZ!'

You can experiment with the layout – different sizes (640 x 480 pixels vs 800 x 600 vs 1024 x 768, etc.), shapes (4:3 old TV size vs 16:9 widescreen size), quality (standard definition vs high definition). You can also experiment with the content – different lengths, using text over the video (voiceover vs subtitled),etc.

Here's an interesting statistic to help you fine-tune your videos. According to MarketingSherpa's Online Advertising Handbook, a video outperforms a picture (86 per cent to 73 per cent) and video that is accessible directly on the page performed slightly better than video that expands out of the page into a pop-up box (88 per cent to 86 per cent)

Up to now, I've only referred to video because audio can be used in almost exactly the same way. The only caveat I'd personally apply to audio is that it should be of good quality. Getting a microphone from £30 to £50 should give you good quality and using free software like Audacity (audacity.sourceforge.net) will give you all the capabilities you need to record and edit it. There is nothing more off-putting than having to strain to hear what someone is saying. It's less relevant for video because the visuals can 'carry' the sound quality. There are plenty of audio sites you can upload and link your audio files to, the best known being iTunes.[4]

So, there's plenty to test and play with but remember it doesn't have to be perfect because even a rough and ready piece of multimedia will undoubtedly have more impact on your prospects than not having one at all.

[4] An excellent example of how to use podcasting to maximum effect is www.boagworld.com (which discusses all things web designer-y).

We're not completely finished with multimedia though, as you will read below...

Testimonials

Testimonials are one of the most powerful elements you can add to your website. They create a sense of confidence about what you do, and, in raising your visitor's confidence about your business, will make them read your website with more care.

The big problem with acquiring testimonials is businesses often take a formal approach to trying to get them and hence you see so few of them. Most of the time they rely on their clients writing them, which rarely happens because most customers are too busy to spend the time doing it. The alternative is that the business writes the testimonial and the customer signs it. There's nothing intrinsically wrong with that approach except that by the fifth time they're all starting to look very similar!

So, here's a technique which overcomes the above and is also dead simple. Phone your clients and say you're doing a bit of research and as they are one of your best customers you'd like to get their honest feedback on your product or service.

Make sure you note down the key themes of what they say and then read it back to them. Now ask them if you can use their comments on your website and in your marketing. Next you quickly write up what they said and email it to them for them to check over.

Do this with five customers and you will get five very natural and completely different testimonials.

This approach has another advantage, which is if your customer has a problem or complaint it gets flushed out with you well before they decide to go to another supplier.

Once you've obtained your handful of testimonials, get them onto your website in key locations. Put them on your home page, product and/or service pages, buying pages and so forth. And don't be afraid to use the same one more than once.

A drawback to any written testimonial is in proving its authenticity. In other words, how do you prove to a sceptical audience that you didn't just make it up? Well, there are a couple of techniques you can use that will address those concerns.

The first is adding an audio testimonial to the written one. So, not only can your visitor read it but they get the chance to listen to the customer saying it. The audio could also provide more detail on how good they found your service to be or it could even be a full-scale interview or just the testimonial as it was written.

You could visit your customer with a Dictaphone or do the interview over the phone. (AudioBoo, at audioboo.fm, will allow you to do this via your iPhone or Android phone and link the audio directly into your website.) Once the recording is complete you can download it to an audio file. All you then need to do is use your CMS (or web designers) to upload it onto your website.

How you go about recording a phone call is pretty straight-forward and there are lots of companies that can do it for you without you needing any recording equipment. (A web search for 'recording telephone calls service' will find them for you.) Some also allow your customer to leave a recorded message.

Another great technique is to get a photograph of your customer and put it next to the testimonial. If you can take a photo of your customer using your product, or with you or your staff in it, or even doing something daft involving your brand name, that all adds to the veracity of the testimonial.

If you want to take this to its ultimate level, video-record your customer giving you an endorsement. Obviously, this takes a bit more preparation and you will have to find a customer who would be comfortable doing it. However, if you can make it worth their while (with a bottle of something, a donation to their favourite charity or even helping them do a video for their own website) then you should find some willing participants.

The great thing about going that extra mile is that your competitors probably won't – which makes you instantly stand out from the crowd.

Guarantees

Along with testimonials, guarantees are one of the most effective ways of increasing your conversion rate on your website. A guarantee in marketing language is known as a *risk reversal*. In other words, you are taking the risk away from your customer when they buy from you, and by doing so you eliminate one of the major buying objections your potential customer may have.

Using a guarantee on your website is especially powerful because it provides that final push your visitor needs to feel confident enough to get in touch or buy your product directly, there and then. And confidence is a big factor in people's purchasing decisions on the Internet. The more confidence you give them, the greater the likelihood they will buy from you.

Here are some approaches to guarantees you might consider.

Guarantee Your Work

- If our repair fails in the first 90 days, we'll do it again for free.
- If our cleaning fails to meet your high standards of excellence, we'll do it again free of charge.

Guarantee your Service

- If our engineer is more than 10 minutes late for an appointment, the next hour's work is on us.
- If our technicians are not the most cheerful, pleasant people you've ever met, have a bottle of champagne on us.

Guarantee your Product

- If you don't like it within the first 30 days, we will give you a 100%, no-hassle refund.
- If our XYZ breaks within 5 years, we'll replace it for free.

That's called a limited guarantee, but you could extend it to a lifetime guarantee.

Although it's not directly seen as a guarantee, you could also make an introductory offer, the classic one being a 30-day free trial or something simple like 'No set-up charge.'

The best-known (and perhaps, most powerful) risk reversal is the money-back guarantee.

Money-Back Guarantees

Money-back guarantees often put business owners off because they fear that all their customers will take advantage of them but this really isn't the case. It's ludicrous to think that if you sold 100 products you would have to give the money back to 100 people or even 50 people; the real-life statistics aren't anywhere near that figure. Think of it like this: if you offer a money-back guarantee and that increases your sales by 50 per cent, even if your return rate goes up to 5 per cent overall, you've still increased your sales by 45 per cent.

Use your existing return or refund rate as a guide to how often your guarantee is likely to be used.

Another way of viewing this is that there will always be people out there who will try to take advantage. A guarantee isn't going to make any difference as they'd try it on whether you had one or not. I bet you've experienced this already – it's just part of the cost of being in business.

Don't forget that your visitor may have five or ten other websites offering something similar to you, so your guarantee helps differentiate you from your competition while simultaneously boosting your prospect's confidence in your business.

If you're still unsure that this is a workable guarantee, do a web search for 'money back guarantee' and see just how many companies are flourishing using this technique.

ECOMMERCE SITES

If you're running an ecommerce site then there are four primary areas you can focus your conversion strategies on: the product gallery page, the product page, the basket page and the payment pages. But, before we take each in turn, let's consider the ecommerce process itself.

Most websites have some kind of sales 'funnel' or timeline that describes the process of moving a visitor from prospect to customer. In the offline world the funnel might be as simple as that shown in Fig 4. It could, of course have more stages to it (call, letter, call, meeting, proposal, presentation, etc.). The steps are not what's important; what is, however, is the fact that the number of people who start out as prospects is never equal to the customers you eventually acquire. The difference between the two is known as the *attrition rate* or *shopping cart abandonment*.

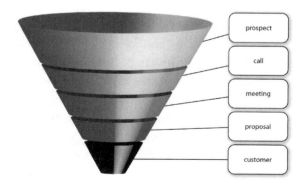

prospect

call

meeting

proposal

customer

Fig 4 Standard offline sales funnel

On an ecommerce site, the steps a visitor has to take to become a customer is your sales funnel. At each point, people will drop out of the process for one reason or another. Your job is to minimise the drop out.

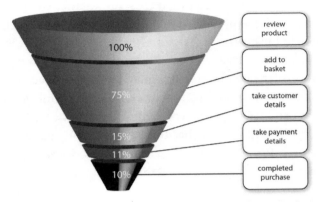

Fig 5 An ecommerce sales funnel

If 100 people review the product but only 10 buy it somewhere along the line, you lost 90 per cent of your prospects. Knowing where the drop-out occurs allows you to focus your attentions on the page (or pages) which are causing the trouble. If, for argument's sake, 75 people add the product to their basket but only 15 people move on to entering their details, then the problem lies with the basket page. Could delivery cost or scheduling be a problem? Have you emphasised the product's value enough? Is it clear what they have to do next? The questions for why a page is failing become the tests you apply to improve its performance.

Knowing not just the *overall* attrition rate but the attrition rate *at each step* your visitor takes is vital to boosting your conversions.

Now let's take a look at some of the techniques you can employ to reduce your attrition rate and increase your conversions.

The Product Gallery Page

A product gallery page is simply the first page your visitor gets to which lists all the products. Often these pages show categories of product first before listing the actual products. This page then allows you to click on a product to view its details.

Typically, the product gallery page is the first sight your visitor has of what you've got on offer, so being obvious and simple is the key – clear headings and pictures with obvious places to click to see more.

These pages are more about enticing the customer to look at your product in detail rather than selling it to them. The selling should principally be left to the product page itself. However, these pages need to be functional and make it easy for your visitors to get to what they want.

Here are a few simple suggestions to help you improve the visitor experience on these pages and reduce the dreaded Attrition Rate!

1. Give your visitor the option of sorting the items, for example, by brand name, price, colour, size, application, etc. Don't forget ascending and descending options.

2. If you fancy a really advanced option, consider sorting the products by most popular, what the visitor's Facebook friends are buying, what people with similar interests were thinking of buying.

3. Combine your sorting facility with the ability to narrow the search by brand name, price (or price bracket), colour, size, application, etc.

4. The reverse of this is to provide a 'View All' option. The reasoning behind this is that some visitors won't want to have to keep clicking on 'Next Page' to see the next set of products. Instead, they'll want to see them all in one go and skim down the page. This can be especially useful if you've got more than two pages of products.

5. Add a Sale or Special Offer category into this page for your bargain hunters.

6. Offer an internal site search to assess what people are doing. With site searches you'll be able to identify what keywords your visitors have been typing in. Two key areas you'll want to focus on are the top searched-for words that did have results (i.e. a page was found on your website with that keyword in) and the top searched words that did not have results (i.e. no pages were found). Both of these give you an insight into your visitors' wants and, therefore, tell you what you must to do meet them. So, if your website sells clocks and you notice lots of searches for 'clock repairs' you know there's a market for a clock repair service!

Site searches should not be underplayed on ecommerce sites. MarketingSherpa's 2007 Online Shopping & Research Survey identified that 27 per cent of shoppers typed the product name into the site's search box – 4 per cent ahead of those people clicking on a product from the home page.

Fig 6   A product gallery page

The Product Page

First let's assume that you've done the obvious things to make your product page as appealing as possible. These include: a clear, zoomable picture of the product, good product copy, delivery times and, of course, its price. Now let's take a look at some of the specifics.

Buy Now

Daft though this may seem, you wouldn't believe how many websites make you search for the 'BUY NOW' button. Put it right at the top (and at the bottom if your page scrolls) but make sure it's instantly visible when a visitor lands on the page.

Try different wordings on the button: 'Add to Basket,' 'Get it Today,' 'Order Now,' 'Buy.'

Only Just

The psychology of people who are surfing on the net is that they believe the Internet provides them with cheaper prices. Whether this is true or not is irrelevant. It is the perception that people have of the Internet and it is a psychology which you can capitalise on.

Using words like 'Only' and 'Just' in front of your price gives your visitor the perception that you are offering a great product at a steal.

And while we're on the subject of price... be proud of it! Don't hide your price as though you were embarrassed. Place it in large and clear text right next to the product.

Nail Them to the Page

When people are searching to buy, they want as much confidence about the product and your business as possible. It's strange then that so many websites fall short of providing good-quality, relevant information on their products pages when there is so much to be gained. Imagine how well your sales team would fare if you only gave them half the product information? Well, remember that your product pages are your 'salesmen on the screen.' You've got to give them every opportunity to close the sale for you.

Giving your visitor lots of relevant information means there is greater likelihood that you will overcome any resistance they may have to buying from you. That's why you must give them everything you can to minimise their objections: PDFs to download, manuals, customer comments, case studies, videos of the product in action, podcasts, photographs from every angle, close-ups, specifications, FAQs and so on.

Remember, the more information and help you give out upfront, the more sales you will make!

The Big Little Things

Even the little things can make a difference and sometimes a huge difference. Here are a few for you to try:

1.   Give the product a more exciting headline than just its name
2.   Put the price next to the 'Buy Now' button
3.   Put a quantity box next to your 'Buy Now' button so your visitor can easily buy more than one of your products
4.   Put delivery information next to the 'Buy Now' button
5.   If you are selling below RRP, display the RRP with a strikethrough and show your lower price in bold. For example,

~~RRP £19.99~~ I **Our Price £15.99** I You Save £4.00

Or you could soup it up a little to look like this:

£15.99 Free Delivery
RRP £19.99 I You Save £4.00 (20%)

6.   Use any appropriate logos to indicate that you provide a secure shopping experience. Your payment provider will provide you with one (Sage Pay, World-Pay, PayPal, etc.). You can also get listed (and use their logo) in safe shopping directories like www.shopsafe.co.uk.

Voucher Codes

Vouchers and discount codes can be a great way to entice people to buy. Essentially, you are rewarding your customer for being a customer, continuing to buy from you, referring you to other people and so forth. It plays to the 'something for nothing' psychology we all love when we go shopping – 'Buy 1 Get 1 Free' is a perfect example of this. (Very often, the offer is costed back into the sale but it's nice to feel we're getting a bargain nonetheless.) For example, having a voucher which rewards your visitor with a discount will help you incentivise people to buy your products.

You should make it clear where your visitor has to enter these codes and ideally have them both on the product and basket pages.

What you offer in the voucher is up to you but here are a few ideas to get you thinking:

1. Free delivery (on this purchase, on purchase for X length of time, on orders over £X, etc.)
2. X% off your next purchase (pick a percentage that's easy to calculate for your visitor and show the new price plus the saving)
3. £X off your next purchase
4. A voucher for another company (for example, £50 Amazon voucher)
5. 2 for 1, 3 for 2, etc.
6. Free gift, or other related product (like batteries for toys or SD cards for cameras)
7. 'Enter the voucher and we'll donate £X to our favourite charity'
8. Free X-day trial of another service or product. For example, a 30-day free trial at your DVD rental club
9. 'Buy Now, Pay Later on orders over £X'
10. Points for your VIP member's scheme (see point 5 below)

Obviously, you don't just hand over the code, your visitor has to do something first. For example:

1. **Email** – Ask your visitor to join your email marketing in exchange for a voucher code. You could also send out vouchers via email to people already on your mailing list.
2. **Referral** – Ask for a referral. For every referral that purchases, you give your customer a voucher.
3. **Third-Party Sites** – Get your voucher listed on one of the many Voucher Code sites like www.voucher-codes.co.uk and www.myvouchercodes.co.uk.
4. **Competition** – For example, get your visitor to hand over their details to a system which picks a voucher winner every X sales the site makes.
5. **Points Scheme** – Give your customers points for

every purchase they make and then offer vouchers to boost their points. Your customers sign up to the scheme (handing over their details so you can continue to market to them) and redeem cash value for points, which they can use to buy more products from you.

Ideally, give your voucher codes an expiry date. This puts a sense of urgency in your customer's mind and focuses them on using the voucher before they lose it! There are also a couple of ways in which you can use expiry dates in combination with your vouchers. For example,

1. **Time-Limited Seasonal Offers** – 'Buy before [31st March, Friday, Valentine's Day, etc.] to get our special spring saving price of £X'
2. **Early Bird** – 'If you are one of the first 100 to sign up you will get your gizmo for only £X – a saving of X%!'

Accessory Upsells and Related Products

The product page and basket page offer a great opportunity to add to the value of your sale. So, for example, if you are selling children's toys, it makes sense to offer the option to buy batteries for appropriate toys. If you sell washing machines then offer repair insurance. If you sell pianos then offer a piano stool. If you sell beds then offer a mattress.

These are all upsells but you will notice that they are more like accessories for the product. In other words, they are things you might not realise you need until after you've bought the product. (Hence you are adding value to your customer's experience.) If your ecommerce store presents these 'essentials' to your visitor then you remove the risk that your customer goes and buys the accessories elsewhere.

This is distinct from offering Related Products, which are products that are separate to the product your visitor is looking at. So if you sell necklaces then offer earrings that complement them. If you sell house insurance then offer life insurance. If you sell baths then offer the matching suite of wash basin, shower, etc. If you sell software training for Microsoft Word then offer training for Excel, PowerPoint and Outlook.

You can also test putting a 'Buy Now' button right next to the products so your visitor doesn't have to jump to a different page to add the item to their basket.

Do remember that in all instances you need to have pictures of the items and not just a text description and they should ideally be expandable into larger photos so your visitor can see exactly what they are buying.

By placing accessory upsells, related products or even bundles of products on the product pages, you guarantee that a percentage of your visitors will buy them. The fact is upsells work which is why you'll notice that McDonalds and Burger King always ask if you want to 'Go large for X pence' because they know that a certain percentage of their customers will say yes. A certain percentage of *your* customers will also say 'yes' to upsells.

The Basket and Payment Pages

The basket page is where your visitor goes to begin the checkout process. It provides the facts about the purchase and its value but its primary aim is to get the visitor to the next step. The payment pages are where your visitor gives you the necessary personal, delivery and payment details to complete the transaction.

Both pages should be simple, and without unnecessary copy and distraction but both still need to sell the reason why the visitor should buy from you.

Improving your basket and payment pages can be hugely rewarding. MarketingSherpa's 2007 Ecommerce Benchmark Survey identified that 57 per cent of respondents said improvements to their shopping cart's design and/or functionality was 'very effective,' with internal search coming second at 46 per cent, and product copy coming third at 43 per cent.

Here are a few ideas you can apply to these pages to help increase your conversions.

Reassuring Messages

I've always thought it a bit odd that most ecommerce sites stop selling when visitors get to the arduous point of having to enter their details and going through the rigmarole of becoming a customer. When you get to the basket page it all seems to become very formal – as though accountants had designed it.

Odd because it's at exactly that point that most people need more reassurance, not less. So use everything at your disposal: guarantees, free delivery, 'the 5 reasons why you need this product', contact numbers, product FAQs, secure shopping logos, customer reviews, etc., to help them overcome any barriers in their minds about making the purchase with you.

Catching the Drop Outs

It's inevitable that as people progress through the process of buying, some will drop out – there will always be an attrition rate. But can you do anything about those who leave the process? Yes, you can!

The first thing you need to do is make sure you've captured their email addresses. Now this is a personal choice but I think there is a strong argument to make the first page in your payment process an email capture page. There should only be the email capture field with a pre-ticked message stating you may wish to contact them, and a returning visitor login (so they can get back into their basket). If anyone drops out of the process you've now got their email address which leads us on to the next stage.

With an email address (and knowledge of the contents of their basket) you could ask them:

1. What did you do to upset them?
    a. Price
    b. Delivery
    c. Decided on another product
    d. Session timed out while they were hunting for their credit card
    e. And so on
2. Would they like to continue the purchase?
3. Would they like an alternative product? (and offer them some)

Just getting a few of the drop-outs back on board will give you a 'recovery' percentage and that gives you a boost in your profits. If you can improve the recovery percentage by improving the email then you're continuing to increase the number of conversions from your website.

Also consider testing capturing their mobile number instead so you can call or text them directly.

Getting People to Do Something They Might Not Want to Do

Handing over their details, going through the pain of writing out credit card details, filling in a survey, opting in to a mailing list, divulging personal information (date of birth, partner's name, etc.) – none of this is easy for your visitor. Nor is it fun, plus it can be coupled with the worry of what might happen to those details once they've been submitted. This creates a big resistance to action in your visitor's mind. However, the solution is simple: incentivise, incentivise, incentivise.

If your website is asking your visitor do something boring, repetitive or worrisome, offer something in exchange for their effort.

For example:

- Complete your first purchase with us and get 10% off.

- Let us know your email and postal address and we'll give you £10 to spend in our store.

- Tell us about a friend or family member who might love our products and we'll give you XYZ.

- Fill in our buyer's survey and get FREE DELIVERY.

The trick is to make it clear at the point your visitor begins the 'painful' process that there is something pleasant waiting on the other side apart from just the product they are buying.

The Confirmation Email and Beyond

Once your customer has completed the purchase they should receive a confirmation email indicating what they've purchased, the delivery time, possibly an attached invoice and a big thank you.

This is also a terrific marketing opportunity. You can use this moment to offer them a voucher, an upsell, an unexpected gift (I particularly like that approach), etc. You should also continue to email them as part of your email marketing plan, periodically offering help, upsells, related products and so on.

■ *ORGANISING YOUR CONTENT*

Let's take a look at how you might want to organise the information on your webpages. This is sometimes called 'visual hierarchy' and describes how to think about finding the most effective positioning of information on the screen for your reader.

But first take a look at your competitors' websites from the point of view of a client. How many times do they put vital information at the bottom of the page (like the price)? How often does a meaningless graphic fill useful space at the top of the page? Is the call to action immediately visible? I can almost guarantee that you will be able to pick substantial holes in your competition. Here's how we stop them doing the same to you.

The first barrier to overcome is what is known in marketing terms as 'the fold'. Imagine you are reading a broadsheet newspaper on a train. What you, and almost everybody else does, is fold the paper in half and read the top half first. In other words you read the most important information first (above the horizontal fold). What lies beneath remains hidden until you flip or unfold the newspaper.

In website terms it means that all the critical information you want the reader to see should be above the scroll-line (the fold). The last thing you want is to have your telephone number tucked away at the very bottom of the page or the 'Buy Now' button out of sight, forcing your visitor to scroll down to find it. Let's remember that when it comes to the Internet, we are all lazy. We want all the essential information right in front of us without us having to do a thing. So, make sure your website has the vital information above the scroll point. Do remember that screen sizes vary, although the standard now being set is 1024 x 768 pixels. (If you're feeling really thorough, you can use your web statistics to determine the average screen resolution of your user and use that as a basis for your scroll-line.)

Interestingly, while it makes sense to keep the most important information at the top, the introduction of scroll wheels on mice has helped visitors access 'out-of-sight' information. (One could also argue that those who take the trouble to scroll are more committed buyers.) Here is some great research by ClickTale on scrolling habits of browsers: blog.clicktale.com/?p=19. You might also want to take a look at Jacob Neilson's article on this subject: www.useit.com/alertbox/9712a.html.

So there are two perspectives, both valid and both worth testing.

Now let's prioritise some of the content on your landing pages. Here's an example of webpage features that need to be immediately visible:

- call to action
- compelling headline
- benefits
- contact details
- guarantees
- pricing
- product imagery
- video or audio content
- your navigation system

What is less important may include:

- animated graphics
- artistic graphics
- any additional information not directly connected with the thrust of the page (for example, if you had written an article relevant to the content of the page, you wouldn't want its link to feature prominently at the top of the page)
- comments from visitors
- data tables
- detailed product descriptions
- links to other pages

Ultimately, you must choose what is important. However, do it from your prospect's perspective. What do they need to see in order to choose you? The interesting thing about this subject is that it tips over into a discussion about relevance because as you review your website, you may identify things that from your prospect's perspective are not relevant.

For example, you may have testimonials from satisfied clients at the very top of the page. This may seem an obvious place to put them – after all, the first thing you are doing here is establishing your credibility. However, if this is on the product page, you can bet that the principal interest your prospect has is in the product first and whether it's right for them. At this point, it's too early to tell them how great you are because they haven't even worked out whether you can meet their needs.

Wrapped up in the positioning of your content is your page's layout. One page layout which has particular merit is the 3-column approach. It is basic but effective because it divides primary information from secondary information and functionality. Imagine the far-left column contains your navigation, the central column contains all the key information you wish to present[5] and the far-right column contains information which is of secondary importance.

The far-right column gives you the ability to put 'panels' or discrete blocks of information that relate to the page but aren't central to the offer. For example: downloads, news items, related pages, sign-up forms and so forth.

The advantage of this layout is that it organises the content in a very obvious way, so that your visitors know exactly where to look when they need to get more information but aren't distracted from the principal focus of the page.

[5] The reason for putting the primary information in the centre of the screen is that eye-tracking studies have shown that it is the first place people look when they first visit a page, then to the left of the screen and finally to the right.

ACTION THINKING

What's the most important point about marketing? Simple, that the person you're marketing to takes the action you want them to take. Without them actually 'doing something' at the end of your marketing, the exercise is wasted. This is even more important on the Internet. Imagine investing all your hard-earned time and cash attracting visitors to your website, only to discover that none of them act on your sales message. Ultimately, this chapter is about helping you maximise the conversion actions your visitors take, but in this last section I wanted to give you the reasoning which underpins everything I've suggested.

It stems from a very simple idea, namely that you have in mind a specific action you want your visitors to take before they leave. Yet oddly, very few websites make any clear attempt to direct their visitors to what they want them to do or to try and control where their visitors go.

Remember, you want your visitors to take an action on your website which leads them to the specific outcome you want.

Now, from a commercial point of view it might be something as simple as getting your visitor to buy online or begin an offline communication with you. However, people rarely come to a website with the sole intention of buying or giving up their contact details. They may be right at the beginning of their relationship with you and that's probably the vast majority as your website will be the first place they visit to find out about you. So, you can't just jump right in there and expect the sale – there are a number of steps that precede that. If you like, you must help your visitor jump the hurdles in their mind in order to get to that final decision of becoming a customer or highly qualified lead.

Let's take the example of someone visiting your website who's not been there before. Typically they're going to want to see if you can solve their problem so they might look at your services. Then they might want to see some case studies or read more about your product. They might have a look at your FAQs. Then they might sign up for a free report or perhaps, when they've jumped all the hurdles in their minds, then buy, or directly inquire about, your product or service. The fact is that in their heads they have a set of questions that they need answering. Your website has to do its best to answer those questions without knowing what they are.

Now some questions can be very simple, like 'How much does it cost?' But sometimes the questions aren't questions, they are objections, like 'That's too expensive.' These can be hard enough to answer even if you are talking to the customer there and then, so you can imagine how difficult it becomes for your website to anticipate an objection and then overcome it.

The questions in their minds and the answers you provide, determine the journey they take through your site. If you fail to answer a question then you run the risk of your visitor going elsewhere. Now most websites do two things: first, they totally ignore this idea and have dollops of information scattered all across their site leaving it largely to luck as to whether the visitor stumbles across what they're looking for; second, they make no attempt to guide people in the right direction. The combination is lethal, and so they make sales more by accident than judgement (if they make any at all).

Let's deal with the first problem. All of your visitors are coming to your website with an unknown bunch of questions or objections in their heads that need answering before they are going to commit to a sale. How do you find out what these questions are? Easy, speak to your existing customers or take a survey

6 There are lots of survey systems on the market (www.surveymonkey.com, for example). Many can seamlessly integrate with your website.

of visitors to your website.[6] Ask them what they would expect to see, ask them what questions or concerns they have, and find out how they would like the information presented – as text, a table, graphic, a PDF, a podcast, an online screen presentation, etc. You'll begin to see a pattern emerging and that pattern will tell you exactly the type of information you need to be presenting on your website.

Now, let's deal with the second problem – stopping your visitor from random roaming. Visitors are like cats: the last thing they are likely to do is be predictable. They all want to do their own thing and none will do the same thing twice. This means that if you could trace the path people take through the average website, you would probably find it looking like something a three-year-old would doodle over your coffee table.

If you are going to try and get people to do what you want them to do then you have to make it really clear what it is you want them to do and not leave it to chance. In other words, you must learn the ancient art of cat-herding. The only real way to herd cats is not give them a choice but to file them towards your objective. The same goes for the visitors to your website.

So, if someone gets to the 'Buy Now' page, don't give them the opportunity to veer off the page to read an article. If they get to your newsletter sign-up page, don't show them a tasty link to a special offer. When they reach the bottom of your sales page, tell them exactly what you would like them to do next: get in touch, fill in the form, listen to the podcast. Remember you must tell them what you want them to do next.

Offering people hundreds of choices on your home page or any other page for that matter isn't going to help them. It's basic human psychology that the more choices you present to people, the less likely they are to take the action you want them to take.

Incidentally, there is a school of thought that says that more people will take the action you want if it is the only one you present to them. In other words, fewer people will take the option you want them to if you present lots of options. It's just like the famous Henry Ford misquote: 'You can have any colour as long as it's black.' This technique works extremely well when you want your customer to take the final action. For example, in the case of an ecommerce store, when your visitor is providing their credit card details, you won't want to distract them with any other options, links to other pages, downloads, etc.

Although you can't guarantee people's behaviour on your site, you can influence it. That's why it's best to direct people to the places you want them to go because people will naturally gravitate towards the things that look most interesting. This means that the more appealing you make something to click on, the more likely your visitor is to click on it.

For example, don't just say, 'Contact us today.' Say, 'Contact us before 4 p.m. and we'll guarantee next-day delivery.'

Finally, it's been pretty much universally agreed upon by usability experts that people don't want to click more than three times in order to get to the information they want. So when you are structuring the information on your website to funnel your visitor, make sure that all the things they want to see first are no more than three clicks from their landing page. (This is particularly important if you are running an ecommerce store.)

Remember, making your visitor take action is fundamental to your website's conversions and, ultimately, to its overall success.

THE STRATEGY

No matter how much traffic you are sending to your website, you will want to convert the absolute maximum you can into customers. This is even more critical if you are paying for the traffic through AdWords and other pay-per-click systems. However, the approaches I have demonstrated in this step need to be seen within a wider idea. The idea is that your website is a laboratory in which you are making gold. In order to find the perfect formula you will need to experiment – you simply can't assume that your website is the best it can ever be the day it goes live. Almost nobody instantly discovers the 'gold formula' but testing and experimenting gives you the means by which you can wring every last ounce of value from your website.

Very few actually do this and almost none will go to the lengths described in this chapter. However, we know that in order to produce exceptional results we need to be the exceptions to the rule. So, test and experiment away and have fun in the process, because the results will make you smile!

CHAPTER

Get Lasting Traffic to Your Website

▣ INTRODUCTION

In this chapter we're going to unravel one of the most exciting and yet misunderstood subjects on the Internet, namely, Search Engine Optimisation (SEO). It's a subject that is littered with misinformation, confusion and controversy – the Internet's equivalent of a soap opera.

If you've done any research on this subject then you probably already know just how much of a minefield it is. So, the purpose of this chapter is to cut through the chaos and give you a clear set of things you and your web designers can do to get you rocketing up the search-engine rankings. I'm going to give you the facts and we're going to put to rest some of the myths that, if you believe in them, could seriously hamper your website's success.

▣ WHAT IS SEARCH ENGINE OPTIMISATION (SEO)?

Let's firstly get on top of what search engine optimisation actually means.

I'm going to use Google as my default example because it typically attracts more than 90 per cent of the search engine traffic in the UK. I'm not suggesting that you don't need to consider the other players (Bing, Yahoo!, etc.) but I am saying that it's more efficient to nail Google first. (Remember the 80/20 rule.) You will also find that many of the techniques for getting to the top on Google apply to the other search engines as well and so a strong position on Google will more than likely result in a strong position on the others.

If you look at a standard Google Search Engine Results Page, down the left-hand side of the page you will see what are known as the natural or organic listings. These are the search results that

Google thinks are most relevant to what you typed, in descending order of importance. These are free listings in which your website will naturally appear if it is relevant to the keywords typed in.

Obviously, it makes sense to get as close to the top of the organic listings as possible because it costs you nothing to appear there. Imagine your website appearing at the top for a major keyword relevant to your industry – this is the Holy Grail of SEO, and what we call 'owning the keyword.' It may take a year, two or three but you can do it. (After all, the company that's currently there already did it!)

Being listed at the top can result in a huge increase in the number of visitors to your website and will hugely magnify your website's profitability. So, it doesn't take a business guru to spot that this is a smart thing for you to do.

There's one other little psychological quirk about being in the No. 1 slot: people's perception of the top listing is that it must be a quality brand and, therefore, they are more likely to make a purchase from the top website than the one in tenth place. Part of this has to do with people's confidence in Google producing the most relevant results and so some of this 'brand confidence' rubs off onto the top spot. You could almost view it as Google voting for your company.

However, there is huge competition on the Internet for popular keywords and phrases and you often find that getting listed in a visible place is difficult and time-consuming, especially for fledgling websites. But there is hope in the form of a suite of techniques I am going to show you.

Before we begin, though, here's one thing to consider: most people think that Google ranks their entire website. And indeed that is partly true – Google will assess your entire website, but only one page at a time. Google actually ranks individual pages, not whole websites. A good example of this is Wikipedia: individual pages of Wikipedia are ranked and appear at the top of the search results. They take you to the specific page that relates to your search – you'll notice that you don't get taken to the Wikipedia home page. This is because each page is ranked according to how specific and relevant Google deems it to be. This concept is important because it limits your expectations – you're not trying to get your entire website to pole position, just the page that is most relevant to the keyword typed in.

Ultimately Google is trying to mimic a human being in terms of identifying the most relevant information. This is really important because many think of Google as a system to be beaten through the application of technology and covert techniques. In reality, this couldn't be further from the truth. Google is trying to organise, catalogue and present information on the web as if it were a human because it's us humans that are going to use it. Therefore, the best way to succeed with Google is to be as human and as natural as possible (a point we'll keep returning to throughout this chapter). In fact, any attempt to unnaturally 'push' your website up the rankings will probably trigger an alert with Google and result in your ranking being dampened.

And finally, if you are running a Google AdWords campaign, you should know that the results of your campaign will have no bearing on your SEO. So, if you are getting lots of traffic to a particular landing page, Google will not include that in their judgement of that page because you've paid for the traffic and so won't account for it when assessing your position in the natural rankings. In fact, AdWords and SEO have little to do with one another so it's best to think of them as two separate entities.

Now let's dive in and discover exactly how Google ranks websites.

■ HOW ARE YOUR WEBSITE'S RANKINGS CALCULATED?

In the early days (between 1994 and 2000) search engines suffered from a significant problem: you'd type in a perfectly innocent phrase like 'san francisco holiday' and you'd see a whole slew of results which had nothing to do with either San Francisco or holidays, and were often less than savoury! So the results you got back were completely irrelevant to the search you entered. This eroded people's confidence in the results and caused user disenchantment and ultimately led to the demise of many search engines.

It was the concept of relevance that was fundamental to Google's success, as it instilled confidence in users – every time they searched for something they ended up with results that were useful. At the time this was a major breakthrough. Google had solved this problem using a process based on the *citation method*.

Sergey Brin and Larry Page, founders of Google, were Stanford graduates and came from an academic background. It was this background that led them to the principle which underpins Google's ranking methodology. In academia if you publish a paper, article, book, etc., others may refer to it in their own publications. This is known as a citation. The more people who cite your work the more popular it becomes and thus the more important it is deemed to be. In the end, with enough citations, you will be crowned king of the subject and all will use your text as the standard on the subject – you will have become the authority. This is why *The Origin of Species* is the standard text on Darwinism – because it has received so many citations.

So, Larry and Sergey used this system as the template for how they would rank websites on the Internet. Your ranking for any particular keyword would be determined by how many times your webpage had been referenced by other people.

So, let's take an example, let's say that you sell widgets. A blogger tries out your widgets and thinks they are the best in the world so he writes up a report on his website. At the bottom of that website is a link to yours. Now here's the really key bit. The hyperlink to your widgets page does not read <u>www.greatwidgets. co.uk</u> instead it reads '<u>best widget company</u>'. Google picks up the fact that this link is pointing to yours and marks you as having one link coming into your website called 'best widget company.'

At the same time, you also send out an article to an article website and a few more bloggers pick up on you, plus some people on Twitter too. All that generates more interest and soon you have a number of links pointing to your widget page. But the key is that all the links are called 'best widget company.' Now when someone types in 'best widget company' into Google, Google then ranks the webpages according to a multitude of criteria of which one of the most important is the number of quality citations each webpage has received.[1]

Now this leaves us with two really important points. The first is that backlinks, as they are called, coming into your website must be the same as (or synonyms of) the keywords you want to be searched against; the second is that the number of backlinks coming to your website from external websites largely determines your position on Google's search results page.

Google achieves the monumental task of assessing all this by sending out the Googlebot, a piece of software that crawls the entire web, building an index of every single webpage on the

[1] I have simplified this for the purpose of explanation but as you will see during this chapter, Google takes more elements into account when determining the position of your website. For now, you've got the Google basics.

Internet. The Googlebot will regularly (and automatically) crawl your website to make sure it has got up-to-date information about you.

There's one final point which adds some finesse to the system, and that is something called Page Rank (PR). Our example assumes that every webpage has equal importance, but in reality that is not true – you wouldn't ascribe the same importance to the BBC home page as you would your local taxi firm's home page. If your webpage is cited by a page which itself has a large number of links pointing to it then your page gets some of that value. This is *link juice*. The more important a webpage the more link juice it has and so if they link to you, some of that link juice gets poured onto your webpage.

Google ranks PR on a scale from 0 to 10. So, let's say a webpage has a PR of 5 linking to your webpage. This would be a more valuable link to acquire than a link from a webpage with a PR of 4. And a link from a webpage with a PR of 6 would be better to acquire than a webpage with a Page Rank of 5. You get the idea. Interestingly, Google's Page Rank scoring is exponential, which means that Google determines a PR of 2 to be twice as important (or valuable) as a PR of 1 and a PR of 4 is twice as important as a PR of 3. Unfortunately, it also means that it becomes twice as hard to move your PR from its current one to the next.

For example, the BBC News home page currently has a PR of 8, so a link from this page to your website would be worth significantly more than a link from the ITN news page which only has a PR of 6.

Bear in mind one other factor: I am comparing pages which Google deems to be of equal relevance. In other words, if you are a flower arranger and you get a PR 5 link from Steve's Garden Centre, that's an 'on-topic' backlink. If you had a backlink from a NASA webpage it probably wouldn't be on-topic. So even if you were in receipt of a PR 10 backlink from NASA, Google would not perceive it as more relevant than the PR 5 link from Steve's Garden Centre – in reality, the NASA PR 10 link would be *less valuable* than the PR 5 link.

Fortunately, Google has a tool which tells you exactly what the PR of any webpage is. You can find this by downloading the Google Toolbar (toolbar.google.com) and enabling the Page Rank function in the Options menu. You'll see a small graph on the toolbar which, if you hover your mouse over, will reveal that page's Page Rank score. Here's Google's home page PR shown on the toolbar.

Fig 1 The Google Toolbar showing a Page Rank score

THE TARGET PAGE

Now before you begin to define the keywords or search terms[2] you want to be found against, you'll want to consider which page your visitor is going to land on when they click on your listing. Therefore, within your website will be target pages that you will wish to SEO for. Specifically, these will be the pages which your visitor will get to click on from the SERPs for a particular search term they enter.

Here's a quick diagram to clarify this (Fig 2).

So, you can see that, at least in the first stages of SEO, you optimise one search term for one webpage. You don't optimise several of your webpages for one search term because you'll end up diluting your efforts. By focusing all your attention on one webpage per search term you focus and magnify your effectiveness and so give that page the maximum 'thrust' up the ranking. Equally, don't try to SEO multiple search terms for one page as that will also dilute the efficiency of your SEO.

Pick the most appropriate page on your site for your search term. I'd recommend that the page meets the following criteria:

1. The page must naturally have the correct content for the search term. (Do the themes and topics identified by your search term already exist as pages on your website or do you need to create pages for them?)
2. Have a reasonable amount of content instantly visible.
3. Be navigable to (that is, not be a webpage that doesn't appear in your primary navigation or is buried deep in your site.).
4. Is 100 per cent relevant to the search term (don't try to SEO a page on 'cat pants' for the search term 'dog pants').
5. Provide a fulfilling experience for the visitor.

Now your choice of webpage may be influenced by the search

[2] Throughout this chapter I refer to both 'keywords' and 'search terms' – they are, principally, one and the same. Technically one could argue that a search term is only ever typed into a search engine whereas a keyword can be used anywhere (in your website, in hyperlinks to your website, in search engine listings, as search terms typed into a search engine and so forth).

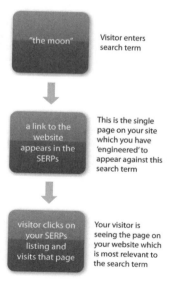

"the moon" — Visitor enters search term

a link to the website appears in the SERPs — This is the single page on your site which you have 'engineered' to appear against this search term

visitor clicks on your SERPs listing and visits that page — Your visitor is seeing the page on your website which is most relevant to the search term

Fig 2 The target page

terms that you are able to SEO for (you'll see why below). However, in the meantime list out the primary contenders on your site that fit the above criteria. We'll match them to the right search term later on.

■ PICKING THE PERFECT KEYWORDS FOR SEO

Keywords (or search terms) are fascinating creatures. They are almost organic in their behaviour – growing, changing and multiplying on the Internet – and we humans are their parents. They are also much misunderstood and outwardly chaotic and complex – much like the average human!

More than 70 per cent of the Internet's websites are found using search engines and, therefore, using keywords. So, quite simply, if you want to be found, then picking the right kind of keywords is essential.

Keywords are the bedrock of any SEO campaign. It is your choice of keyword that will determine whether you get a flood of visitors to your website – or a trickle. It will also determine the nature (or type) of visitor – whether they are ready and primed to receive your sales message or whether they are passersby who have no intention of spending any money with you.

Choosing Keywords that Pinpoint Your Customer

Let's take an example to illustrate this. Imagine that you sell insurance. The obvious keyword to optimise your website for would be 'insurance.' Now let's see how many people type 'insurance' into Google every day. I used the Google Keyword Tool to look this up and discovered that this search term is entered into Google about 364,000 times each day in the UK alone. Wow! If you had just 1 per cent ($\approx$4,000) visiting your website daily you'd be very happy. However, there is a sting in the results and it's this: Google's results tool includes all the searches that contain the keyword 'insurance' and not just 'insurance' on its own. This means that not only do you get people who only type in 'insurance' but you also get those that type in 'industrial insurance' (which you may not sell), 'insurance careers' (people looking for jobs), 'insurance ombudsman,' and even 'insurance exams'! (If you've read Chapter 5, 'Get Instant Traffic,' then you'll understand that this is the same principle that governs Google AdWords too.)

So at first glance 'insurance' would be a terrific keyword to optimise your website for but, on further examination, it would also attract a huge volume of traffic from people who are not your target market and not likely to become paying customers. So, optimising for this keyword would be taking a scatter-gun approach to your SEO and, therefore, not great use of your energies.

There is another reason that choosing really broad terms may not yield results and that's simply because of the amount of competition from other websites. If you take a look just under the search bar on a Google Search Engine Results Page, you'll see how many websites Google deems to be relevant to that search term. The screenshot shows you the count for 'insurance.'

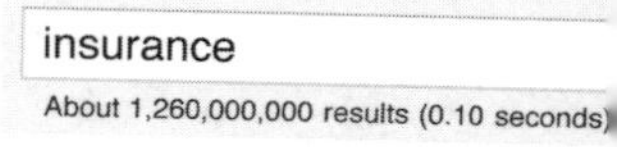

insurance

About 1,260,000,000 results (0.10 seconds)

Fig 3 The number of webpages competing for the term 'insurance'

It's one of the peculiar facts of life that people (and, therefore, businesses) like to take what appears to be the easiest route despite, in reality, it being the hardest. Most don't think beyond the 'generic' single keyword and never consider that they would be attracting unproductive visitors. They charge headlong into highly competitive terms and almost never see a return because the competition is too fierce and too well established. Even if they did, they'd be attracting a vast number of useless visitors. Strangely, I've seen this time and time again and, between you and me, long may it continue! The more of your competitors putting their resources into the wrong keywords, the more space it leaves you on the profitable ones.

Okay, so if the major or generic keywords are a no-no, where do you begin?[3] Well, a lot of keyword choice is about understanding the psychology of your visitor. The great advantage you have is that you are already a 'visitor' to lots of other websites and so you understand the psychology (it's just that you may not have noticed it). So, let's use an example to dig a little deeper into this subject.

[3] If you are already running a Google AdWords campaign then use the conversion data to guide you in choosing your keywords. See 'Why You Should Use AdWords Before SEO,' page 156, for the details.

Imagine that you're looking for one of those new-fangled flat-screen TVs and that I have a website which sells Sony LCD TVs. So you type in something like 'lcd tv' and Google brings up a gazillion results. Guess what? I'm not anywhere to be seen and I'm happy about that. Why? Well, I know that if you've typed in 'lcd tv' you are probably still trying to find out more about the subject – you're researching and learning. The truth is your search hasn't got specific enough for me to be interested in you yet. (That sounds mean, doesn't it, but remember I'm ruthlessly chasing the people who have both a clear need and are ready to buy.)

A little while later you try a different keyword, 'sony lcd tv.'

Now we're getting somewhere. You've narrowed down your choices to a specific manufacturer. This is great news for me because I now know that you have at least decided to look at something specific I have to offer. Sure, you may type in 'samsung lcd tv' next but that doesn't matter because I know that your interest in Sony is worth my pitching to you. Would I want to appear in the listings against that keyword? Yes.

So now you've reached a point where you've done the research, decided on the TV and you want to get down to the details. This time you type in 'sony kdl-55nx813.' Guess what, that's one of the TVs I sell. Your search is now so specific that my listing in Google takes you straight to the page that's all about the Sony KDL-55NX813. Your search defines not just what you want, where you are in the buying process but also the type of person you are:

1. You've been highly specific, which means you've already narrowed your choices and pre-qualified yourself for my service; and
2. Because you've done that it means you are close to making a purchase.

If you were to add the words 'buy,' 'price,' 'cheap,' 'delivery' and so on to the end of your key phrase, then you would give away the fact that you're right on the verge of buying and so even more relevant to me. You can see that the more specific you make the key phrase, the more targeted the market you attract.

Naturally, you expect there to be fewer people typing in a long or specific phrase than those who only use one or two words (and yet 14 per cent of people type in 5-, 6- or 7-word key-phrases). That's obvious, but what seems less obvious to the majority of businesses is that although you get fewer people visiting your website, it is far more likely that they will buy.

This whole concept is known as the long-tailed search. Essentially, the longer the phrase used the more specific the requirement and therefore, the closer they are to the sale.

Another lovely little addition to the search term is a geographic location. So, if you're in Birmingham then someone searching for 'insurance birmingham' is a much better bet than someone who just types in 'insurance.'

Choosing the Wrong Keywords

Now is a good time to consider some of the classic mistakes people regularly make when choosing keywords to SEO for their website.

You already know why you shouldn't choose single keywords for your SEO project but here are a few more.

The first is optimising your website for your company name. That's fine if you are a household name but for the majority of businesses their prospects have never heard of their business name until they first visit their website. Consider this: the main purpose (and indeed power) of Google is to bring visitors to your website who are *new* to you. If they're typing in your company name then they already know you.

The only time this is a good thing is if it's important that you manage your brand identity or your business name has keywords describing what you do.

The second keyword cock-up is to choose complex terminology or words and phrases that may only be used by a small group of people. For example, few people (other than botanists) type in 'betula pendula pruning' – the rest of us would type in 'silver birch pruning.' The upshot of Search Engine Optimising for such search terms is that you would find yourself at the top of one of Google's SERPs for a phrase that hardly anyone ever types in!

The third is to use your competitor's keyword choice as a template for yours. There are two key things to note about this: firstly, you don't know that they've got their keyword selection right; and secondly, you ideally want to be finding keywords and phrases that have lots of traffic but few of your competitors and so, by extension, you don't want to automatically choose keywords your competitors are already listed against.

Choosing The Right Keywords

The right keyword satisfies three criteria:

1. It must be relevant to your product or service.
2. It must be attracting a good volume of traffic.
3. There can't be too much competition for it.

So, the first thing you need to do is identify a bundle of keywords relevant to your product or service.

Step 1: Choosing Relevant Keywords

We've already covered exactly how to do this in Chapter 5, 'Get Instant Traffic to Your Website.' If you need to reacquaint yourself with this, please review pages 114–136.

At the end of this process you should have a list of anything between 50 and 150 keywords. Put these into a spreadsheet (all in Column A).

Step 2: Choosing Keywords with Traffic

It's hardly worth going to all this effort if you end up optimising for keywords that don't actually attract any traffic. So you need to know that the keywords you have chosen will generate traffic to your website. Go to the Google Keyword Tool (in your Google AdWords account) and paste the keywords from your spreadsheet into it. Make sure you choose the 'Phrase Match' option as this gives you the middle ground of traffic volumes between Broad and Exact matches.

This will give you an immediate insight into whether the keywords you've chosen are going to generate traffic for you. Next, using the 'Download' button in the Keyword Tool export your keywords into your spreadsheet. Once you've done that remove all but the 'Local Monthly Searches'[4] column so that you're left with Column A as your keywords and Column B as your search traffic. Here's what it should look like:

[4] In this example I am assuming that you only want traffic from your country and not the world. However, if you are a multinational business you may be more interested in the 'Global Monthly Searches' results.

A	B
Search Term	**Local Monthly Searches**
Keyword 1	4,400
Keyword 2	90,500
Keyword 3	27,100
Keyword 4	40,500
Keyword 5	12

You can also use Wordtracker's free keyword tool (freekeywords. wordtracker.com) to give you an alternative measure of traffic for comparison purposes. (Putting the two traffic values side by side helps you 'moderate' both, so a more reasonable average can be determined.)

Step 3: Choosing Keywords with Little Competition

Now we're on to working out competitiveness. This is interesting stuff because keywords are not all equal – some are more popular than others, not necessarily in terms of the number of times they are typed in but the number of webpages clamouring to be seen against them. Here's that screenshot again to remind you where to see how many webpages are referenced against a search term.

In other words this is the number of webpages containing the keywords or phrases in the search. (In the case of my industry the search term 'web design'[5] generates a staggering 297,000,000 results!) Enter the results for each keyword into column C of your spreadsheet.

However, we're also after the number of *directly* competing websites. A directly competing website is one that has links pointing back to them from other websites which have the exact search phrase in the link text. In other words this is the number of websites which have links coming into them where the text is the same as or semantically similar to the search term you typed in. To work this out enter into the Google search box:

insurance

About 1,260,000,000 results (0.10 seconds)

[5] Don't forget to put quotation marks around your search terms or else you'll include search results that just contain the results ('web' and 'design') and not *only* 'web design.'

allinanchor:type your search term here

Using our example, I've added in the number of competing webpages into the 'Results' column and using the allinanchor technique added those under the 'Directly Competing' column:

A	B	C	D
Search Term	Monthly Searches	Results	Directly Competing
Keyword 1	4,400	847,000	401,000
Keyword 2	90,500	10,900,000	9,050,000
Keyword 3	27,100	37,200,000	3,222,000
Keyword 4	40,500	15,500,000	7,270,000
Keyword 5	12	448,000	357,000

Step 4: Find the Gap – The Science

Now you need to calculate where the opportunity gaps are in this keyword list. Essentially, we're trying to identify keywords with reasonable levels of traffic and not too much competition. We

can do this using an equation known as the Keyword Effectiveness Index (KEI).[6] To do this you'll need to take the Number of
Searches and square it, then divide this result by the number of
results. This is the actual formula:

$$\text{Keyword Effectiveness Index} = \frac{\text{Number of Searches}^2}{\text{Results}}$$

In column E row 2, enter the following formula:

    =(B2^2)/C2

Now copy the formula down for all of your keywords and you'll
get results like the ones below:

A	B	C	D	E
Search Term	**Monthly Searches**	**Results**	**Directly Competing**	**KEI**
Keyword 1	4,400	847,000	401,000	22.86
Keyword 2	90,500	10,900,000	9,050,000	751.40
Keyword 3	27,100	37,200,000	3,222,000	19.74
Keyword 4	40,500	15,500,000	7,270,000	105.82
Keyword 5	12	448,000	357,000	0.00

Essentially, the higher the KEI the better, as that indicates that
they are popular terms but with less competition. The drawback
to KEI is that it makes no reference to the quality of the competitors in the listings. For example, even with a high KEI, you could
be up against a few heavyweight websites that have excellent ranking and whom you'd find difficult to oust.

So, we're going to add in another technique, devised by David
Viney, which does take account of the 'quality' of the competition
(at least to a degree) known as the Keyword Opportunity Index
(KOI). It does this by including in the equation the actual number
of Directly Competing websites and not just the total number of
results.

Here's the formula for working out KOI:

$$\text{Keyword Opportunity Index} = \frac{\text{Number of Searches}^2}{\text{Directly Competing}}$$

In column F row 2, enter the following formula:

    =(B2^2)/D2

A	B	C	D	E	F
Search Term	Monthly Searches	Results	Directly Competing	KEI	KOI
Keyword 1	4,400	847,000	401,000	22.86	48.27
Keyword 2	90,500	10,900,000	9,050,000	751.40	905.00
Keyword 3	27,100	37,200,000	3,222,000	19.74	227.93
Keyword 4	40,500	15,500,000	7,270,000	105.82	225.62
Keyword 5	12	448,000	357,000	0.00	0.00

Again, the higher the value the better the keyword choice. This method certainly refines the results and shows that in our example above, keyword 3, which had a low KEI, actually has a far more promising KOI.

This begins to give you a sense of which keywords you can optimise for and which would, at least in the early stages, be more difficult.

Once you have completed your table you will begin to see those keywords which look like good candidates for SEO. Use both KEI and KOI to help influence your judgement. You are looking to pick between five and ten search terms to optimise. (Anymore and you'll probably be distributing your efforts too thinly.) In SEO, focus is the key.

Step 5: Find the Gap – The Art

Now that we've just delved into some of the science of SEO, we can move on to the art of SEO. By that I mean that choosing your keywords is also informed by more imprecise, intuitive measurements. (In fact, it's the human judgements which are probably of greater value.) You will need a little experience to hone your instincts but to begin with just go for it and don't worry too much about whether you've made the perfect keyword choice. This next phase will help you make those instinctive decisions.

We're going to use a tool called 'SEO for Firefox' – a great little plug-in for your Firefox browser which shows you some great statistics about the entries in the SERPs.

Firstly, make sure you've got Firefox loaded and then search for an add-on called 'SEO for Firefox.' Once you've installed it you'll spot that at the bottom of the status bar is a tiny 'SEO' button. Click on this (if it's greyed out) and then search Google using one of your selected search term candidates. Underneath each of the entries on the SERPs you'll see some additional statistics. The screenshot below (for the search term 'the moon') shows what you'll see (please note that I have turned off some of the less relevant data for the purposes of clarity).

Moon - Wikipedia, the free encyclopedia
en.wikipedia.org/wiki/**Moon** - Cached
The Moon is Earth's only known natural satellite, and the fifth largest satellite in the Solar System. It is the largest natural satellite of a planet in the Solar System ...
Orbit of the Moon - Moon (disambiguation) - Moon landing conspiracy theories - Io
#1 I PR: 7 I Google Cache Date: Sep 8 2011 I Traffic Value: 636,801,966 I Age: I Y! Links: 234,843,615 I Y! Page Links: 10,160 I OSE links to page: ? I OSE links to domain: ? I Yahoo position: 1

The Phases of **the Moon** for Kids - Time
www.woodlands-junior.kent.sch.uk/time/**moon**/phases.html - Cached
The revolution of **the Moon** around the Earth makes **the Moon** appear as if it is changing shape in the sky. From Earth we see **the Moon** grow from a thin crescent ...
#2 I PR: 5 I Google Cache Date: Sep 8 2011 I Traffic Value: 45,645 I Age: I Y! Links: 82,926 I Y! Page Links: 838 I OSE links to page: ? I OSE links to domain: ? I Yahoo position: 70

Google **Moon**
www.google.com/**moon**/ - Cached
A photographic map of the equatorial region with pan and zoom capability, showing locations of the Apollo landings.
#3 I PR: 7 I Google Cache Date: Sep 9 2011 I Traffic Value: 130,206,623 I Age: I Y! Links: 1,256,096,729 I Y! Page Links: 21,276 I OSE links to page: ? I OSE links to domain: ? I Yahoo position: 8

Fig 4 A Google SERP showing SEO for Firefox in action

An examination of the listing gives us the following information:

1. The Page Rank
2. When Google last cached the page
3. The page's Traffic Value (if you click on 'Traffic Value' it reveals more information about the domain, its traffic, competitors and performance).
4. It's age (clicking on 'Age' takes you through to web. archive.org otherwise known as the Way Back Machine where you can see old versions on the website although typically only the Home page.)
5. The number of backlinks coming into the domain (click 'Y! Links' to reveal more information)
6. The number of backlinks coming into the page (click 'Y! Page Links' to reveal more information)

Now you've got the information, let's do an analysis of the key findings.

Just take a look at Google's SERPs for your search term. Begin your analysis by assessing who is in the listings. So for example if you distribute widgets on behalf of another company and you spot that the top few entries in the SERP are from the manufacturer (www.widgets.co.uk), that's a signal that it may be difficult for you to get above the actual manufacturer from the listing. So, the website's significance in relation to the search term has a big part to play which makes total sense – if you wanted to be listed against the key phrase 'google' then you're going to have a tough time upstaging Google's own entry! Conversely, if you're Google then you would expect to be listed at the top of that search term because of your relative significance.

So, if you are facing some big hitters in your industry then remain wary of the search term. Meanwhile, consider reviewing the following statistics from SEO for Firefox:

Page Rank

Compare the Page Rank of the target page on your website with that of the first ten results in Google. How do you compare? If they all have several PR points above the PR of your intended target page then it may be too difficult to break into this search term and you may want to try a variation of your chosen keyword.

If they have lower PRs than you then this represents a plus point for the search term.

Y! Page Links

Next review how many inbound links they have pointing to this page. Tens, hundreds, thousands?

Don't forget that Page Rank will influence the number you need to acquire. You may need a lot fewer than the current website on first position if you can source a number of links from websites with high Page Ranks. Equally, you may need a whole bunch more if you are only getting links from websites with low Page Ranks.

So with that in mind it's tricky to definitively state the number of links the competition may have beyond which make search engine optimising for a search term an impossible task. However, if the top listings are showing thousands of page links and you're starting with zero, the task would be too daunting and you should look for better search term opportunities.

If you sense that there might be an opportunity here, click 'Y! Page Links.' This will take you through to Yahoo!'s Site Explorer, which will list the links coming into this listing.

Fig 5 A screenshot of the Yahoo! Site Explorer

Again take a look down the listings to see if the webpages linking to the listing are from big-hitting domains as this would suggest that the page linking to this listing has a high PR. Of course, the only way you can properly identify their PR is to click on the entry in Site Explorer and manually review it using the Google Toolbar.

By going through this process (admittedly a time-consuming one) you begin to build up a picture of the competition's backlinks. So what's the ideal you are looking for? Here it is in a nutshell: Small number of backlinks from unknown domains with low PRs.

The latest update is that Yahoo! Site Explorer is to become part of Microsoft's Bing Webmaster Tools. At this point no information has been released as to whether the functionality and data of Yahoo! Site Explorer will be maintained when it is moved. However, should SEO for Firefox not be able to get the Y! data from it's new location at Bing, there are a couple of alternatives which do a similar job:

1. Open Site Explorer (www.opensiteexplorer.org). If you register (for free) you can use the system as much as you like but there are some limitations on the detail of information you get back. (You can access this data directly from SEO for Firefox by clicking on 'OSE links to page' and 'OSE links to domain' entries.)

2. Ahrefs (ahrefs.com). This site also gives you similar information. As above they offer a limited service – a free account gets you up to fifteen requests per day.

If you'd like to stay up-to-date with this development, please sign up to my VIP Update at www.jedwylie.co.uk.

Other Factors

At first glance you may look at the total number of links coming into the domain (Y! Links) and be put off (especially if it's in the thousands). However, it is worth bearing in mind that not all the link juice coming from each of the links into the domain will be directly benefiting the page you are competing against. Only some of the juice derived from these links will be flowing to that page through a process known as 'link dilution.' (Think of this as a watering can: the total amount of link juice heading to the domain is the reservoir in the can but the link juice is ultimately distributed out to each page like the streams of water coming from the spout.) So it's best to use the Y! Links number as just another factor which contributes to your overall assessment of competitiveness.

Other factors to consider are whether:
1. The page title contains the exact search term
2. The page name contains the exact search term
3. The search term is explicitly used on the page

If the listings are not demonstrating one or more of these then there's room for your target page.

Now do you have enough information to make a decision about whether your chosen keyword represents an opportunity? If not then keep reviewing the SERPs until you start to feel a pattern emerging. You may want to grade your results so when you begin the SEO process you can start with the easy, quick-win search terms first.

I realise that this looks like it's a lot of work but the fact is that unless you take the time to get the keyword choice right, you could be investing even more time pursuing hopeless search terms which you may never get listed against. So, getting it right at this stage could (and should) profitably set you up for a long time to come!

The Final List

Once you've completed your keyword research, simply draw up a list defining the keyword and the target page. Something like this:

Search Term	Target Page	Grade
Search Term 1	www.jedscompany.co.uk/product1	Easy
Search Term 2	www.jedscompany.co.uk/product2	Mid-range
Search Term 3	www.jedscompany.co.uk/product3	Easy
Search Term 4	www.jedscompany.co.uk/product4	Difficult
Search Term 5	www.jedscompany.co.uk/product5	Easy

Now you have your definitive list in place which you should refer to as often as possible so you maintain your focus both on the search term and its associated target page.

ONSITE AND OFFSITE SEO

You're at the point you can really start making some impact on your rankings. Your SEO activities will now be divided up into onsite work and offsite work, and so the remainder of this chapter will be dedicated to these two pursuits.[7]

Don't forget that you are SEO-ing for a particular set of search terms – not the entire website. So, when you consider the activities below see them in the context of targeting those search terms. Once you start engaging in these activities not only will your ranking increase for your target search terms but because you are increasing the exposure of your website you will also see an overall increase in ranking for other, perhaps unexpected, search terms.

In the final analysis, every link to your website – be it contributing to your search engine ranking or not – is a highway for traffic to drive down and visit you. Thus, even if you get one or two fantastic links which generate a lot of traffic for you, you shouldn't disregard the cumulative effect of having lots of 'lesser' links pointing to your website!

As a relevant aside, every two years SEOmoz does a survey of the top search engine specialists to identify the major ranking factors for websites. You can find the latest results at www.seomoz.org/article/search-ranking-factors. This is an excellent piece of research that will help you focus your SEO efforts and direct you towards those activities which yield the greatest SEO effect. Check it out.

[7] An interesting observation about Small-Medium Enterprise websites is that you'll find that about 80 per cent of your effort in increasing your ranking is offsite (link-building, press releases, forum work, and so forth) and 20 per cent will be onsite (improving your copy, creating internal links, page titles and so on). Curiously, if you are running a large and well known website you'll probably find that it'll be the opposite with you spending 20 per cent of your time on offsite work and 80 per cent on onsite work.

ONSITE SEO TECHNIQUES

Onsite work is activity that takes place on your website; it includes:

1. Packing your website with great content that people will want to link to
2. Optimising your target pages for the keywords you have identified
3. Making sure that your website is as search engine friendly as possible

So, let's get started.

Content is King

This is the easy bit – simply write great copy. Write copy that is going to inspire people to link to you. That's it. No magic, no sleight of hand, no brown envelopes under a park bench for Google. Just write great copy that people will love to link to. (Once again you can see the concept of 'value' surfacing.) The idea is that you should give as much value as you can on your website and that by doing so you create an inspiring visitor experience, one that naturally leads to websites (or people) wanting to link to you.

Put differently, supply copy to your visitor which creates a demand of interest.

Ultimately, your job is not to satisfy the search engines but the people who are visiting your website and having great content will do just that – content is king and quality is queen.

Below are some pointers to help you write good Search Engine Optimised copy.

Have a Policy and Glue it to Your Forehead

The biggest gripe most professional SEO experts have with their customers is that they don't generate content. So why is the continuous creation of content important for your SEO ranking?

Well, the relevance of a piece of information tends to have a lifespan. The news is a perfect example of this. You would hardly be interested in the BBC News website if it hadn't been updated for a week because the content on the page would have lost its relevance.

Now you might think that not every page on your website is like a news page and, therefore, doesn't need to change. For example, your product page may not vary from one month to the next. However, there will always be an information 'flux' for such a page no matter how static it may seem. For example, the price may change, people may say different things about it, how people are using it may vary, and so on. To keep it fresh, you could use a Twitter feed to the page, write new articles about the product and reference them on that page, you could link to your blog or vice versa, and so on. If you are updating the page with this new information then it indicates to the search engines how significant this information is.

So, information's lifespan is directly related to its relevance and interest; therefore, it clearly makes sense to keep every page as up to date as possible with fresh information – don't let the information go stale or you'll lose ground with the search engines.

The key to this is to make a promise to your website that you'll keep it up to date. But beyond that I recommend defining a more formal programme of updates. These could include:

1. Adding new content pages
2. Adding new content to existing pages
3. Rewriting existing copy
4. Updating your blog
5. Adding Twitter/Facebook/LinkedIn feeds
6. Adding in feeds from your blog

All fairly obvious stuff admittedly but the important thing is to make the commitment to update the copy on a regular basis – weekly if you can and fortnightly if you can't! It's worth considering that doing this sends a clear message about the value you place on your website not only to the search engines but to your visitor too.

Keyword Density

A few years ago much play was made of the 'density' that keywords should have on the page. This meant how many times you needed to repeat the keywords in the body copy before the search engines accepted that this page was genuinely about the search term used. The average figure bandied about was 5 per cent of the total text. However, keyword density is less important these days when compared to other ranking factors. The trick is to let the occurrences of the search terms appear natural and not forced (as following the 5 per cent rule would do). Yes, you do want use your key terms in your copy but no, don't try to cram your copy with them.

Search engines also have spam filters which detect if you are over-emphasising a search term. These filters identify unnatural language patterns and if triggered, will dampen your ranking. So, behave naturally, write for your human visitor and the search engines will be much happier.

Keyword Phrasing

When you're writing your copy take care how you phrase your keywords. For example, if I wanted to optimise for the keyword 'dog pants' I could happily swap out the keywords for synonyms 'canine underwear' without Google marking me down. Why? Because it recognises that we humans don't always describe something using the same words and phrases – it's more natural for us to use alternatives in our writing.

However, don't dilute your keywords by introducing new topics between your core keywords. For example 'dog collars and pants' would syphon some of the keyword value away from the core search term as we're now discussing collars as well as pants. (Amazingly someone has actually invented dog pants!)

Remember, natural language usage is all part of a well-crafted website which gives your visitor a great experience, so getting that fundamental element right will result in Google rewarding you with better rankings.

Headings

You will want to use the search terms in your headings as well as your body copy because this emphasises the significance you place on them. However, you don't need to keep repeating the same search terms over and over in headings, subheadings and sub-subheadings. Instead, the search engines are looking for more natural patterns. For example:

Heading 1 – Exact search term match ('Dog Pants')

Heading 2 – Synonym ('Canine Underwear')

Heading 3 – Rephrased search term ('Pants for Dogs')

Your headings should be denoted as H1, H2, H3, etc in your website's code. So ask your web developers if, when you enter a heading into your pages, it will correspond to 'H1 tags' in HTML. They'll be impressed! (See Coding Considerations, page 275.)

Resource Naming

Apart from your copy, each of your webpages is likely to have other resources, such as images, hyperlinks, PDFs, Word documents and so forth. Each of these has a filename so if you are looking to add a bit of link juice into the page you can name these resources using the keywords you are optimising for. For example, if you are about to upload a PDF catalogue of your latest selection of dog pants, then calling the PDF 'Dog Pants Catalogue' would be a smart SEO move. But don't confine yourself to uploads; you can also change the name of the images, sound files, video files (and so on) to be keyword-rich.

While we're on this subject let's also look at alt-tags and titles. These are the little pop-ups that appear under your mouse when you move over a page resource. Alt-tags appear over images; titles appear over text links. These useful text pop-ups help people (and search engines) clarify the nature of the resource. Your CMS should give you the ability to name your resources using alt-tags, thus giving you a great opportunity to add your search terms in. (Don't forget that you can use synonyms – be natural, even with your alt-tags.)

Fig 6 An Alt-Tag in action over an image

Fig 7 A Title in action over a hyperlink

Internal Links

Just take a moment to consider that your visitors are going on a journey through your website. As they progress, you are going to show them points of interest en-route. Your design accounts for a lot of the visual signposting but you also signpost your visitors using hyperlinks in the body text of your page.

This gives your visitor the option to get further information, to go deeper into your website and have an even more relevant experience – search engines love that! So, creating natural hyperlinks which encourage 'relevant' movement around your website is a real winner. Plus it has the advantage of keeping the visitor on your website for longer – length of visit is one of Google's ranking criteria. And don't forget to use both the exact keyword and its synonyms for your internal links.

It's important not to get internal links confused with navigation. Your navigation menu, footer links, breadcrumbs will largely be ignored in relation to internal links because the search engines recognise them for what they are, namely, navigation. You're not directly aiding or adding relevance to the page the visitor is on with your navigation. It's easy to see that there is a qualitative distinction between a link in a paragraph of text to another page which is specifically related to the content and more generalised navigation. In other words, navigation is relevant to where you may want to go as opposed to where you are currently. So, if you're looking to prioritise your efforts, pay more attention to generating and organising your internal links rather than adding lots of different types of navigation all over the place.

One final point, you may find that there are parts of your website which generate links automatically. A typical example is seeing a 'Read More...' link in the articles section of your website. Such links are great opportunities from an SEO angle but the last thing you want is for them to be called 'Read More...' So where you find such links being automatically created, take a moment to see if they can be made more meaningful. Have a look at the example below: the title is being reused as the link to the article. The neat thing here is that the CMS is automatically creating the internal link. So, review your website for opportunities to have the CMS spawn these links for you.

---

5 Ways to Destroy Your Website

Very few of us wake up in the morning and think 'I know, today I'll really put some effort into destroying my website.' In fact, you wouldn't imagine that anyone in their right mind would think that. How is it then that so many businesses still manage to annihilate their website's chances of making money on a daily basis?

Read more: 5 Ways to Destroy Your Website

Fig 8 An automatically generated internal link

Outbound Links

Many web owners panic about linking out from their website to others. However, remember that the Internet is essentially a social network and so it pays to be of a sociable nature – search engines recognise this characteristic and will reward you for adding further relevance to your website. In fact it would be unnatural not to link to an external resource. (The search term equity – or link juice – you've created for that page won't escape down the outbound link to another website.)

If you're worried about your visitor jumping ship to another website then consider these options:

1. Open the link in another browser window (so your website is still in the background).

2. Tell your visitor it's a link to an external website in some text next to the link.

3. Open the content in a modal window.[8]

4. Cite the complete text (along with the link) from the other website in your webpage so there is no need to take your visitor elsewhere.

This type of approach also predisposes other websites to link back to you, which rather neatly leads us on to...

Reciprocal Link Exchange

Reciprocal links are where you link to a website and they link back to you. In the 'olden days' of SEO these were artificially generated as a means of fooling the search engines into believing that you were more popular than you really were. However, it wasn't long before the search engines got wise to this tactic and started to 'downgrade' the value of such links.

But surprisingly, they still do have value if they occur naturally – remember search engines are wise to artificial behaviour patterns. So, for example a hairdresser linking to and from a beauty salon is a perfectly acceptable link (especially if they are in the same town, perhaps less so if they are on different continents). However, a hairdresser linking to and from an estate agent is clearly not natural or relevant. The question is, as always, 'Are we adding relevance?'

Meta Information

Within the HTML code of your webpages are the options to specify information about the pages themselves. These are called meta tags and are so named because they provide data about the page that is not on the page itself.

It's highly likely that your CMS will enable you to enter this information directly for each of the pages on your website. This will give you the flexibility to change them from their original state to a more Search Engine Optimised state. If your CMS does not give you this facility then you will need to compile a list of page names with their new meta information and hand this across to your web designers so they can manually input it. Below are the three meta types you'll want to consider: Meta Title, Meta Description, and Meta Keywords.

Meta Title

A Meta Title is the title of the page and is very important to your SEO. The title of your page effectively frames its content as far as the search engines are concerned. This gives you approximately 69 characters[9] (including spaces) to convey the page's meaning.

Typically, most people start by putting their company name first. Obviously that's wrong. Begin with your selected search term first because the search engines will assign a greater importance to the words at the beginning of the Meta Title than at the end. Here's an example of a great usage of meta title:

[9] This figure for Google – meta data length for other search engines may vary.

Fig 9 A Meta Title in action

The search term that they are optimising for is primarily 'Luxury bedding' and secondarily 'luxury duvet covers.' You'll notice that the last keyword in the list is the company name. You would only want to optimise the Meta Title for your company name if your brand name is a search term (Best Kitchens Inc., for example) or you are a well-known brand and that level of brand awareness is important to you.

Another important characteristic of a Meta Title is that it forms the title for the link in the SERPs. Here's the example for 'luxury bedding' as it appears in the SERPs for Google:

> **Luxury bedding** : luxury duvet covers : Sheridan
> www.sheridanuk.com/ - Cached
> Sheridan UK - famous for **luxury** bed linen and superior
> yarns, beautiful textures and enduring quality, has been
> trading in the UK for over 25 years.

Fig 10 Where the Meta Title appears in the Google SERPs

Notice that the key phrase 'luxury bedding' is rendered in bold-face in the listing, making it more prominent. This is also going to incentivise people to click just like they would with an Ad-Words advert. So you can take some of the knowledge and experience you've already gained from AdWords and apply it here.

One final recommendation: Don't dilute the Meta Title with unnecessary words; keep it as concise and as relevant as possible.

Meta Description

Next on our hit list is the Meta Description. This is about 156 characters (including spaces) of text directly beneath the link title on the SERPs. It offers a brief description of the page, but more importantly it offers a *reason* to click.

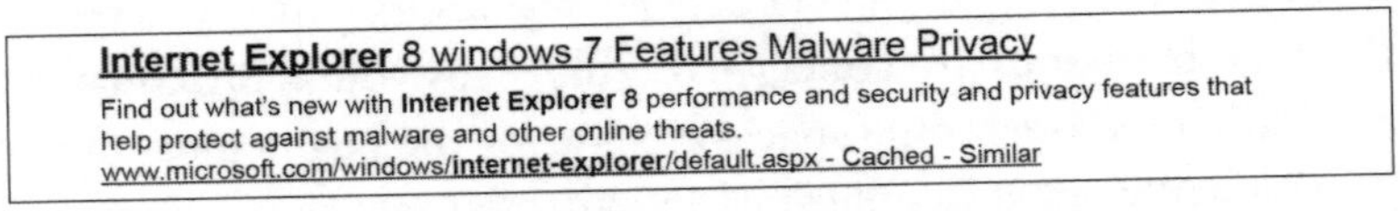

Fig 11 Google SERP showing the Meta Description

> **Internet Explorer** 8 windows 7 Features Malware Privacy
> Find out what's new with **Internet Explorer** 8 performance and security and privacy features that help protect against malware and other online threats.
> www.microsoft.com/windows/**internet-explorer**/default.aspx - Cached - Similar

Looking at the screenshot above gives us a really great example to review. Firstly it states a call to action – 'Find out what's new' – and then continues to provide reasons why the product is great – an excellent use of the space.

Of course, if you've been running AdWords you'll probably know what advert gets the highest Click-Through Rate and, therefore, the kind of text to use here.

Interestingly, despite the fact that you can specify the Meta Description, Google can override it and replace it with text that it feels is more appropriate. However, even if that happens, all is not lost. Simply find that text on your website and change it to something which gives someone a reason to click on your link.

While your Meta Description has no bearing on your ranking it has huge bearing on the likelihood of being clicked on once you are in the rankings.

Meta Keywords

These used to be one of the key determining factors search engines would use to calculate your website's ranking, but no longer. They have pretty much dropped off the criteria for ranking because they could so easily be abused. (All you had to do was enter completely irrelevant keywords and you could end up with a spurious ranking.) So, they have been all but relegated out of the league – use them if you've got time to kill but they have minimal impact and are of questionable value.

Domain Names

Firstly, let's dispel a myth. Google is only going to reference one domain and one website. While you may have multiple domain names, only one can take precedence. So, there is little point buying lots of domain names when only one will contribute to your SEO.[10]

If you do have more than one domain name you must use a '301 redirect' from one domain to your primary domain. Other-

10 You may have other reasons to buy domain names, such as protecting your business or brand name, using them for marketing specific products or services, etc.

wise, Google will think you have multiple websites, all with dupli-
cated content.

So what type of domain name should you choose? Well, the
SEO ideal is to pick the domain name that is a complete mirror of
the search term you are trying to SEO for. Imagine you're a hotel
in the Lake District, someone might reasonably enter 'lake district
hotel' as their search term. If the domain www.lakedistricthotel.
co.uk is available and on your hit list to SEO, then it would be well
worth investing in it as the primary domain of your website. (This
is exactly what the company that owns this domain name did.)

If you're struggling to find a domain name which includes
your search term, try putting hyphens between the words, for
example, www.my-search-term-here.co.uk.

Sand Box

The 'sand box' is where, it is believed, new domains and websites
get relegated while Google figures out what type of site you are
and the sort of traffic you are attracting. New websites can expect
to have their rankings artificially depressed in the sand box. Some
cynics believe this is to help Google sell its AdWords system as
the only means of getting into the listings but my interpretation
is a little more benign.

Imagine moving into a house with ten other tenants and it's
your first day. If the other ten don't know you but they know
one another, then it might take some time before the relationships start to gel with you. This is normal as it takes time for us
to become comfortable with new people in our lives – we like
to weigh them up first. Google views websites in the same way.
It takes time for your website to earn enough points for good
behaviour before being properly ranked. In other words, Google
is assessing the nature of your website prior to giving it a fair and
stable ranking.

Sand box effects are reputed to last anywhere between six to
12 months so don't panic if your ranking jumps about a bit in the
early stages of your website's life.

Domain Age

Domain age adds weight to your ranking. It's a little like having
generations of your family living in your country mansion – the
mansion takes on your name and eventually those around you

recognise it as the seat of your family!

If you've owned a domain for 20 years that will count in your favour more so than if you've owned it for one year. Essentially, it sends a message to the search engines that you aren't a fly-by-night and your business is real and permanent. So, if you have the opportunity to buy a domain for ten years (and some domain vendors will offer this) then do so.

Hosting Location

Clearly it makes sense to host your website in the country that you trade in. Hosting a website in Bahrain when you trade in Ireland is, well, odd and the search engines know it. They will assess your address, the domain owner's address, the top-level-domain[11] of your domain name and so on, in order to get a sense of your physical trading location.

[11] A top-level-domain is the bit of the domain name at the end. For example, '.uk' refers to United Kingdom domains, '.me' refers to personal domains, '.biz' is used for businesses and so forth.

Therefore, a .uk web address will typically appear further up the listings on Google if you are searching in the UK than a domain for another country like .fr (France) or .au (Australia).

The reasoning behind hosting your website in your trading country is, once again, one of relevance. Evidently, those businesses situated in their trading country are better able to serve their customers than those from another country. So, Google always gives preference to the home country's websites. If you are a UK company and you own a .com domain then make sure you've got the .uk domain too and tell your hosts (or whomever you bought the domain from) to make it your 'primary domain.'

Bottom line – keep your website local.

SEO Help from Your Web Designers

Inevitably, there are some technical things that will help your SEO which you probably won't want to get involved with. Enter your web designers.

Sitemaps

Every website needs a sitemap, which is a webpage listing all the pages on your website in a hierarchically organised structure.

Now it's very rare a human uses a sitemap (in fact you wouldn't want them to as it would mean that the information they want is buried so deeply or so obscured that they have to resort to an index to find it!). However, search engines use specific variations of these pages, called XML sitemaps, to make sure they crawl every page of your website.

Making an XML sitemap is a technical process and one that you should request of your web designers. One point to note is that it should be dynamic so that as the structure of your website changes, the XML sitemap changes with it.

When the Googlebot crawls your site it can use the Sitemap to ensure it knows all about the pages on your site. You can find out more about sitemaps at www.google.com/support/webmasters/bin/answer.py?hl=en&answer=156184&from=40318&rd=1.

- Welcome
- Get More Traffic
    - Paid Traffic, Instant Results
        - Golden Adwords Rule #1
        - Golden Adwords Rule #2
        - Golden Adwords Rule #3
    - Get Free Traffic
- Get More Sales
    - eCommerce Success
    - Split-testing for a Pay Rise
    - Powerful Email Marketing

Fig 12 Example of a sitemap

Hosting

Very often web designers host their customers' websites and so you can ask them directly about the technical performance of yours as this will have a bearing on your ranking. What you're particularly interested in is how quickly pages are being served to your visitors and whether there has been any website downtime. Both of these are determining factors in how the search engines view the quality of your website.

As you can imagine the search engines won't rank you very highly if your website is slow or offline half the time.

If you set yourself up a Webmaster account with Google (www.google.com/webmasters/tools), you can see Google's interpretation of how your website is performing by selecting 'Labs' and 'Site Performance.'

Coding Considerations

In all honesty, good coding naturally results in SEO. If your web designers are producing W3C compliant code then you don't need to worry.

For example, your webpage will have headings in the content but the search engines expect to find these headings structured using special HTML code called 'H tags.' An H tag gives your text a specific formatting but also defines its importance on the page (H1 being more important than H2, etc.). In the code you might see something like this:

```
<h1>Dog Pants</h1>
<h2>Where to Buy Dog Pants</h2>
```

All you need to know is that your web designers are following this and the many other conventions laid down by the W3C.

Another important consideration, which I've mentioned before, are '301 redirects.' In simple terms if you have two domain names pointing at one website, Google will regard that as two separate websites (one a duplicate of the other). Duplication of content doesn't help your SEO since Google will ascribe original authorship to only one and not any of the duplicates. (You couldn't just copy a Harry Potter book, change the 'J.K. Rowling' to your name and expect it to be regarded as your work! Likewise only one website can benefit from authorship.) To avoid this your web designers must use '301 redirects' to redirect the traffic from one domain name to another.

Don't forget that if you're redesigning your website make sure your old page names are mapped to new ones (we covered this on pages 79–81).

Link to Us

It's a well-known tactic in referrals marketing to 'ask for the referral' right upfront (even before you do the work). This works well because it places in the mind of your customer the notion that you want a referral right from the outset. Oddly almost no one ever asks for the link 'referral' off their website which, I think, is a missed opportunity. If you don't ask people to link to you then you don't even indicate it's something you want. So at the bottom or every article, news piece, product or service page why not add a prompt 'Please link to this article.' You can also use Social Bookmarking (see Social Bookmarking, page 286) to help the process along.

Why not go one step beyond that and create a 'Link to Us' page? On this page you can display links which other web masters or visitors can easily copy. The trick to this page is to only choose those pages which are your target pages for your chosen search terms. So don't reference every page, just the ones you are optimising.

The link should be properly formed with the search terms used in the link text. For example:

<u>Dog Pants from John Wilson & Co.</u>

Or if you fancy providing a bit more information:

Get the Exciting New Dog Pants from John Wilson & Co.

A neat trick to engineer your linking a bit more is to rotate the links so you only display one at a time but each time a new visitor sees the 'Link to Us' page they get a different link. This means all your link requests have an even chance and not just the most exciting-looking or popular ones.

Offering Reasons to Link to Us

Consider offering an incentive or reward to those who link to you:

1. A free report or piece of research
2. A discount on a purchase
3. A small free gift
4. A reciprocal write up of their website
5. Some free help or consultancy

Frankly, anything you can think up which has some value in the eyes of those who may wish to link to you.

And why stop with a 'Link to Us' page? Why not request a link on your...

1. Email signature
2. Reports
3. PDFs
4. Presentations
5. Exhibition documentation
6. Invoices (and offer a discount if they link to you)
7. Letterheads
8. Business cards
9. Purchase orders
10. Compliments slips

The list is endless!

OFFSITE SEO TECHNIQUES

So begins the second half of your SEO project – acquiring links from external websites, otherwise known as offsite SEO.

Much of your offsite activity will be around generating backlinks and ideally from webpages with the highest possible Page Rank. However, even if the links you do acquire have low Page Ranks they can still be of value because the ultimate goal is to get people to visit your website and even low PR pages can do that!

Let's begin with something completely obvious and that's getting Google to recognise that you've even got a website.

Getting Listed

Many propose submitting your URL directly to the search engines for them to crawl and index your website. Personally, I suggest a different approach. Given that the Internet is a social network and links count as votes, why not get voted in?

What I recommend is that you ask for links from your clients, suppliers, Facebook supporters, Tweeters, even your web designers (who will, no doubt, want to add you into their portfolio pages anyway). You could even add your listing to an online directory if you can't convince a human to do it on your behalf (see Directories, page 284). As you gather these external links the search engines will regard your website as voted into the system.

Think of it like this: Google will naturally give more weight to someone voting you in rather than you telling Google directly that you exist. However, if you would prefer to let Google know anyway then you can use the Google Webmaster tools to do this.

The next step is for you to find sources of backlinks so you can get people linking to your target pages. Below is your guide to offsite link acquisition.

Being Unusual

Begin by being unusual.

If you want people to spot you amongst the chaos and mayhem of the Internet you need to be different. There's little point being silent and behaving just like everyone else – that's not how you get noticed. Remember that people will only link to your website's content if there is something they perceive to be worth linking to. (Relevance and interest is very much in the eye of the beholder!) And so the key to attracting backlinks is to be different. Look for what everybody else is doing and find the gap (or, if you're feeling radical find what everyone else is doing and do the reverse).

What you're looking for is an angle – to take a view on something in your industry which is separate and distinct from the approach of your competition.

This is often referred to as link baiting. Put differently it is the act of generating content which generates interest which then leads to people linking to your website.

Here's my advice to help set you up with this.

1. Be open to all ideas no matter how mad they may seem.
    a. Remember the Nescafé romance? (103,000 YouTube hits)
    b. Or the Crazy Frog? (14.5 million YouTube hits)
    c. How about the Smash Mash Potatoes Robots? (250,000 YouTube hits)
    d. The Compare the Meerkat adverts (639,000 YouTube hits)

    On paper they must have looked like insane ideas but they captured the imagination of the public and were extensively discussed, remembered and were advertising genius because they were so unusual.
2. Be conscious of and purposefully ignore your prejudices. We all have them and especially about what we think our target market will accept. (Who would have thought that a fake gorilla playing the drums would appeal to Cadbury's chocolate-eaters!) Put aside what you think you know and only work with the absolute facts about your marketplace.
3. Don't be afraid. It's often fear that stops businesses from doing extraordinary things. It's unlikely you'll destroy your business no matter how 'far out' the idea is.

Once you've started to establish your angle you can begin to put the materials together to express it, for example by writing articles, reports, podcasts and videos and/or taking a particular stance using social networking sites, etc.

Now you are in a position to publicise your difference and unique standpoint across the Internet. What follows are some of the techniques you can use to help you do this.

Social Connections

A big component in link acquisition is forging relationships with people whom you can help and who can help you.

There are a number of such relationships you may want to cultivate so let's take a look at each in turn.

Bloggers

Bloggers are a great source of backlinks and given their proliferation it's highly likely that there is a keen blogger in your industry.

However, before you ask for the link directly it makes sense for you to introduce yourself and your company. You can do this by becoming one of their commentators and contributing to their feedback. If you can't effect an introduction by interacting on their website then simply email them. If you don't get a response by email then send a letter or give them a call. But start with an introduction and a solid reason why you would like them to link to you. (If you begin by asking for the link its unlikely the blogger will respond.)

You could send your product in for them to review or offer them your service free of charge in exchange for a review. Don't be frightened to do this – many will be, worrying that they may get an appalling write-up. A simple way to mitigate this possibility is to send the product or offer the service with some background information: a 'how to use and understand the product/service' guide, its key benefits, known problems, plans for improvement, etc. This helps frame your offering and manage any negatives your blogger may identify. So, help yourself by helping them as much as possible. Even if you do get some negative coverage, don't panic – a little bit of bad in a good article makes it more believable! For example, ten five-star reviews sounds engineered, nine five-star reviews and one three-star review sounds more 'real.'

Remember to give the blogger the pre-formed link to the specific page you want your 'link juice' to flow to – don't leave it to chance.

Plus, you don't need to confine yourself to bloggers; consider online newspapers, independent journalists, ezines, and trade journals.

If your attempts at getting a write-up or straightforward link fail, you may want to consider a more commercial arrangement with your blogger:

1. Suggest they keep the product.
2. Offer them something over and above the product or service you have given them.
3. Pay them.
4. Request an advertising link.
5. Consider a more formal joint venture with them.

6.   Ask if they would be a paid guest writer for your
blog/articles/news section or vice versa.

Remember to put your effort only into those bloggers who have a
good Page Rank on their websites.

Now, what if there isn't a prominent blogger in your sector?
Well, that means you can seize the opportunity and become
that blogger! Set up your own blog (this takes five minutes with
Google's Blogger (www.blogger.com) or Wordpress (wordpress.
com), start writing and start backlinking to your own website.
However, a quick word of caution: you'll find that the more impar-
tial your blog, the more attention it will attract so if you do decide
to write your own be careful not to make it too commercially
biased in favour of your business.

Leaders

In most industries there are often a few outspoken people for
whom a lot of respect is held. For example, in Internet marketing
there are Dan Kennedy, Seth Godin, Chris Cardell, John Jantsch,
Rich Schefren, etc.

These are deemed to be the leaders of the market. They are
the people that others follow and listen to. (Every market has
them and if yours doesn't then I would strongly suggest that you
become that person.)

Now it's not just a question of picking anyone as there is often
a huge amount of 'information noise' on the Internet (especially
on Twitter). You need to look for people who are emitting quality
signals and not gibberish. Look for those who have a following
and are being commented on.

If you can find an angle to engage with one or more of then,
simply by association, you can develop backlink traffic. Let's take
an example.

Imagine that your industry leader has a blog, speaks at confer-
ences, is an active Tweeter, writes for an industry magazine and
has maybe even published a book. Now, it's pretty unlikely that
they are going to pay any attention to you, especially if you are
new to your industry's social network. Even if your company has
been around a long time you still may need to establish some
'social' credibility before you engage your leader. By social credibility I mean that you must develop a 'voice' – an angle – a posi-

tion which you can write against. So, establish your 'take' on your industry and begin to write about it. (See Being Unusual, page 278.)

You could start by commenting on your leader's blog; re-Tweet their Tweets and add you own. These are soft methods to introduce yourself. You could then begin to expand into writing your own articles which are continuations of something they wrote on or you could passionately agree (or disagree – more on that in a minute). You could ask your industry magazine to publish your take on their comments or write an open letter to your leader. The actual route you take will be dictated by where and how your leader operates on the Internet.

At a suitable point you can address them directly and ask for the link. The attractive thing about this approach is that while you'll probably get the link to your website you can also cultivate a whole slew of other opportunities with them:

1. Would they consider a joint venture?
2. Would they be prepared to write a feature on your company?
3. Would they write an email to their email list about your business?
4. Would they be prepared to refer you?
5. Would they endorse your product/service for use on your marketing?
6. Would they pay a special visit to your premises?

Once the leader starts to comment about you and links to your website, others will naturally follow and so will come a flood of interest (and backlinks) to your website. And thus the act of engaging a leader will benefit you far more greatly than just the link they provide.

There is a combative approach that may suit some and that's to find something that the leader is saying and take an oppositional stance to it. You deliberately take a confrontational position with the aim of creating controversy. The idea is that controversy will lead to others backlinking to you (either in agreement or disagreement). It's a risky strategy and wouldn't be my personal first choice: even if you are the righteous David facing down Goliath, you could find that Goliath still wins, no matter how wrong they are!

Social Enablers

This group is made up of people who bring other people together. They may be administrators for particular subject areas on threads in forums (or indeed be the owners of the forum). They could also be group leaders for LinkedIn, avid commenters on other websites, emailers and so forth. They are people who facilitate a central point (or nexus) of connections to and for others. Influence them and they can influence others through those connections.

Manage the social enablers with the same techniques you would for bloggers and leaders.

Forums

Forums are one of the oldest 'gathering places' on the Internet and many have very established and committed audiences. As such, they can be great places to elicit traffic and establish quality backlinks. Here are a few guidelines to help you get the best out of forums and acquire good traffic and links.

For starters read the forum rules. Some forums have specific rules regarding how they allow commercial companies to promote themselves, so please read these first. If you do decide to register, do so transparently. In other words, don't pretend to be someone you're not or hide the fact that you work in the industry. This can be very embarrassing if you get found out and the administrator decides to make an example of you!

I would recommend that you follow the Internet rule of giving great value and carefully observing the forum's rules.

Some forum owners may attempt to sell you advertising space so be prepared to field that or, ideally, offer them something that is of equal value to them. For example, consider offering them some form of content that they would not normally be able to get – a video or podcast, etc. You could even suggest that you 'guest' for them on a regular basis. If you can define and provide some content which lifts their content above their competitors then you will undoubtedly have the ear of the forum owner and they will be happy to return the favour with a link (or series of links).

Some forums allow you to add a signature to your comments and within this signature you can place a link to your website. This can effectively give you more backlinks to your target page. However, it's unlikely that the page you are posting your comments to has a high PR so you might need quite a volume of these backlinks before they have a noticeable effect on your SEO.

Some forums only allow you to add a signature after a certain number of posts, some do allow it but only if you are an advertiser and some do not allow it at all if you're a commercial enterprise. (Again, the forum rules will help you out here.)

Some forums may attempt to funnel the commercial content into specific 'divisions.' For example, AVForums (www.avforums. co.uk) has 'Owners' Forums' where owners of a particular make of product can interact with the manufacturer. The manufacturer, in turn for helping their customers, gets the opportunity to pitch directly to them in the forum. However, these sub-forums only exist where the manufacturer is already an existing advertiser.

Remember your fall-back position: if all else fails, take out some advertising so you can get preferential treatment from the forum owner. You'll often find that the forum's rules only allow signatures and backlinks with paid advertisers.

Directories

12 When I took the screen-shot of the Dmoz home page it had a PR of 8/10 and the 'Retailers listing' (Business > Retail Trade > Retailers) had a PR of 4/10 – still very good and worth listing against.

Directories are listings of websites organised into categories. Dmoz is such an example.[12] Submitting your website to such directories can be a great way of getting backlinks.

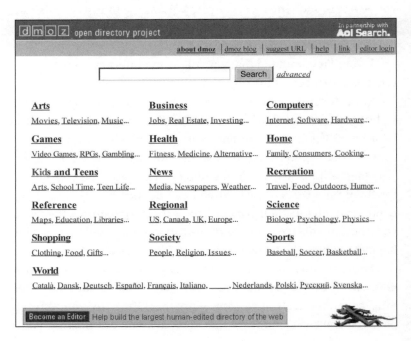

Fig 13 Home page of Dmoz – an example of a directory

However, don't be beguiled by their home page PR as your listing probably won't appear there. Instead drill down to the page where your website would be listed and look at its PR. (The PR for these directories changes all the time so it's best to Google 'directories with high page rank' as there will already be pre-compiled lists of them for you.)

There are also directories you can pay to be listed in, Yahoo! Directory being one (dir.yahoo.com). I looked up the Web Designers listing and that's got a PR of 5, which is excellent (especially given how far down the hierarchy it is). However, while a guaranteed listing is $299 per year there is the free option available via the 'Yahoo! Directory Submit' under 'Suggest a Website.' Some directories, like Yahoo!, are edited by humans, so don't expect your listing to appear overnight.

You may find that the best directories to be listed in are your own trade or association directories. Not only will they have relevance to your target market directly but could have good PR.

Twitter

If you're not familiar with Twitter, think of it as a normal blog, but with each entry having no more than 140 characters (roughly one sentence). It's a sort of text messaging service for the Internet. You can follow other people's Twitter pages and they can follow yours. As you gain more followers more people read your 'tweets.'

There may be many reasons why you want to tweet but SEO can be a compelling one in its own right. After all, your Twitter page is effectively another website from which you can link to your website. The higher the PR of your Twitter page, the stronger the backlinks to your website.

Plus if you can create a buzz on Twitter then the word about your business will get about, your tweets will be re-tweeted and the backlinks will be propagated beyond your Twitter page.

You can be up and tweeting in just a few minutes. However, don't expect instant results. You will need to tweet for some time (and consistently) before other tweeters will pay attention to what you're offering. Remember the Internet Golden Rule: Give as much value as you can.

Here's an example to get you thinking. The *Guardian* newspaper's twitter page (twitter.com/guardian) has a PR of 6, so getting a link to your website from that page is well worth the effort. Imagine posting something of current interest which then gets re-tweeted by others, eventually ending up on the *Guardian*'s Twitter page – you've just got yourself a very juicy link!

It doesn't take long to review who the movers and shakers are in your industry plus you should look for press Twitter pages on specific subjects. For example, the *Independent* newspaper has over 16 Twitter pages on different subjects and 27 journalist-specific Twitter pages. Once you have them identified you can start to interact with their Twitter pages.

Twitter is very much a personal choice. If you're the type of person (or you know of one in your business) who would enjoy this form or social networking then absolutely go for it. But don't make a half-hearted attempt at it or it'll probably be doomed from the get-go.

Social Bookmarking

Social bookmarking is a peculiar but powerful addition to your backlinks campaign. If you're unfamiliar with how it works let me briefly explain. Most of us tend to bookmark websites we like – we save them to our 'favourites' list so we can quickly access them without having to enter the URL into the browser each time. You can store these on your browser or on the Internet using a social bookmarking website. These websites allow you to store and organise your 'favourite' lists of websites.[13] Each of the bookmark pages can be made publicly available for viewing so others can access the bookmark lists. What's interesting from an SEO perspective is that, because the links can be publicly accessible they are effectively 'backlinks' to websites – each one representing a vote for the webpage they are linking to.

[13] You can see a list of sites at en.wikipedia.org/wiki/List_of_social_bookmarking_websites.

One such website is Digg (www.digg.com). Whenever someone 'Diggs' your webpage they have effectively voted for it, which causes it to move up the Digg ranking. The more Diggs given, the more popular the page is deemed to be. Interestingly, because so many people use Digg, it's highly likely that if your webpage gets to the top of the pile, or onto any of the section home pages, you will receive some substantial volumes of traffic. (In fact, there have been instances where Digg traffic has 'taken down' the target website through the sheer volume of traffic visiting it.)

In order to elicit such attention you could join a few of the social bookmarking websites and start linking to your own website.

You could also get colleagues, friends and family to do the same. However, there is no substitute for actually writing some amazing content that inspires other people who don't know you to bookmark your webpage. This is more to do with creating a buzz about a subject based on your content rather than engineering one.

To make it easy for people to bookmark your content you can add a social bookmarking 'widget' to your website so all your visitor has to do is click on the relevant button and they will automatically be sent to their favourite bookmarking website and so help spread your content across the web.

Fig 14 Social bookmarking 'widgets' to add to your website

For example AddThis (www.addthis.com) or ShareThis (www.sharethis.com) will give you a variety of social websites and button styles to choose from as well as give you some analytics on how people are using them. There are many others to choose from and a web search for 'social bookmarking widget' is a useful starting point. However, remember to apply these widgets only to relevant pages of your website (so, *not* your home page, contact page, etc.).

Article Sites and Lens Sites

Article sites are effectively content warehouses where you can post articles you've written; they can be a terrifically effective means of getting backlinks to your site. You write an article and submit it directly to an article site and syphon the link juice from the article site directly to yours.

Let me cite an example. WebProNews (www.webpronews.com) is a generalised article site covering a variety of online topics. The home page has a PR of 6, as does its Technology section home page. So appearing on either of these pages would be beneficial. (Obviously you'll find that the actual article page itself will have a much lower PR.)

You can then submit your work to article sites which have a good PR and will help contribute to your overall ranking. Bear in mind that if Google discovers duplicate content (that is, the same article on multiple article sites) it won't necessarily show the duplicates on the search results, although typically it won't discount the link value that they provide to your website either.

However, don't be beguiled by 'article spinning software', which essentially takes sentences and paragraphs and rearranges them so they don't resemble the original. I regard this as 'junk' SEO and don't recommend it at all, as you could end up with completely mangled versions of your original.

Look for article sites that are specific to your industry and focus on your niche. These will have a higher overall relevance to your reader and, therefore, to the search engines. If you land your article on a site which is highly generalised, you may find that the actual Page Rank is seriously diluted. Remember then to check what the Page Rank is for the average article in your category before you go to the effort of writing something exclusively for that site.

To find article sites, Google 'article websites with good page rank' but remember to check the PR yourself as it may have gone down (or up).

There is another alternative to the classical article site and that is the 'lens' page. A lens is a single webpage which focuses on one subject, any subject, and is so called because each author has a different focus to their page. A terrific example of a lens website is Squidoo (www.squidoo.com) – the originator of the lens idea.

Squidoo gives you the ability to create a webpage on whatever you like. Each author's lens page is categorised to give some organisation to the site and so in this respect it is more like a directory site combined with an article site with the flavour of an encyclopaedia!

You can backlink to your website directly from the lens page and so as your lens accumulates PR, that will filter through to your website. The better the content of the lens page, the more of a buzz it creates, the more people link to it and so the more link juice lands on your site.

In addition you can monetise each page with Google AdSense. This places Google AdWords adverts on your lens which, when visitors click on them, earns you revenue. Squidoo claims that some of its authors generate up to $10,000 per year.

(I, somewhat randomly, clicked on 'How to Grow Crystals' from the home page and was taken to a lens with a very respectable PR of 3.)

Another website which delivers a similar approach and is well worth reviewing is HubPages (hubpages.com).

Google Places

You may have noticed that Google shows local businesses, points of interest, etc., on searches that contain a geographical reference (or if the search results would benefit from displaying geographic results). Here's an example below for my search term 'entertainment london':

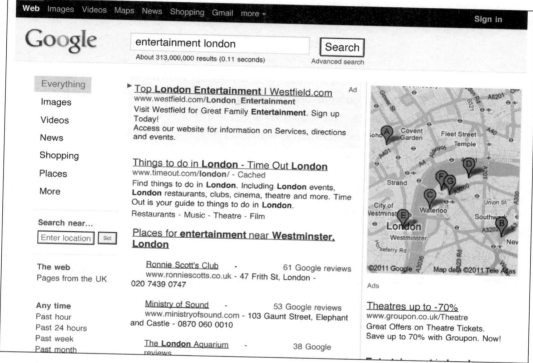

What is immediately apparent is that Google places far greater emphasis on these 'Places' than on the organic search results. (Even the AdWords advertising has been shunted down the right hand side of the page in favour of a map.)

Fig 15 A Google SERP showing how Google integrates local information

Getting listed here can be highly advantageous because your position in the search results is more a function of being listed using Google Places than conventional SEO. Plus, if you are a business which only attracts customers from a certain radius then this can be a very welcome boost to your local traffic.

So, how do you get listed on Google Places? Well, for once, it's remarkably easy! Search for 'google places' and log in using your Google account (the same one you use for AdWords). Next, click on 'Add new business.' You are then asked to fill in some basic information about your company:

1. Name, email, web address, etc. (If you can, sculpt your Description around your chosen search terms.)
2. Whether you service your customers at your premises or theirs
3. Your opening hours
4. Payment options
5. Photos
6. Videos
7. Additional details

Once you've submitted this information Google may send a postcard to your business address, to confirm your location.

By the way, just have a quick think about the photos and videos sections. I've already discussed the value of video and here is yet another great example of a multimedia opportunity. You can take the same video you've already put together for your main website and upload it here – something your competition probably won't do!

Google then takes what it believes to be relevant copy from your website and displays it against your listing.

Fig 16 A Google Places SERP

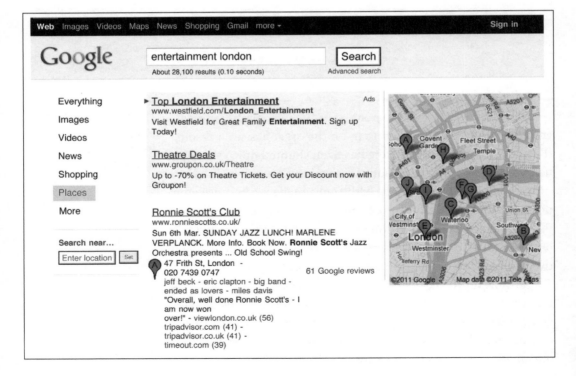

You'll also notice that people can add reviews to your listing which, as you can imagine, can be something of a mixed blessing. However, you can always give yourself a boost here by getting some of your customers to write up some reviews for you to help the process along.

Wikipedia

Many companies see Wikipedia as a great opportunity to write about themselves. After all, many of Wikipedia's entries appear at the top of the SERPs. However, Wikipedia states that 'you are strongly discouraged from writing articles about yourself or organisations [...] in which you hold a vested interest,' which is fair enough given that it has grown its reputation on impartiality and objectivity.

However, that said, it doesn't stop you from posting an article which relates to something you do. For example, if you sell a product which uses a new form of technology you can create an article about the technology, if not the product. You may then be able to backlink to your site as an external reference. I recommend that you follow Wikipedia's guidelines, because if you don't, you will probably find that your article (and hard work) just gets deleted.

Here are a couple of links which you may find useful:

1. Wikipedia's guidelines for organisations: en.wikipedia.org/wiki/Wikipedia:FAQ/Organizations
2. How to write your first article: en.wikipedia.org/wiki/Wikipedia:Your_first_article

Buying Links

Buying links is not my preferred approach. Sure, lots of companies offer this service but Google tries to do everything it can to spot manufactured link-building because it's contrary to all its core principles. One of the techniques Google uses is to identify how many and how quickly the links are built. If, for example, Google suddenly spots a significant increase in the number of websites linking to yours (because you've employed a company to perform a link-building campaign) it may regard that as unnatural and, potentially, ignore those links. Remember you shouldn't (and can't, if Google has anything to do with it) manufacture relevancy.

Some less-than-scrupulous companies will acquire their links from 'bad neighbourhoods' because it's quicker and cheaper than acquiring them from legitimate sites. These are sites on the Internet which contain spam, huge numbers of irrelevant links and even viruses and illegal content! Even so, if a website links to you Google won't penalise you for it – so don't panic if you find a link coming from a 'dodgy' site. However, if Google begins to see that you are repeatedly being linked to from such websites, it may hand it over to its human quality-control department.

If you do fancy parting with your cash I would suggest a softer approach. For example, sponsoring a blog article entry ('This Page Has Been Sponsored by Dog Pants, Purveyors of the <u>Best Dog Pants</u> on the Planet!') Or advertise your website link using a banner or sponsor a charity. I suggest beginning by asking for links for free or by offering something of value other than hard cash. However, if you really want the link and the page it will appear on has a great PR and is relevant, then paying for it may be the only option.

THE STRATEGY

If Google AdWords is the 100-metre dash, SEO is definitely the marathon. SEO is a long-term activity and as such puts many people off by the absence of a 'quick-fix'. I think it's the combination of a concerted effort and the lack of instant results that causes so few to ever finish the race. This is where the 'dabbling' mentality is at its most dangerous because the effort:reward ratio is so skewed in the early stages. This is a marketing activity that you will definitely need to set aside regular weekly time for. Don't give up on it though – it may take a long time to break the finishing tape time but the rewards will also last a long time.

Your SEO activities do more than simply get you further up the rankings; they get you noticed at all sorts of levels because SEO is fundamentally linked to public relations. The more popular you are, the more links you will acquire. So if you get your Public Relations right your SEO will be bolstered, and vice versa. This is a connection rarely made in the SEO world and as such leaves many companies resorting to buying links in a 'brute force' approach.

Finally, don't be afraid to get yourself and your business out there on the Internet. Remember that you're an expert in your field, you and your business have a lot of value to give, and it's only right that the entire world knows about it!

CHAPTER

9

Analyse and Grow

■ INTRODUCTION

Welcome to the last leg of our strategy. This chapter will give you an insight into your visitor's behaviour in such detail that you might just blush.

One of the amazing aspects of the Internet is that so much of it is measurable. And by that I mean you can get access to the who, what, how, when and why of what's happening on your website. And by piecing those elements together you can gain a whole new understanding of your visitors' desires, needs and habits.

Whatever the nature of your business, in order to measure and maximise your success effectively, you must have access to the basic information about how many people have visited, what pages they viewed, what sites they came from and what searches they did to find your website. These are referred to as web statistics or web metrics and although it may sound like I'm about to embark on a math lesson, these are easy to understand, strangely fascinating and key to your ongoing success.

Fundamentally, you are trying to measure how people behave when they visit your website. Understanding their behaviour patterns gives you the knowledge to shape your website into what they want to see, in order for them to take the action you want them to take. In other words, you are using the data from people's behaviour to give them more of what they want that benefits both you and them.

How you get access to this information is very simple; there are lots of products that will measure what's happening on your website and report it back to you. However, I recommend one product to begin with – partly because it provides you with a huge array of incredibly useful reports but also because it is free. It's developed by Google and is called Google Analytics.

Google Analytics is an online tool that records how people are interacting with your website. It saves this information in logs which it then interprets into reports and graphs. All you need to do is add some code that Google gives you to each page of your website that you want 'measured' and Analytics takes care of the rest.

GETTING THE MOST OUT OF YOUR ANALYTICS

Clearly your goals for the site will be dependent on the type of site you are running. If it's a lead-generation website, your interest will be focused on getting enquiries, sign-ups, etc. If you are running an advertising website, your interest will be in getting as much traffic to the site as possible and having visitors click on your advertising messages (commercial forums are great examples of this). If you are running a customer support site, your focus will be giving customers the quickest and most appropriate routes to the answers they want.

Knowing what your core objectives are is fairly obvious stuff. However, what can be less obvious are the metrics which you need to measure in order to determine your success. Let's take two examples to illustrate this.

If you are an ecommerce shop, then your interest will be in online sales. So let's ask a few questions which may help us reveal what the customer is doing and, therefore, how well the website is doing:

1. How many visitors did you have last month?
2. How many of those bought from you?
3. What was the average order value?
4. How many customers purchased more than one item?
5. What was the overall profit per visit?

If you are a lead-generation site then you might ask:

1. How many visitors did you have last month?
2. How many of these left their details?
3. How many signed up to your email marketing?
4. How many converted into customers?
5. What was your profit per lead?

By asking these questions you begin to get a sense of your website's performance. These are 'top level' questions. However, they only give you a measure of performance and not how to improve it – that's down to your marketing tests. Analytics can help you answer the questions that contribute to the 'why' you're doing how you're doing! For example, you might see that lots of people buy in response to a particular offline advertising campaign, or that more purchases are made by mobile devices, or that media-rich pages outperform pure text pages, etc. You can then tune your website accordingly.

So, analytics help you marry the behaviour patterns of your visitors with the objectives of your site. For example, if you see that the majority of visitors are interested in one specific page of you site, you can expand upon it, offering more information and details. If, for example, you see that the majority of enquiries come after your visitors have seen a video, you can emphasise the video on the site. If you spot that lots of visitors are reviewing your site using iPhones, you can optimise your site to look great on these devices.

Not having access to this information reduces your ability to increase your success because it leaves you guessing. Analytics takes that guesswork away and turns it into solid data against which you can make informed judgements.

If you have set your website goals and objectives, then you can begin to 'ask' questions of the data you get back in order to interpret it correctly. Let's expand on this idea a little...

Using Questions to Help Your Analysis

There is a real risk that after an hour of using Analytics you'll go 'data blind.' Looking at the vast arrays of tables, graphs, numbers, averages and so on can begin to leave you, well, either needing a holiday or a straitjacket and, in certain cases, both.

This is perfectly normal if you haven't properly defined your key objectives. Let me explain. Just looking at data hoping that some marketing revelation will appear in front of you is unlikely to happen. It is unlikely because unless you are looking for something specific in the data, you're just going to be haplessly reviewing the metrics. However, if you look at a report with a key objective in mind then you will filter what you are looking at to meet the criteria of your question.

For example, let's imagine that you have opened up a new shop in Birmingham. You've done some online advertising and maybe put an advert in the local press. Now, while you will be able to measure your online advertising using all the reporting methods in Google AdWords, it is much harder to measure the success of offline advertising. Here's where Analytics comes to the rescue:

The question you are posing is, 'How effective was my offline advert?'

Let's say your advert went in on 1 March. You now set Analytics to display data from 1 March onwards. Next you focus on how much traffic has come from Birmingham using the Map Overlay report. You see a big spike on 1 March and a few days afterwards. Analytics has also tracked the traffic on the specific landing page you sent visitors to and also how many left their contact details. So you now know exactly how many people responded to your advert, which you can then measure against the total circulation of the local paper and, hey presto, you've got the answer to your question.

By beginning your analysis with a question, you are far more focused and can analyse the data more quickly and with a greater sense of purpose. Plus, if you know what you are looking for, you are less likely to be blinded by the data.

At the beginning of each report section in this chapter, I give you an example question applicable to that report. These are meant as gentle nudges for you to write your own questions.

Structuring Your Analysis

Remember, the best way to review your analytics is in relation to questions, objectives and goals. However, it also helps to have a structure to how you go about this.

A simple structure to help you stay focused comes from Webtrends' Executive Pocket Guide to Smarter Marketing. It simply suggests this: Report, Analyse, Decide, Act, React, or RADAR. So:

1. Review the reports
2. Analyse in relation to the question you are posing for that report
3. Decide what to do next
4. Act on that
5. React to the results you get

I recommend keeping a Testing Diary in which you detail all the changes and marketing tests you are making to your website. This gives you a reference point from which to analyse the results of your efforts. It also gives you a place to record the results and write down the decisions you then took. Now this level of organisation might sound terribly boring but believe me, organisation is one of the foundation stones to website success. As your site expands and your tests increase in number, you could easily get lost in the reports and data if you haven't kept a record of what you have done and why.

SETTING UP GOOGLE ANALYTICS

The first step is to create your Analytics account. Go here to begin: www.google.com/analytics. If you already have a Google Account (which you will if you've started your Google AdWords campaign), then you can simply sign in as normal.

Next you will go through the sign-up process which will see you providing:

1. Your website's URL (you can also set up multiple domains later on, if necessary)
2. An account name
3. The country and time zone you're in
4. The terms and conditions (you'll also find the option to stop sharing your analytics data with Google, if you're feeling so inclined!)
5. The final page gives you the code you need to copy into your website and looks something like Fig 1 (if you click on the Advanced tab)

Analytics asks you, 'What you are tracking?' and in most cases it will simple be 'A single domain (default).' However, depending on the size and complexity of your site you may have:

1. 'One domain with multiple subdomains' (for example, shop.jedscompany.co.uk, support.jedscompany.co.uk, etc.)
2. 'Multiple top-level domains' (for example, www.jedscompany.co.uk, www.jedscompany.com, www.jedscompany.net, etc.)

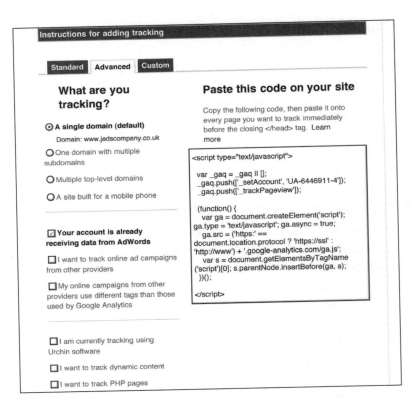

Fig 1 Google Analytics' tracking options, and the code you need to send to your web designers

The remaining options down the left-hand side are not applicable to the average website. However, you may want to check the AdWords campaign checkbox so the data from AdWords can be integrated with your Analytics data.

Copy the code out and give it to your web designers so they can insert it into every page of your site.

Eventually, you'll see a page resembling Fig 2. Once your designers have applied the code, the exclamation mark triangle will be replaced with a green tick indicating that Analytics has begun receiving and analysing data.

Editing Profile Information

Next let's edit some of the settings for this domain by clicking on 'Edit' under the 'Actions' column. You will then see a screen like Fig 3. While most of the information here is straightforward there are a couple of points to note:

Your home page appears when you enter your domain name (www.abcdomain.co.uk) on its own and also when you specify the

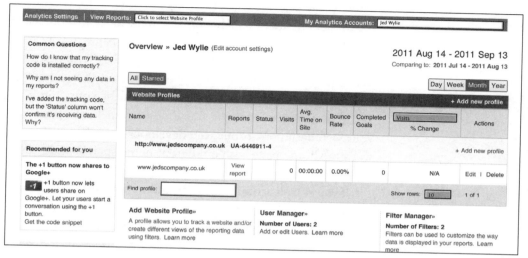

Fig 2 The 'home page' to Analytics

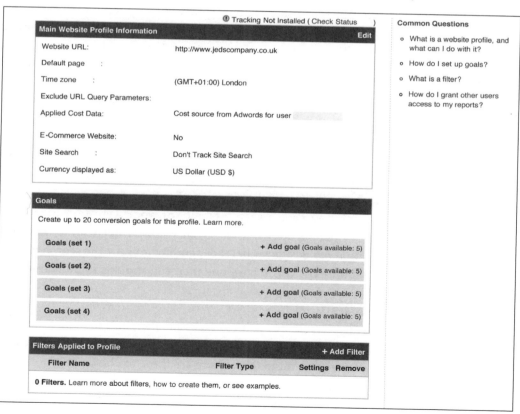

Fig 3 Editing the settings for your domain

actual home page file itself, typically by typing in /index.html after the domain name (www.abcdomain.co.uk/index.html). Analytics will initially separate these into two separate pages in your results, but this isn't particularly helpful given that they both point to the home page. You can combine the two using the Default Page setting by typing in the explicit filename of your home page. If you're not sure what the filename of your home page is, ask your web designers. (Your web developers may have set up your website's home page with a different name such as index.htm or index.php.)

If you run an ecommerce shop and want to see the ecommerce reports you will need to switch the field 'E-Commerce Website' from 'No' to 'Yes.' You will also need to perform a technical task in order for the reports to show data. This involves your web designers taking some special code that Google provides and putting it in the Receipt or Thank You page after the transaction has been completed. You can point your web designers in the right direction by getting them to visit www.google.com/support/analytics/bin/answer.py?hl=en&answer=72289 or search Google Analytics' help database for 'required ecommerce fields' and also 'how do I track ecommerce transactions.'

One word of caution: Do make sure that you have tested that Analytics is producing the correct information. You will need a test account with your shopping cart vendor (WorldPay, PayPal, etc.) to make sure that the data is being correctly displayed on the reports. You may well require your web designers' assistance especially if your shopping cart has been developed by them.

If you have a search facility on your website, you can track how people are using it. Again you may need some input from your web designers here, depending on how the search has been set up – but if you have one then you should certainly track it!

Goals

Analytics allows you to track specific goals for your website. A goal is achieved when your visitor takes a specific form of action you wish them to take. There are three to choose from:

1.   URL Destination
2.   Time on Site
3.   Pages/Visit

Fig 4 is a screenshot showing you a new Goal:

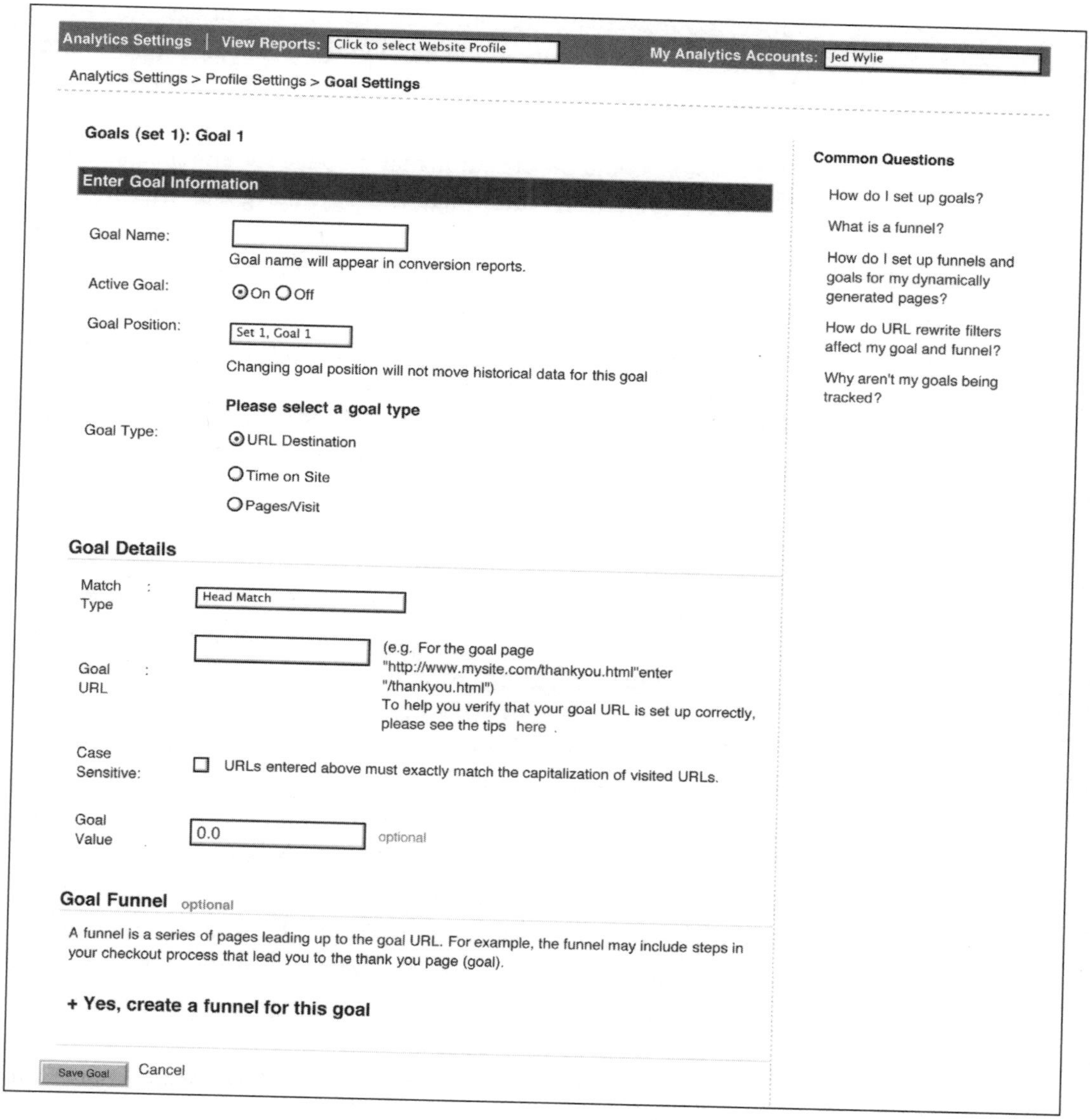

Analytics Settings | View Reports: [Click to select Website Profile]

My Analytics Accounts: [Jed Wylie]

Analytics Settings > Profile Settings > **Goal Settings**

Goals (set 1): Goal 1

Enter Goal Information

Goal Name:
[   ]
Goal name will appear in conversion reports.

Active Goal:
⊙ On ○ Off

Goal Position:
[Set 1, Goal 1]
Changing goal position will not move historical data for this goal

Please select a goal type

Goal Type:
⊙ URL Destination

○ Time on Site

○ Pages/Visit

Goal Details

Match Type :
[Head Match]

Goal URL :
[   ]
(e.g. For the goal page
"http://www.mysite.com/thankyou.html" enter
"/thankyou.html")
To help you verify that your goal URL is set up correctly,
please see the tips here .

Case Sensitive:
☐ URLs entered above must exactly match the capitalization of visited URLs.

Goal Value .
[0.0   ] optional

Goal Funnel optional

A funnel is a series of pages leading up to the goal URL. For example, the funnel may include steps in
your checkout process that lead you to the thank you page (goal).

+ Yes, create a funnel for this goal

[Save Goal] Cancel

Common Questions

How do I set up goals?

What is a funnel?

How do I set up funnels and
goals for my dynamically
generated pages?

How do URL rewrite filters
affect my goal and funnel?

Why aren't my goals being
tracked?

**Fig 4 Setting up the
different types of goals
for your domain**

The 'Goal Name' and 'Active Goal' fields are self-explanatory but we're interested in the 'Goal Type' field and the three choices available. Let's now look at each of these in turn.

URL Destination

A typical goal for a website is to get the visitor to land on a specific page. Often these are the pages that signify the user has completed an action on the website. For example, when a user completes an enquiry form they'll be taken to the Thank You page – visiting that page represents the completion of one of your website's goals. If you run a lead-generation site then the goal could be completing an enquiry form. If you run an ecommerce store then a goal may be for a user to see the Receipt or Order Confirmation page. Or the goal could be the confirmation page for an email signup.

Once you have identified the various goals you want to achieve, you can then enter the URL for the pages that represent the completion of those goals in the 'Goal URL' field.

You can also identify the value that achieving one of those goals represents to you. Let's say that you know for each new subscriber to your e-mail marketing list your business will generate £5 of revenue. You can then enter this into the 'Goal Value' field and Analytics will calculate the goal value in your reports. For example, if each customer nets you £100 and you convert one in five leads you know that each lead is worth £20 to you. This then becomes your Goal Value.

A note on 'funnels.' In most instances it is unlikely that your visitor will land on your 'goal page' straightaway. They will typically have navigated their way through your site, seeing several pages, before eventually arriving at your goal. A funnel is a route that the visitor could take in order for your goal to be achieved. Let's take a simple example. Imagine that on your home page you have a link to a membership club that you have started. That link takes you to a page which describes all the value and benefits of that club. At the bottom of the page is a form which people can fill in to join. Once they click on the Submit button they are taken to the Thank You page, and the goal is completed. The two pages that would make up the funnel are the home page and the membership page.

The number of steps in your funnel will typically reflect the complexity of the goal. For example, if you're asking someone to buy from your site then there are probably many more pages that they would need to visit before completing the transaction (category page, products page, basket, credit card details, etc.).

So when you have set up your funnel(s) the 'Funnel Visualisation' report will tell you how many people completed the funnel, how many abandoned the funnel and where they went (page 329.)

Time on Site
Time on Site is an interesting goal to set up because it helps you

understand how much information people are absorbing and whether they are interested in your website's content. This is particularly relevant if you are running a news-style website, a forum, a blog, or similar.

Pages/Visit

If you want to measure the depth to which a visitor is using your site then you can set a goal for the number of page visits. If a browser is visiting a good number of pages then that indicates they are both engaged with the site and demonstrating a more considered interest in what you have to offer. For example, you would naturally expect this to be higher for news and article sites than more classical business websites.

You can specify up to 20 goals (four sets of five goals). That should be enough. However, if you want to set up more, the easiest (though most cumbersome) solution is to set up a new profile and add the additional goals in to your second profile. Alternatively, you could try to combine goals if you can see some commonality between them. For example, if you've got ten Thank You pages all essentially measuring the same key objective then you can consider them as one goal.

Filters

The final element to editing your profile information is filters. Filters allow you to exclude or include data in your reports and in doing so weed out or focus on relevant data. Below is a screenshot for setting up a new filter:

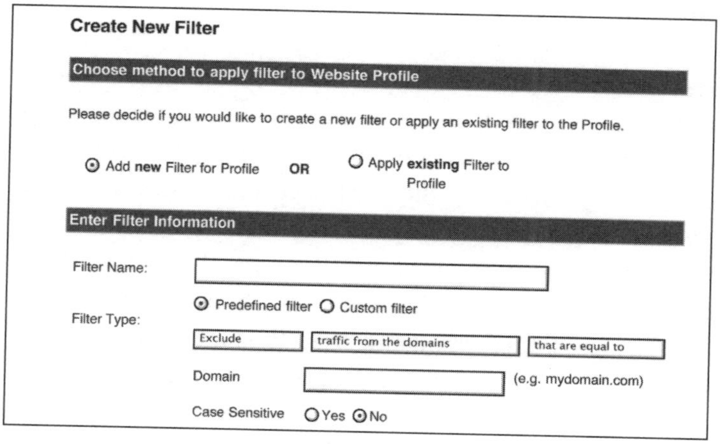

Create New Filter

Choose method to apply filter to Website Profile

Please decide if you would like to create a new filter or apply an existing filter to the Profile.

⊙ Add **new** Filter for Profile   **OR**   ○ Apply **existing** Filter to Profile

Enter Filter Information

Filter Name: [   ]

Filter Type: ⊙ Predefined filter ○ Custom filter

Exclude | traffic from the domains | that are equal to

Domain [   ] (e.g. mydomain.com)

Case Sensitive ○ Yes ⊙ No

Fig 5 Setting up a filter

There are two filter types, either predefined or custom. Let's take a look at each in turn.

Predefined Filters

Analytics gives you three predefined filters which are very useful:

1. 'Exclude: traffic from the domains...' – here you can exclude traffic coming from a specific website such as a sister company or traffic coming from your own domain.

2. 'Exclude: traffic from the IP addresses...' – here you can exclude a specific IP address or range of IP addresses. This is useful if you want to exclude visits from your company's computers. You can find out what the IP address of your computer is by going to www.whatsmyip.org. If you are on a large network you will probably want to ask you IT manager what the IP ranges are so you can exclude them. Some ISPs will change your IP address from time to time so you can either:
   a. Keep checking to see if it's changed
   b. Request a static IP (one that won't change) from your ISP

   You can find out more about excluding your own traffic from the Analytics reports at www.google.com/support/analytics/bin/answer.py?answer=55481

3. 'Exclude: traffic to the subdirectories...' – here you can exclude particular subdirectories from the reports such as www.mydomain.co.uk/secret-files.

You can also set Analytics to 'Include only...', effectively reversing the above.

Custom Filters

If you have a specific requirement then click on 'Custom filter' and you'll be presented with lots of options allowing you to exclude or include specific data such as the city the visitor is from, a particular screen resolution, a specific page and so on.

One useful filter is 'Search and Replace'. If you have long, unreadable URLs on your website you can choose 'Request URL' from the 'Filter Field' selection and enter the long URL in 'Search String' and then enter a more meaningful one in 'Replace String'.

This will make your reports a lot easier to read.

Remember that any filter you apply is for the *entire* web profile, which will most likely be for one domain but could be multiple domains if that's what you specified during the set-up.

The Dashboard

Once you've set up your profile you can return to your Analytics home page and click on 'View report' for the profile you wish to review. This will take you to the Dashboard. Below is a screenshot:

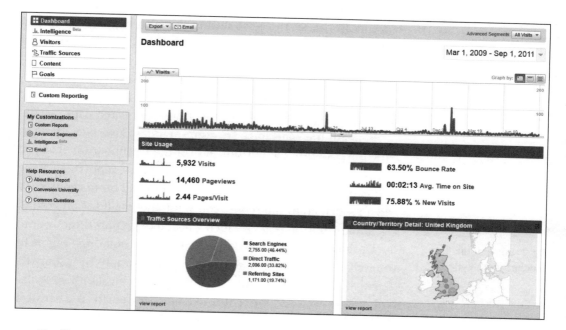

You'll notice on the top right hand-side you can alter your Settings, access My Account, request Help, and Sign Out.

On the orange bar beneath you can alter the Analytics Settings for this profile, jump to different reports with View Reports, and, if you have multiple accounts, jump between them using My Analytics Accounts on the far right-hand side.

Moving on to the body of the page you can see the date range (top right) which you can adjust by clicking on the down arrow next to it. Modifying the date range will show you only data for that time period. (Interestingly, if you check the box 'Compare to Past' you can specify a time period with which to compare against your date range. This is great if you want to compare Christmas

Fig 6 The Analytics Dashboard

traffic from the previous year, for example. However, the time-frames have to be the same – so a week with a week or a month with a month – obviously you can't compare a day with a year.)

Using comparison data is critical for comparing the performance of your various marketing activities. Let's imagine that you run a radio advert in your hometown. It runs three times a day, seven days a week. You would want to compare the number of visits, their locations, the times they visited the site, etc., with a similar timeframe prior to the advert running. This helps you understand whether your radio advertising was successful. (When you link in the idea of goal-setting this also begins to help you understand the value of your offline marketing in relation to your online goals.)

Moving down you can see a graph which indicates the activity of that report (in this case, Visits). Below that is the Site Usage area containing 'sparklines' – mini graphs of related data.

Beneath the sparklines are some standard overview reports. Now the cool thing about this part of the Dashboard is that you can move reports around (click and drag), delete reports (click the 'x' box on the top right of each panel), and add more reports. To add a report, go to the report you want and you'll see an 'Add to Dashboard' button (Fig 7), which will add the report directly onto the Dashboard. You'll also notice that you can email any report to yourself (or anyone else for that matter) simply by using the 'Email' button at the top of each report; you can set up a regular schedule or even add the report to an existing email. You can also Export the reports to PDF, CSV and XML.

Fig 7 Some of the nice touches in Analytics

Customise the Dashboard to show the key metrics you identified at the beginning of this chapter, and so give yourself an at-a-glance view of the information critical to you.

■ THE ANATOMY OF REPORTS

Each report, while containing different data, is presented in broadly the same format. Clicking on each of the menu headings on the left-hand side (except 'Intelligence') will take you to an Overview page, which gives you headline information of the contents of that section (Fig 8).

You'll find all the remaining detailed reports under the main section. Fig 9 is an example of a standard report. You can see the ever-present timeline at the top and the table below. You'll notice that at the top of the table you can see headline information such as 'Average Time on Site' and the 'Bounce Rate.' Beneath these is a table with individual lines of data you can drill into by double-clicking.

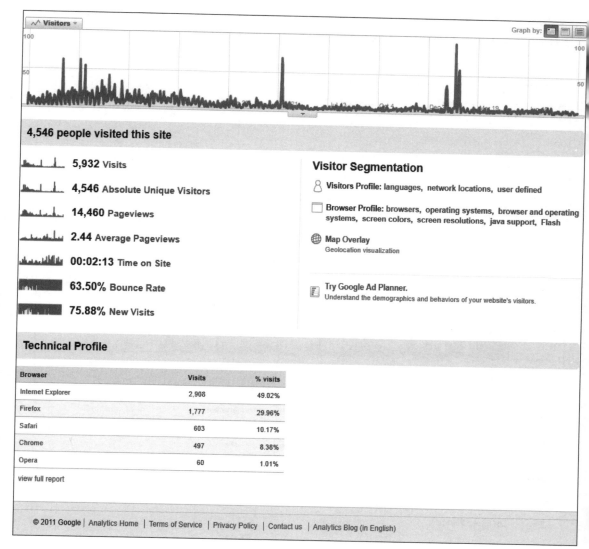

Fig 8 A standard Overview page

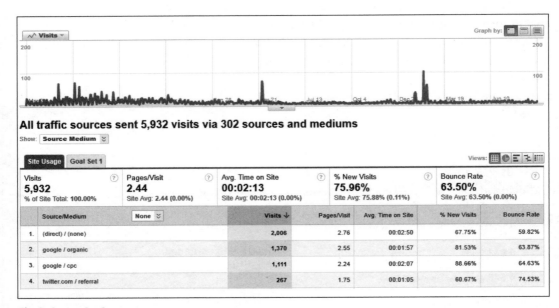

Fig 9 A standard report
page

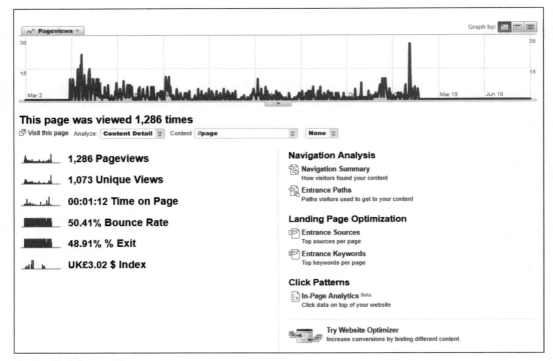

Fig 10 A page-specific
report

I've chosen the Top Content report and clicked on 'Home Page' to see specific data about that page. The resulting report can be seen in Fig 10.

You can get even more information about this page by choosing the various options down the right-hand side (these are replicated in the 'Analyze' drop-down. You can also click on the 'Content' drop-down to choose another item from the top ten pages so you don't have to keep switching back and forth between pages. Finally the drop-down next to Content gives you segments of the data including: keyword, where visitors are from, their technical details (browser type, connection speed) and so forth. Watch out for these drop-downs as they can give you access to more information. However, they're only displayed if it's relevant to the report.

One final but useful item to note is the 'Visit This Page' icon and text next to the 'Analyze' pull-down – sometimes you'll find it necessary to have a look at the page whose data you are reviewing. Also if you ever see the icon next to it in a table you can click on it to take you to the relevant page.

Now you've got a sense of the interface, we'll discuss each of the reports in turn. Let's begin with your visitors.

■ VISITOR REPORTS

The visitor reports give you information about the type of visitor, their loyalty to your site, their location and technical status. You can use these reports to help you identify the characteristic segments that make up your visitors. For example, how many people are viewing your website from a mobile device? Are you getting significant numbers of people from one particular location? Do very few of your visitors return to your website?

Map Overlay

Sample question: Is our marketing effective in specific locations?

The Map Overlay report tells you what parts of the world people are visiting your website from. You can drill down to various levels of detail simply by clicking on the relevant country in the map. (I clicked on the UK to bring up the screenshot in Fig 11.)

You can change the 'Detail Level' for the data by selecting 'City | Country/Territory | Sub-Continent Region | Continent' from the main report page. This updates the table beneath.

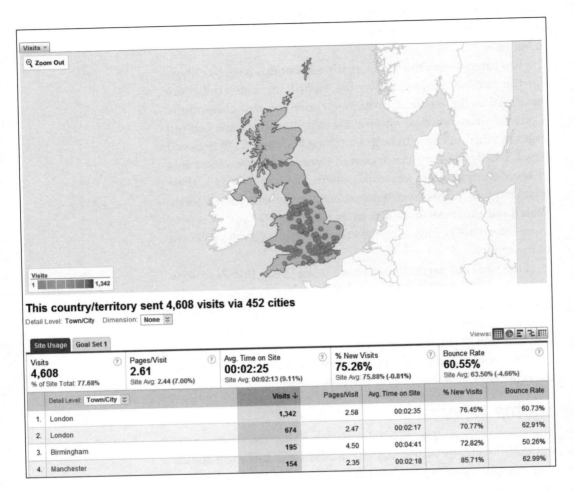

This country/territory sent 4,608 visits via 452 cities

Detail Level: Town/City   Dimension: None ⌄

		Visits ↓	Pages/Visit	Avg. Time on Site	% New Visits	Bounce Rate
1.	London	1,342	2.58	00:02:35	76.45%	60.73%
2.	London	674	2.47	00:02:17	70.77%	62.91%
3.	Birmingham	195	4.50	00:04:41	72.82%	50.26%
4.	Manchester	154	2.35	00:02:18	85.71%	62.99%

**Fig 11 The Visitors Map
Overlay report**

If you are a geographically bound business (let's say you supply catering equipment for local events) then it might be useful to identify local traffic coming to your website. This report could also give you an insight into hotspots of traffic coming from specific areas. For example, suppose you're exhibiting at the National Exhibition Centre and you notice that during the exhibition lots of people are accessing your website from that location. You could then modify your website to offer a giveaway at your stand, directions to your stand, a link to Foursquare (foursquare.com), events going on at your stand during the day, and so forth.

New vs Returning

Sample question: Do I get more signups to my email marketing from new visitors or returning visitors?

The new-vs-returning report is particularly useful. It defines for you the number of new visitors to your site versus those that have already visited at least once before. Return visitors indicate that your website is enjoyable, trusted, useful and has a high perceived value. (This could be a function of other marketing activities, for example, driving your existing customer subscriber-base to your website.)

An interesting nuance is to see how many new visitors completed your goals vis-a-vis returning visitors.

Fig 12 Report showing how many new vs returning visitors completed a goal

In the screenshot above you'll notice that I have clicked on the 'Goal Set 1' tab and selected 'Goal Conversion' from the second column. Now I can see that the vast majority of conversions arise from new visitors. At first glance this may seem counterintuitive. However, the results are dependent on the type of website you are running. In this case, this website has a large amount of pay-per-click traffic focused directly on signup landing pages. However, this report also reveals that nearly 20 per cent signed up after a second look.

Languages

Sample question: Could there be a specific interest in our business from people whose first language is different from ours?

This report defines the language in use on your visitor's browser. This can give you an insight into your visitor's country of origin. It can also help identify opportunities for you, especially in countries which have many diverse languages, such as America or Switzerland. Knowing your visitor's language will help you identify further potential marketing opportunities.

Visitor Trending

These reports give you a stronger insight into how your visitors are behaving on your site once they get there.

Visits

Sample question: Is there a specific time/day that we should be focusing our online pay-per-click campaign?

The Visits report enables you to see the volume of traffic coming to your site by hour, day, week and month.

The results of the report are fairly self-explanatory but if you consider the question above then they can become rather useful. Imagine that you are an ecommerce store selling home furnishings. You might notice that you naturally acquire traffic in the evenings between 6 p.m. and 9 p.m. You may also notice that Sundays have higher traffic levels than Saturdays. From this you could deduce that more people are actively looking for your type of products at those times. The next step would be to focus your online marketing at the productive times and throttle back on what you spend in the remaining times.

Absolute Unique Visitors

Sample question: Can I get an accurate picture of the actual number of people visiting my site?

This report effectively filters out those people who have visited your site more than once, giving you a more realistic impression of the number of individuals visiting your site. You can use this figure to input into your other ROI equations and gain a more accurate result than if it were based on all visits. For example, your site may attract 1,000 visits monthly but only 800 of those are unique. If you are calculating customer ROI, let's say, it would be more accurate to use the unique visits rather than the total number of visits.

There are a couple of additional factors worth considering. Firstly your date range may affect the results. For example, if somebody visits your website every day for a week then as long as your date range includes the entire week they visited your site they will be marked as one absolute unique visitor. If your date range included only half the week and you compared it with a date range of the other half then the same person would be counted twice. The second criterion is that they visited your site from the same computer.

Pageviews and Average Pageviews and Depth of Visit

Sample question: Are people taking a really good look around our website or are they just skimming and disappearing?

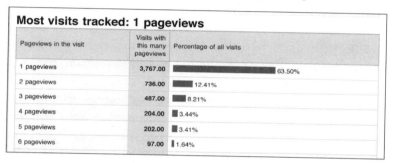

Pageviews in the visit	Visits with this many pageviews	Percentage of all visits
Most visits tracked: 1 pageviews		
1 pageviews	**3,767.00**	63.50%
2 pageviews	**736.00**	12.41%
3 pageviews	**487.00**	8.21%
4 pageviews	**204.00**	3.44%
5 pageviews	**202.00**	3.41%
6 pageviews	**97.00**	1.64%

Fig 13 Depth of Visit report

Pageviews represent the number of times pages have been viewed on your website. Apologies for the obvious statement but views can be confused with visits – a visit is a session which includes multiple pageviews. Ideally, each visit should result in multiple views because you'll typically want your visitor to navigate around several pages on your website. Again, both the 'Pageviews' and 'Average Pageviews' reports allow you to review the information by hour, day, week and month. However, the 'Average Pageviews' report is worth reviewing: this tells you just how interested people are in the material you are providing. A greater number of pageviews, we can assume, is related to a sustained interest in what you have to offer. You can also see if there is a correlation between the 'depth' of visit and specific marketing activities you've got going on. For example, if you've just been interviewed on the local BBC radio station you might expect the average pageview depth to increase immediately afterwards as people want to find out more about you from your website.

Now compare this with the number of pageviews you would expect when giving away a free report. It would be perfectly normal to assume that because you are taking people to a landing page where they can sign up for specific information, their focus is going to be on getting that information and reading it rather than reviewing your website. In a sense, it could be argued that the more specific the intention of the visitor, the fewer pageviews they make.

You can find out the exact breakdown of your visitors' depth of visit by choosing the report under 'Visitor Loyalty' called 'Depth of Visit.'

Visitor Loyalty

This group of reports helps you identify how your returning visitors are behaving.

Loyalty

Sample question: Are we engaging our visitors through our website's content on an ongoing basis?

Here we can see how many times return visitors, erm, return. If you can see that your visitors are returning a healthy number of times then that's a positive reflection on your marketing, brand penetration, perceived value to the visitor and so on. If you find that the vast majority of visitors are leaving on their first visit, never to return, then that would indicate there is a huge opportunity for you to address these people by improving your website's offering, like introducing email marketing, for example. While you can never please all of the people all of the time, every attempt you can make to minimise the one-hit wonders will increase your return on investment.

Recency

Sample question: How regularly should we update our website's content?

This report enables you to identify, of those who returned, the time period between visits. This can be useful if you are trying to identify how frequently you should update the information on your website. For example, if you find that most people who return do so within one week, there would be little point updating your home page any more frequently. Conversely, if you are not updating your site as often as people are returning to it then people may perceive it to be stale.

Length of Visit
Sample question: How interested are our visitors in what we have to say?

This is measured in seconds (somewhat unhelpfully as, off the top of my head, I have to calculate that 1,800 seconds is three hours when reviewing this report).

Again this provides us with more proof of how interesting and valuable your website is perceived to be. Essentially, the longer people are on the site, the more attention they are paying to what you have to say.

Browser Capabilities

This section (and the two report groupings beneath, i.e. network properties and mobile) are of particular interest to you if you are about to redesign your website or are in the process of evaluating its technical performance.

Browsers, Operating Systems, Browsers and OS
Sample question: Does our website look perfect under all conditions?

These three reports in combination tell you specific information about the types of systems your visitors are using to view your website. Let's begin with browser software.

As you know there are many different browsers and each of them has, over time, released various versions. Unfortunately, not everybody has the latest version of the browser, which means that your website must be compliant with several versions of the same browser, at the same time. The browser report is thus particularly useful in identifying whether you are receiving significant traffic volume from a specific browser type for which your website has not been optimised. The easy way to check this out is to first ask your web designers precisely what browsers they optimised your website for; and secondly, use third-party software – such as Browsercam (www.browsercam.com), for example – to assess your website across a variety of types and versions. If it looks 'broken' (i.e. the layout is jiggered) then you know you've got a problem which your web designers need to resolve.

Below is a screenshot of the Browsers report, which details the breakdown of browser software in use by your visitors:

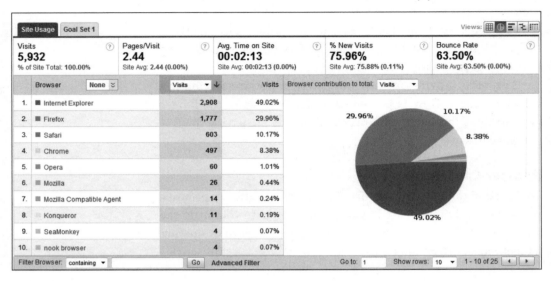

Fig 14 The Browsers report

If you click on the browser name, Analytics will show you the version numbers of that browser being used to you view your website. As you can see from the screenshot below, the vast majority of people are viewing this website in Internet Explorer version 7.0 – two versions behind the current one. By reviewing Analytics, we can determine whether it is worth investing in making the website compliant with a particular browser version.

Fig 15 Drill-down into the Browsers report showing the version numbers of Internet Explorer

	Browser Version	None	Visits	Visits
1.	7.0		1,229	42.26%
2.	8.0		1,121	38.55%
3.	6.0		512	17.61%
4.	9.0		46	1.58%

Typically you would expect browser testing and compliance to be done by your web designers. So, this is information to feed back to them so they can ensure your website looks perfect under all conditions.

You can extend exactly the same principle to the Operating Systems report and the Browsers and OS Report.

Screen Resolution

Sample question: Are we making best use of the real estate on our visitor's monitors?

Another design consideration is the screen resolution that your visitors view your website in. Although studies suggest that the majority of people use screen resolutions of 1024 x 768 pixels or greater, it's best not to make assumptions. Use this report to define the actual resolutions in use.

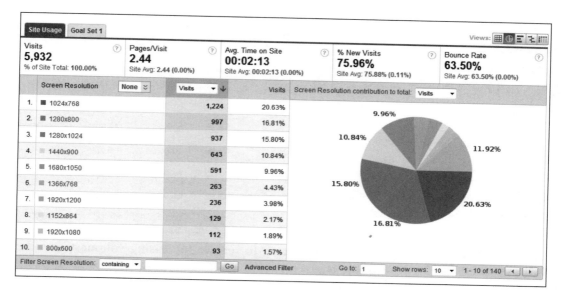

If your current website is a few years old it may well have been designed for screen resolutions of 800 x 600. If you now notice that very few people are viewing your website in that resolution (and you are planning an upgrade), you can design the site from the outset with the more typical resolutions in mind.

Fig 16 Screen Resolution report

Mobile > Mobile Devices

Sample question: How much 'on the move' traffic are we receiving and should we optimise our content for that market?

More and more handheld and mobile devices are now able to view websites, meaning that there is a strong possibility that yours will be viewed by one of them at some point soon, if it hasn't already. This report helps you identify just how many people are viewing your website on the move. This is important as you may need to get your web designers to format your site specifically for these devices. However, you don't have to do this until you feel you are receiving enough traffic to warrant it.

Site Usage	Goal Set 1				Views:	
Visits	**Pages/Visit**	**Avg. Time on Site**		**% New Visits**		**Bounce Rate**
88	**1.92**	**00:01:23**		**93.18%**		**67.05%**
% of Site Total: 1.48%	Site Avg: 2.44 (-21.22%)	Site Avg: 00:02:13 (-37.66%)		Site Avg: 75.88% (22.81%)		Site Avg: 63.50% (5.58%)

	Operating System	None	Visits	Pages/Visit	Avg. Time on Site	% New Visits	Bounce Rate
1.	iPhone		42	1.60	00:01:04	90.48%	78.57%
2.	Android		14	1.79	00:02:12	100.00%	57.14%
3.	iPad		13	3.46	00:02:06	100.00%	30.77%
4.	BlackBerry		8	1.25	00:00:51	87.50%	87.50%
5.	Windows		3	1.00	00:00:00	66.67%	100.00%
6.	iPod		3	1.33	00:00:32	100.00%	66.67%
7.	Samsung		2	5.50	00:04:46	100.00%	0.00%
8.	SymbianOS		2	1.50	00:00:33	100.00%	50.00%

Fig 17 The Mobile Devices report

If you are starting to receive increasing volumes of traffic from this sector then you might want to pitch directly to them. For example, let's say you run a restaurant. You're getting 10 per cent of your traffic from mobile sources. This would indicate that people are out and about looking for a restaurant to eat in at that moment. Your website could detect that your visitor is using an iPhone and pop-up a special offer, 'Show us your iPhone and get a free desert tonight only!' Remember that the more relevant and focused the pitch, the more likely the return.

■ TRAFFIC SOURCES REPORTS

This suite of reports helps you get a handle on where your visitors are coming from. The Dashboard gives you the usual at-a-glance metrics but the real fun is in the following reports.

Direct Traffic

Sample question: How successful is our offline marketing in getting people to visit our website?

This is the total number of people who typed your web address directly into their browser, clicked on a Bookmark link or clicked on a link in an email. This can sometimes be seen as a function of how well your branding is recognised in the market but could equally relate to offline marketing factors such as an advert in a paper, flyers posted through people's letterboxes, direct mail marketing and so forth.

Fig 18 Direct Traffic report

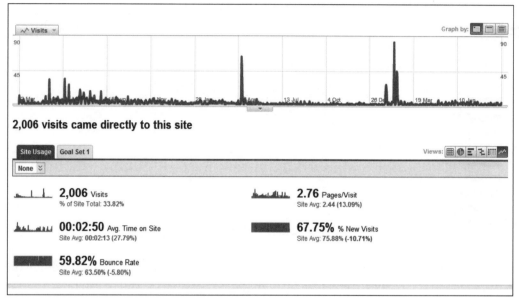

Referring Sites

Sample question: Who is giving us lots of good-quality traffic?

When your traffic visits your website via a link from other websites they are known as referring sites. This report gives you an insight into who is sending you traffic and its overall quality. Let's consider a few things.

Firstly, the number of referring sites is both a reflection of your SEO activity and the quality of your content. (As you know, the better the content, the more widely known and linked-to your website will become.) You can also detect the quality of the traffic by reviewing the 'Avg Time on Site' and 'Bounce Rate.' You're looking for visitors spending a long time on your site and a low Bounce Rate. If you spot a referring site which is sending you lots of poor-quality traffic, then review the site and its link to you: Can you get it changed to be more relevant? Can you ask to have some qualifying copy around the link? Can you change the link to refer to a more appropriate page? Would you want it removed?

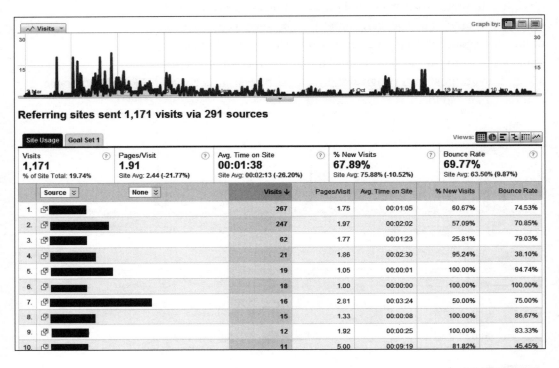

Fig 19 Referring Sites report

Conversely, if you spot a referring site which is sending you lots of great traffic, it might be possible for you to establish a more formal relationship with them. Take a look at Social Connections, (page 279 onwards in the previous chapter) to give you some ideas.

Search Engines

Sample question: Where should we focus our SEO activity?

This report details where your search engine traffic came from. You'll probably find that in the majority of cases the top referrer will be Google, followed by Yahoo! and Bing. However, what's more important is not the top players (because that will be heavily influenced by your SEO activity) but those beneath. For example, are you getting a goodly amount from a less well known search engine, is a particular search engine generating a lot of Goal conversions (click on the tab next to 'Site Usage'), does one search engine have a particularly low Bounce Rate, and so forth.

You can click on any of the listings to drill down to find out what keywords were typed into the search engine. You can then map those against any Goal conversions.

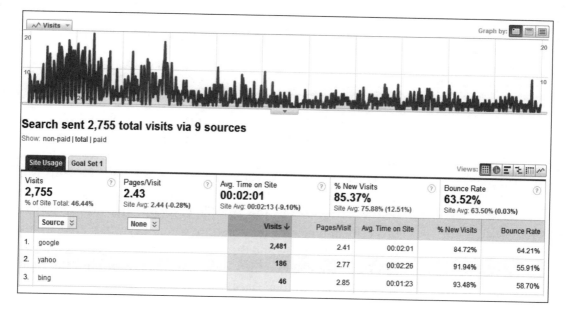

Search sent 2,755 total visits via 9 sources

Source	Visits ↓	Pages/Visit	Avg. Time on Site	% New Visits	Bounce Rate
1. google	2,481	2.41	00:02:01	84.72%	64.21%
2. yahoo	186	2.77	00:02:26	91.94%	55.91%
3. bing	46	2.85	00:01:23	93.48%	58.70%

If you can see good traffic with solid conversions coming from a particular search engine you can then focus some of your SEO activity on that source.

Fig 20 Search Engine Traffic report

Keywords

Sample question: What keywords are earning us the most money?

Here you can see what your visitors typed into the search engines in order to access your website. If you are running a Google AdWords campaign then you can select 'non-paid' just above the tabs. This filters out any paid-for keywords, leaving you with only the organic keywords.

You should instantly get a feel from the top few keywords what's driving the traffic to your site. Scan each keyword in turn and assess its Bounce Rate and Goal Conversion. Ultimately, it's the latter which counts but certainly you should do everything to try and reduce the Bounce Rate.

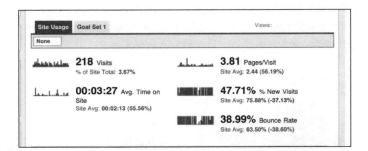

Fig 21 Keyword report showing data for a specific keyword

Next, click on a keyword and select from the Segment drop-down under 'Site Usage,' 'Landing Page.' This then tells you those pages which your visitors landed on using this keyword. Next click on the Goal Set tab to reveal your Goal conversion data. This will then tell you how much money you made from each landing page that was triggered by this specific keyword. This now gives you two critical pieces of information: which keywords are earning you the most money, and the landing pages responsible. Now you can focus your SEO efforts even more tightly around the right keywords and landing pages.

CONTENT REPORTS

Firstly, well done for getting this far. You probably need a cup of tea, coffee or perhaps something stronger by now! I realise that this is quite intense and quick-fire stuff but stick with it because I can guarantee there will be some nuggets of gold lying around in the data – you've just got to spot them. Let us proceed to the last third of this chapter.

Content reports analyse your website's pages according to their content and can give you some useful metrics with respect to site performance. The overview dashboard does the usual job of synthesising some of the more relevant data for you.

Top Content/Content by Title

Sample question: [Exception: Here you need to compile several questions – I have provided a few examples in the text below.]

This report simply details a number of key metrics per page. Initially you see the report showing the pages with the most to least Pageviews. Most of the time you'll find that your home page will be in the top three but what is of particular interest are the other pages in the top 20. Begin your analysis by looking for any

Content Performance					Views:	
Pageviews **14,460** % of Site Total: 100.00%	**Unique Pageviews** **11,595** % of Site Total: 100.00%	**Avg. Time on Page** **00:01:33** Site Avg: 00:01:33 (0.00%)	**Bounce Rate** **63.50%** Site Avg: 63.50% (0.00%)	**% Exit** **41.02%** Site Avg: 41.02% (0.00%)	**$ Index** **UK£7.85** Site Avg: UK£3.00 (161.63%)	

	Page	None	Pageviews	Unique Pageviews	Avg. Time on Page	Bounce Rate	% Exit	$ Index
1.	⬚	▉	1,286	1,073	00:01:12	50.41%	48.91%	UK£3.02
2.	⬚	▉	1,060	993	00:02:50	83.64%	65.09%	UK£2.44
3.	⬚	▉	678	510	00:01:20	42.16%	32.89%	UK£3.44
4.	⬚	▉	606	440	00:00:48	21.62%	11.88%	UK£4.29
5.	⬚	▉	461	334	00:01:21	56.34%	31.89%	UK£4.04

oddities; for example, if you spot pages that are being seen more times than you'd expect, these indicate content that your visitors are interested in.

Fig 22 The Top Content report

Next look for how long visitors are staying on particular pages. Are they leaving before they've had a chance to absorb the content? Are they staying longer than you'd expect? In either case what is it that's causing that effect? (As an aside, a quick way to tell how much of your video content is being viewed is to compare the length of the video with the average time on the page – if you have a five minute video but people are only spending an average of two minutes on the page, then you know that they're probably not seeing the entire video.)

Bounce Rate is a big factor to review here. Using Google's own language, 'Bounce Rate is the percentage of single-page visits or visits in which the person left your site from the entrance (landing) page.' And: 'Use this metric to measure visit quality.' So, a low Bounce Rate indicates that the page is relevant and interesting to your visitor and a higher bounce rate indicates the reverse.

You can also combine the Bounce Rate with the % Exit to give you a broad idea of page quality. For example, a high Bounce Rate and % Exit would be a pretty catastrophic sign for the page quality! However, if you are taking your visitors to a 'single action' page (like a name squeeze page) then you would expect to have a high Bounce and % Exit rate. In such a situation, you should use the Goals reports to identify the performance of the page.

Another useful metric is to see how your visitors got to the page and where they went next. To do this, click on the page you want to analyse, then click on 'Navigation Summary' and you'll see a report which details the top ten pages seen prior to and after the one you're assessing. You can also see how many visitors entered or exited at this page versus those that were passing through it. Again you are looking for patterns here: Was there a high proportion of people who went to another page which detailed further information? Did the visitors go to a sales page having been motivated by this one? Did they come from a sales page but veer off to this one, and so forth.

If you see the same page as both the entrance and exit page, don't get too worried – it could be because someone refreshed the page or clicked a page link that refers to itself (like clicking on the home page link if you're already on the home page).

Top Landing Pages/Top Exit Pages

Sample question: What did we do to make our visitors leave our website?

Your top landing pages will be typically representative of your marketing efforts: AdWords landing pages, pages that you've specifically referenced on other sites or offline marketing, pages you have Search Engine Optimised, and so on.

Fig 23 Exit Pages report

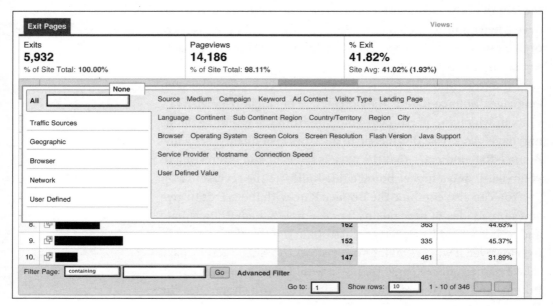

However, it's the top exit pages that are probably of more interest, as they help you identify problem pages. So, just why are they leaving? Well, you can help identify these potential trends by segmenting the 'Top Exit Pages' report. To do this, click on the 'None' drop-down in the Page column and select the additional metric you wish to segment the report by. For example, you might wish to see if a particular keyword or traffic source is driving the wrong traffic to this page. Or possibly you may have a high proportion of people who are from another country hitting the page and discovering it's in a language they can't read.

Using the segmentation facility, you can discover the reasons driving people to leave your website.

In-Page Analytics

Sample question: Where are people clicking on our website, and can we improve our visitor experience by improving our design?

This is a genuinely fascinating utility as it shows you where your visitors are clicking on your website. This gives you an immediate sense of whether the design is optimised. Initially you will see your home page displayed with 'balloons' of data indicating the percentage of clicks made and where. You'll also notice a red bar stating how many of the clicks were made below the fold of the screen as it looks in this window. As you scroll down your website you will see this figure change. To the left are some standard metrics to help support your analysis. You can navigate around your website as normal, reviewing the data as you go.

This provides you with arguably the clearest indication of how your visitors are navigating around your site and what's getting clicked on and what's being ignored. For example, if everyone's clicking on your video but no one's clicking on the call to action at the bottom of the page, put the call to action at the end of the video. There's lots you can deduce from this report but it will all be highly specific to your website. I suggest that you look at each page in turn and simply ask yourself, 'Why are they clicking there?'

As a quick aside Analytics does not differentiate between links that go to the same page. So, two links on the page that go to the same page will have the same data.

■ GOALS REPORTS

This section of Analytics reports on the Goals you created when you were setting up your Analytics account.

Once you click on Goals it will give you the obligatory Dashboard dedicated to the Goals you have set up. In the example below there is one Goal which determines whether a visitor has signed up to the website's email marketing. The screenshot also shows the drop-down list of different Goal metrics you can choose: Goal Conversions, Goal Conversion Rate, Total Goal Value and Goal1 Completions.

Fig 24 Goal Conversions overview page

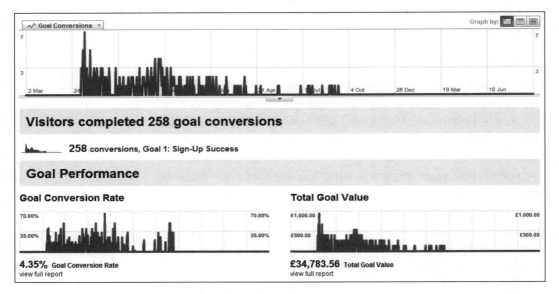

Total Conversions

Sample question: How many visitors are becoming leads or customers and is there a trend?

This report describes the raw number of conversions across your site on any particular hour, day, week or month.

It gives you an immediate insight into the progress of your Goals over time and helps you spot conversion patterns. For example, it's clear from the example above that the conversions become more sporadic towards the end of the graph which indicates that something has changed to reduce the sign-up rate. You could then pin down the dates of certain changes in the process and map them onto the graph to see which change caused the slowdown. You could also do the exact same analysis to identify

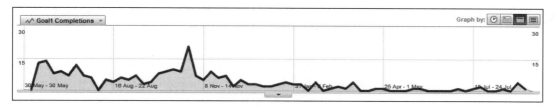

what caused the peak at the beginning of the timeline.

This report doesn't give you the specifics of what's going right or wrong in your marketing campaign but it does give you an indication as to the overall trends and significant changes in conversion patterns.

Fig 25 The timeline graph from the Total Conversions report

Goal Conversion Rate

Sample question: What percentage of our visitors are becoming leads or customers, and how does that map onto our marketing activity?

The Goal Conversion Rate gives you a similar metric but describes it as a percentage of the total number of visits (or more accurately, browsing sessions). This can be fascinating since it gives you a sense of just how successful your site is at converting visitors into leads and customers.

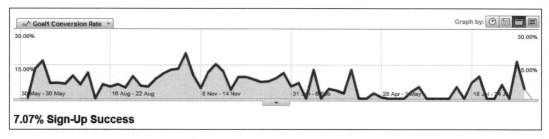

Underneath the graph you can see the average number of sign-ups as a percentage of the total visits. This gives you an at-a-glance idea of how well your website is performing. In our above example the average is 6.87 per cent, which may seem low, but the Internet average is about 1 per cent. However, don't be beguiled by the figure; look to your ROI first. For example, you might expect a lower conversion rate if you are selling a high-value item that yields a high ROI. Conversely, if you are selling a low-value item and your Goal conversions are low then this would indicate that more attention needs to be paid to converting your visitors into

Fig 26 The Conversion Rate report timeline

customers. Remember, it's ROI that determines whether the sign-up success percentage is acceptable or not.

Interestingly, you might find that your sign-up rates changed at certain points along the timeline. When you spot sharp changes or notice emerging trends, you should identify exactly what was happening with your marketing to promote such a change.

Reverse Goal Path

Sample question: How can I control and influence our visitors so that they complete our goals quickly?

This report is simple: it shows the path people took to the conversion point. Firstly you can pick the Goal you want to review by selecting the 'Select Goal' drop-down menu. What you then see in the table is the path your visitors took to get to your goal. This report reveals which route is the most effective and, by extension, tells you where you should be focusing your efforts.

In the example in Fig 27, the most effective route in is straight off the home page to a landing page that is all about the benefits of joining the email newsletter. This is, in fact, twice as effective as the path beneath and gives us a clear indication as to where we should be focusing our conversion improvements. For example, knowing that this page does well in converting visitors might then lead us to trying a split-test on the page – improving the copy, repositioning the sign-up form, adding a video or audio message, and so forth.

This report is a great tool to gather insights into the best and worst routes to conversion and helps you take steps to enhance the best routes and block off or force a re-routing of the worst. For example, if you spot that some of your visitors are getting to your

Fig 27 Paths taken to conversion

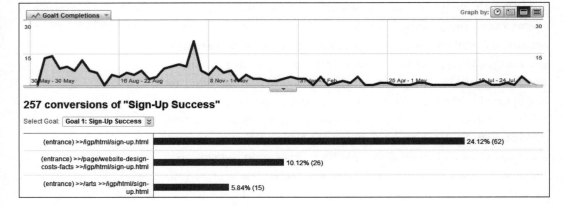

Goal through a circuitous or overly protracted path you might want to flag up a fast-track route or offer them an incentive earlier on in the process. You may even want to use '>>' buttons instead of textual hyperlinks/buttons to direct people to the next page in a sequence rather than leaving it to chance. (The use of '>>' indicates that there's more relevant information next as opposed to a textual description which could be misinterpreted or be deemed as irrelevant by the visitor – this is more of a psychological technique than anything else!)

Goal Value

Sample question: How much money are our Goals earning us?

This report is nice and easy! If you have assigned a value to each Goal, Analytics tots up how much you have acquired by hour, day, week and month by multiplying the number of conversions by the Goal value.

Goal Abandoned Funnels

Sample question: How effective are the steps we have defined in achieving our Goals?

If you have specified the pages in your Goal which form a funnel, then this report allows you to see how many started the process but failed to complete it. If you are getting a large number of abandonments that would signal the need to simplify the process, as typically the quicker you get people to the goal the more will convert. You can do this by clarifying the steps your visitor needs to take, indicating the value of their achieving the Goal, and testing various conversion tactics to reduce the overall abandonment.

Funnel Visualisation

Sample question: Which pages in our funnel need improvement so we can increase the overall conversion rate?

This report gives you a clear visual description of where your visitors come from as they enter the funnel and where they go to. So, on the left-hand side you have the entry points into your funnel, in the centre are the funnel pages themselves, and on the right, where visitors leave the funnel.

This is incredibly useful as it clearly describes where the constraints are along the funnel path and focuses your attention on releasing them. It gives you a clear idea as to how many are leaving and where. This then allows you to pinpoint the exact pages which need optimisation. For example, if you notice that they leave from the Checkout page and head off to a page about your delivery process then you can add that information into the Checkout page and keep them contained within the funnel.

Fig 28 Funnel report

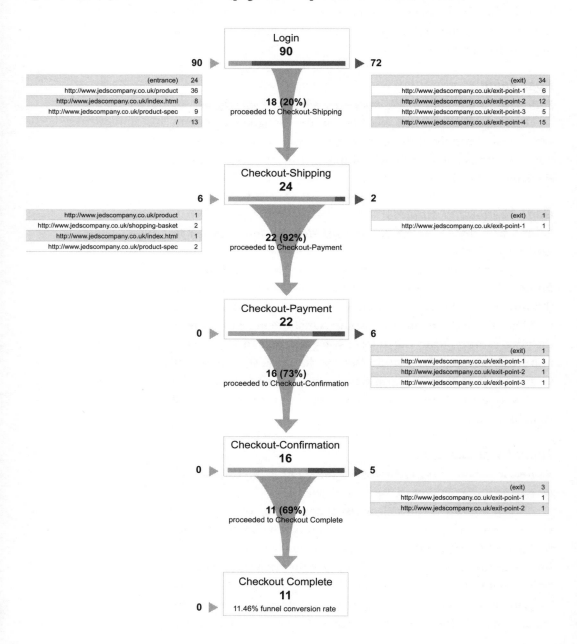

Incidentally, if you look at the very bottom of the funnel it will indicate how many who started the funnel completed the Goal (seen as both a number and a percentage) – a useful metric to measure your future performance against.

ECOMMERCE REPORTS

If you're running an ecommerce website then you will welcome the detailed reports Analytics offers. Each of the eight reports is fairly self-explanatory. However, they give you a terrific insight into your website's commercial performance. (In fact, there is something quite heartening about seeing all your efforts thus far translated into pounds and pence (or dollars and cents, yen or euros). It also provides you with a clear performance indicator: take a snapshot of today and compare that with where you intend to be in a year's time.

The overview dashboard, once again, delivers the headlines and then you can dive off into the various specific reports.

Total Revenue, Conversion Rate, Average Order Value

Sample questions: Are some days better than others at converting visitors into customers? Are we growing our business by offering more value to our customer's basket?

You can use the Total Revenue report to determine your performance by time. For example, you may spot higher revenues over weekends or at certain times of the day or even on specific days. You can also use this report to pinpoint the revenue uplift from your various marketing activities.

When reviewing the Conversion Rate and Average Order Value reports it's best to assess both the overall trends and the detail of how your various marketing tests have been performing – it's certainly a direct measure of the latter. What you're aiming for is to see that trend increasing month on month, proving that your strategy is working.

What's rather interesting is to overlay your Conversion Rate with your Average Order Value and review the differences. For example, if the conversion rate stays flat but the average order value increases then you would assume that your customer's basket size is increasing (well done). However, if it's decreasing then you might want to set about offering cross-sells and upsells to them at the point of sale.

Product Performance

Sample question: Which of our products are doing well/poorly?

Divided by SKU (stock-keeping unit) and category, this report gives you the breakdown of how each product's sales fared. Apart from the obvious value this has, you may want to compare the number of pageviews a product had with its sales performance. For example, sometimes the high-performance products can outshine lesser but better-selling products. Here's how that might work: your top product could have a large number of pageviews in comparison to sales, which would result in a low Conversion Rate (for example, 100 pageviews but only 20 sales), whereas you may have another product which sells less but has a high conversion rate (10 pageviews and 8 sales). In that instance you would want to promote the lower-selling product because its sales would be higher if you could increase the traffic (pageviews) to its page.

This is another example of where combining the information from two reports can help you draw more advanced conclusions than if either one was studied independently.

Visits to Purchase, Days to Purchase

Sample question: How much convincing do our prospects need in order to become customers?

Again two quite self-evident reports but there are some interesting deductions you can make about how your prospects react to your business. If you spot that your visitors are taking several visits to convert, that may not be a bad signal. In fact that may be the direct result of your email marketing bringing them back to the website to deepen their confidence about buying from you. Equally it could be because your offline marketing is working well at keeping your brand in their minds. On the negative side it could also be because you are not presenting all the information they need in one go – something you could resolve by increasing the quality and quantity of information on the page and seeing if, as a result, they spend more time on the page (use the Content reports to determine this from the 'Avg. Time on Page' column in the table).

There certainly is no harm in attempting to reduce both the number of visits and days to purchase. Both can be significantly influenced by a strong email marketing campaign and well-tested landing pages to help overcome the objections in your prospect's mind.

THE STRATEGY

Your website is a laboratory in which you manufacture success. Your tests are what refine the process and your analysis is what guides your improvements. One without the other is about as useful as a fish on a motorbike. However, now you have read this chapter you have acquired the final jewel in your online crown.

There's much more to Analytics than I've been able to describe in this chapter. However, what you've got is more than sufficient for you to make huge gains in your website's effectiveness.

The trick to Analytics is not to be overwhelmed by the volume of data. Split it up into manageable chunks. This keeps your thinking fresh. Combine that with the question-based approach and you'll stay on track.

Remember that this isn't just 'data' – it is the imprint of your visitors. Like an ancient Native American scout, you are deducing what happened from the tracks left behind. Every piece of data is a vote in favour of or against a part of your website. How you interpret that determines the direction you take with your marketing. Use your tracking skills wisely.

A big congratulations to you for completing one of the most advanced aspects to web ownership! Now, there's just one more thing you need to do...

CHAPTER 10

Lights, Camera, Action!

My wife and I are big theatregoers. We both love the anticipation of the event: the energy from the people in the foyer, the hush that rolls across the audience as the lights dim, the emotion that flows from the stage. And, although we've watched a few grim performances in our time, the overall experience is well worth the price. (Frankly, even the dire ones provide some entertainment, although not necessarily in the intended form.)

Now, imagine a world without actors. No films, no TV or radio and absolutely no theatre. Imagine only ever reading *Romeo and Juliet* or having to imagine *Star Wars*. There's no doubt that our lives would be poorer for it. Actors and actresses are vital because they turn meaningful words into tangible action and allow us all to enjoy the result.

I wrote this book to help you but it can only do that if you, like the actor, turn these words into action. The hidden power in information is in the doing and that's where you must become your own Harrison Ford or Katharine Hepburn and act out these pages – transform *Make Your Website Sell* from the script into the film and act out the best website the world has ever seen!

Action leads to change. Act positively on this material now and you will create change and that will lead to business growth, fulfilment and ultimately wealth and freedom.

Writing a Brief

Here's a checklist of information to include in your brief to your web designers:

1. About You
    a. Your company name, web address, address, point of contact/key decision maker
    b. What your business does and its products/ services and size
    c. Attach any promotional material (brochures, catalogues, etc.)
    d. Who are you target markets
    e. Who are your competitors

2. Current Site
    a. Define the goals of your site
    b. Who will come to the site and what will they do once they are there
    c. What you like/dislike about the current site
    d. Percentage turnover of your company it generates
    e. Number of visitors vs number of sales

3. New Site
    a. What you want it to do
        i. What's essential
        ii. What's nice to have
    b. Key reasons for the upgrade
    c. Deadline for launch

4. Technical Requirements
    a. Basic requirements for your website's CMS
    b. Hosting the website
    c. Are there any technical issues they should be aware of (ask your IT support about this one)

5. Budget. This really helps the web design company understand whether they can deliver what you're asking for within your project's financial limitations. Don't be tempted to leave this out as it can create an overly competitive attitude between the web designers, which doesn't always benefit your project in the long run. (Isn't a budget something you'd rather have from your customers also?) You only need to give bracketed figures ($low–$high) to give everyone a sense of your expectations and what they've got to work with.

6. Time scales. You'll need to know that whoever you choose to build your site can do it to the time scales you anticipate. That said, expect some overrun in your project.[1]

[1] It is typical to find IT projects overrunning by 30–40 per cent (ieeexplore. ieee.org/xpl/freeabs_all. jsp?arnumber=1237981).

When you've got them all down, aim to meet with three to four and try to make a decision within a week before you and your team forget who said what!

Sample Project List

Below is a condensation of Chapter 3, 'Plan & Build Your Website,' into a simple set of To-Dos you can use to organise your actions and measure your progress. (Asterisks indicate actions for *you*.)

Pre-Setup Phase
☐ Send out Contract of Agreement*
☐ Contract Signed and Returned
☐ Agree on Approximate Milestone Dates for Each Phase*

Phase 1 (Specification)
☐ Agree on Site Navigation*
☐ Define Accessibility Requirements*
☐ Build Wireframe
☐ Provide Sample Site Content for Templates*
☐ Get Design Team Sign-Off
☐ Get Development Team Sign-Off
☐ Sign-Off*

Phase 2a (Design: Home Page)
☐ List the Sites you Love/Hate*
☐ Have Conference Call with Designer*
☐ Create Logo (if required)
☐ Create Holding Page (if no site exists)
☐ Write Sample Home Page Copy and Send to Designers*
☐ Create 2 Initial Home Page Designs
☐ Feedback*
☐ Create Third Home Page
☐ Revise Chosen Home Page
☐ Feedback – Design Study*
☐ Create Second Revision of Home Page
☐ Sign-Off*

Phase 2b (Design: Inner Page)

☐ Create Inner Page Copy*
☐ Create Inner Page Design
☐ Feedback*
☐ Create First Revision Inner Page
☐ Create Second Revision Inner Page
☐ Create Favicon
☐ Sign-Off*
☐ Hand over PSDs and any Custom Fonts
☐ Check All Graphics are Purchased/Licensed

Phase 3 (Site Build)

☐ Set up Development Hosting Space
☐ Cut Designs to HTML
☐ Ensure XHTML Transitional Standards met
☐ Ensure Accessibility AA Standard Met
☐ Set up Trading Account (ecommerce sites only)*
☐ Develop CMS
☐ Integrate CMS with HTML
☐ Install on Development Server
☐ Basic Training on CMS
☐ Populate Site*

Phase 4 (Testing)

☐ Alpha Test (Internal)
☐ Beta Test (Client)*
☐ Feedback – Usability Study*
☐ Sign-Off*

Phase 5 (Wrap-Up)

☐ Domain and Link Redirect List to New Pages*
☐ Add in Google Analytics Code
☐ Upload Site
☐ Backup Old Site
☐ Change Name Servers
☐ Archive all Base Files
☐ Backup Final Site
☐ Sign-Off*

* Actions for you

Specification Questions

When you get to the point where you are building your specification, your web designers will want to ask you questions to clarify how your website will work. So, in order to give you the heads-up on the type of questions you'll be asked, I've included a list below. Please bear in mind it is not intended to be comprehensive (although it may look it) – it's just intended to sign-post you in the right direction. Many of the questions you'll be asked and ask your web designers will be unique to your project.

Background

Your Website

1. What's your current web address?
   a. List all the domains currently registered
   b. Do you own any other websites that are relevant to the project?
2. What works well on your existing website? Why?
3. What does not? Why?
4. Who are your competitors and what are their web addresses?

Your Customers

1. Who is visiting your website?
2. Who do you want to visit your website?
3. What is the most important thing to them about your service?
4. What kind of information would they like to see before arriving at a buying decision?
5. What information do they not want to see?
6. If they didn't know you, what would they look for to gain confidence about your services/products?

7.   If they didn't know your company, what would be their preferred means of contact (email, telephone, contact form, live chat, etc.)?

Existing Website

1.   What content are you going to reuse?
2.   Is there any key functionality that needs replicating on the new site?

Navigation

1.   Would you prefer the menu to appear vertically or horizontally? (Remember, a horizontal navigation menu will have a fixed width and may not accommodate all your menu items.)
2.   Would you like to use mega drop-down menus? (www. useit.com/alertbox/mega-dropdown-menus.html)
   a.   Do you want dynamic navigation? For example, tag clouds (en.wikipedia.org/wiki/Tag_cloud)?
3.   Do you need to use Breadcrumbs? (en.wikipedia.org/ wiki/Breadcrumb_(navigation))
4.   Mega footers (extended page footers that contain lots of links to other pages in the site – almost like a scaled-down sitemap). They can also include:
   a.   Contact Us details
   b.   Contact form
   c.   Accessibility choices
   d.   Links to Twitter, Facebook, etc.
   e.   Sitemap
5.   How are multiple pages handled?
   a.   At what point does a page become too long and require splitting?
   b.   What navigation is needed to move between split pages? For example, '<Previous | 1 | 2 | 3 | Next >'

Design

1.   What size monitor should the website fit in? (1024 x 768 is the standard, www.w3schools.com/browsers/browsers_display.asp)
2.   What graphics do you have available?
3.   Are any accreditations or logos to be included?

4. Do you have any fonts that would be used on the website? (You may also need to check the licence agreements for your chosen fonts to ensure you have permission to use them on your website.)

Interface Design

1. What accessibility designs need to be added?
   a. Text resize (AAA)
   b. Text only
   c. High contrast
   d. Dyslexia
2. Does the site need to be accessible to mobile devices like Blackberries and iPhones?
3. How should a printed page look?
4. What web browsers does the site need to be compatible with?

Content

General

1. What footer information needs to be included?
   a. Privacy
   b. Legal
   c. Terms of use
   d. Registered office/number
   e. Directors' names
   f. VAT
2. What needs to be multi-lingual? (Specific page content or the whole site including navigation, buttons and other 'textual furniture.')

Content Scheduling

1. What content needs to be scheduled? (For example, do you need news articles to be pre-written but only appear on a certain date? This can be useful if you've got financial information you want embargoed.) If so, the content can be:
   a. Published
   b. Archived
   c. Expired

News/Articles/Blog Items, etc.

1. What order do the news/articles need to appear in (publication date, manual, alphanumeric)?
2. Can they be categorised?
3. Do you want a featured article to appear on specific pages?
4. Can users sign up to news notifications?

Documents

1. Do you want to insert documents into your website?
2. Which icons will be needed for the document types (DOC/XLS/PPT/MP3/SWF(movie)/PDF)?

Videos/Audio

1. How is video to be displayed?
2. Does it require subtitles?
3. How big will the video files be?
4. Are they to be linked to YouTube, TubeMogul, etc?

Forms

1. Define fields for:
    a. Contact Us
    b. Call Me Back
    c. Request a Quote
    d. Request a Brochure
    e. And any other forms your website needs
2. Which fields are mandatory?
3. Is CAPTCHA required?
4. What are the target email addresses?
5. Can these be amended in the CMS?
6. Does data captured by the website need to be stored and exported into CSV, XML, or other third-party product?

Search

1. Is a site-wide search facility required?
    a. Criteria for search
    b. Order of results
    c. Percentage relevance shown?
    d. Does it need to search PDFs, Word, etc.
2. Search facility within CMS?

Ecommerce

Products

1. How do your products divide down?
2. Product fields:
   a. Title
   b. Description
   c. Price
   d. Size
   e. Colour
   f. Weight
   g. Product code
3. How are graphics to be displayed?
   a. Large picture
   b. Zoom facility on main image?
   c. Thumbnails
   d. How many images for each product (e.g. front, back, 360° shot)?
4. How will products be sorted?
   a. By browser choice (price, size, etc.)
   b. Automatically (most popular, date added, etc.)
   c. Defined by category (colour, gifts for him/her, Christmas, seasons, etc.)
   d. 'Show All' facility
   e. Is there a need for a discount feature? If so, how is this to be displayed, for example, strikethrough showing new price?
5. Do you need a 'New Product' flag?
6. Do you offer bundles of products?
7. Will there be Special Offers or Sale or Clearance products?
8. Will sold-out products be flagged or removed when out of stock? Will alternatives be offered?
9. Are there to be any featured products?
10. Will there be any related products links?
11. Are links to products to appear on home page?
12. Will there be customer reviews?

Shopping Basket

1. Is gift-wrapping available?
2. Are there any voucher or coupon schemes?
    a. Buy X for Y
    b. Buy One Get One Free
    c. Percentage or cash discount
3. Are there any areas where you can generate an upsell, i.e. the addition of accessories, warranty, etc.?
4. Will shipping costs be standard or will there be a need for a table of costs dependent on weight/size?
5. What payment types will you accept (MasterCard, Visa, Amex, PayPal, Google Checkout, etc.)?
6. Will you be selling using different currencies?
7. Is the confirmation of order/payment email to be fixed or editable within the CMS?

'My Account'

1. Once your visitor logs in, what information would you like them to view? For example:
    a. Outstanding orders
    b. Order history
    c. Delivery addresses
    d. Billing information
    e. Printable invoice

Content Management System for ECommerce

1. Is an invoicing system required within the CMS?
    a. Can the invoices be created manually with/without linkage to a product?
2. Are any reports required to be generated from the CMS, such as orders received, most popular product, highest revenue product, etc.?
3. Is order tracking available front-end and back-end (open, closed, pending, authorised, dispatched)?

Negative Keywords

Negative keywords are used to make sure that you receive clicks from potential customers only. So if someone types a search term into Google that contains a negative keyword you have defined, your advert will not be displayed. Here's a kick-start list for your campaigns (remember to also include plurals, i.e. review/reviews):

Bargains
bargain
cheap
clearance
discount
discounted
free
freebie
giveaway
inexpensive
liquidation
no cost
odd lots
overstock
remainder
no charge
sample
trial

Price Shoppers
price
pricing
quote

Job Seekers
career
employment
hiring
job
recruiter
recruiting
resume
salary

DIY
how to
make
making
diy
do it yourself
do-it-yourself

Education
class
college
course
education
school
training
university

Reference
about
definition
diagram
example
history
map
sample
what is

Research
association
bad review
book
case study
compare
comparison
define
definition
eg
example
guide
help
image
info
information
instruction
journal
magazine
manual
metrics
negative review
news
picture
poor
research
review
statistics
stats
success story
support
tutorial
user manual
white paper

Acknowledgements

Many thanks go to Martin Liu and his team at Marshall Cavendish for their patience, generosity of time and positivity (and putting up with my incessant questions).

An enormous thank you to our Project Manager, Monique Fitzpatrick, who somehow took on even more work so I would have the time to write, and also to Alistair Spark for his unsurpassed technical input and extraordinary ability to explain the incomprehensible.

Much appreciation goes to my good friend Matt McArdle for all his superb design work, brilliantly done under great pressure (as always).

I would also like to acknowledge Jay Abraham, Chris Cardell, Howie Jacobson, Frank Kern, Jay Conrad Levinson, Glen Livingstone, Perry Marshall, Brian Tracy and David Viney.

To all my family, but in particular to Julie, Elise, Theo and our much-loved and missed son Aaron, and my Dad, Ian – they are the reason I did this in the first place.

Finally I am eternally grateful to my Mum, Dr Vivien Wylie, whose insights and encouragement kept me going.

And if I missed you off, please accept my apologies and thanks!

YOUR VIP INVITATION

Your online journey continues here...

As I write this final page Google has just announced a major update to their search engine ranking system. It will have a profound effect on many of the poorer-quality websites, significantly downgrading their ranking. I would have wanted to include this new and important development but it couldn't be added before the book was published.

But that's the nature of the Internet – it's evolving quickly day by day, leaving many businesses struggling in the wake of rapid change. That's why it's vitally important that you have continuous access to the very best, leading-edge information as it breaks. In fact, I want you to have all the tools you'll ever need right at your fingertips to guide you through every aspect of website success.

So, I would like invite you to join my VIP Golden Circle website. Inside this exclusive website you'll find practical ideas, unbeatable strategies and simple how-to guides, crystal-clear help, and 'quick profit' tips to boost your online profits.

Join and Get Instant Access to:

1. **Video Seminars**: At the heart of your Internet success are these video seminars. Each step-by-step guide delivers critical 'how to' information that will magnify your profits.
2. **Success Papers**: Deepen your success with these profit-focused articles offering you some of the most advanced thinking on owning and growing websites available today.
3. **Toolbox Talks**: These short, to-the-point, 5–10-minute videos show you the online tips and tricks to help you attract and win more business.
4. **Resources Library**: I give you direct access to my top resources, software, people and businesses on the Internet. Each resource will save you time, increase your sales, or simply inspire you!

>>>

Plus when you join you receive:

- Monthly updates – including new Video Seminars, Success Papers, Toolbox Talks, and Resources.
- Regular emails alerting you to new material
- Special member's-only discounts for Jed's internet marketing services
- Your unique Member Login passcode giving you unlimited access to the advanced material on this website
- Unlimited access to every part of the VIP Golden Circle
- *Plus*, use this voucher code 'MYWS-GOLD' and get £14.99 (the RRP of this book) off your first month!

Even More Reasons to Join

1. Member's-only exclusive access
2. Share the material with everyone in your business (one membership per business, not per person)
3. Instant and exclusive 365-day access to cutting-edge and advanced information and knowledge
4. Keeps you bang-up-to-date with the latest developments in the ever-changing world of the Internet
5. Builds up into the most comprehensive resource for creating website success
6. Squeeze every last ounce of value from the materials by instant-ly accessing them from anywhere in the world again and again
7. Easily find the information you need, by topic, by level, by title, by type
8. I have spent over a decade immersed in the practical applica-tion of web design and online marketing. So, what you get is a healthy dose of facts and reality delivered in a no-nonsense, no-waffle manner.

So, whether you're just starting out or you're an Internet veteran, you'll want to get the unique knowledge inside the VIP Golden Circle that will drive your online business to the next level.

Visit **www.makeyourwebsitesell-vip.co.uk**

JOIN TODAY and continue the
most exciting online journey of your life.

If you'd like to hear more from Jed then please join his
FREE VIP Update at **www.jedwylie.co.uk**